Institutions and the Evolution of Capitalism

EUROPEAN ASSOCIATION FOR EVOLUTIONARY POLITICAL ECONOMY

General Editor: Geoffrey M. Hodgson, *University of Hertfordshire Business School, UK*

Mixed Economies in Europe: An Evolutionary Perspective on their Emergence, Transition and Regulation
Edited by Wolfgang Blaas and John Foster

The Political Economy of Diversity: Evolutionary Perspectives on Economic Order and Disorder
Edited by Robert Delorme and Kurt Dopfer

On Economic Institutions: Theory and Applications
Edited by John Groenewegen, Christos Pitelis and Sven-Erik Sjöstrand

Rethinking Economics: Markets, Technology and Economic Evolution
Edited by Geoffrey M. Hodgson and Ernesto Screpanti

Environment, Technology and Economic Growth: The Challenge to Sustainable Development
Edited by Andrew Tylecote and Jan van der Straaten

Institutions and Economic Change: New Perspectives on Markets, Firms and Technology
Edited by Klaus Nielsen and Björn Johnson

Pluralism in Economics: New Perspectives in History and Methodology
Edited by Andrea Salanti and Ernesto Screpanti

Beyond Market and Hierarchy: Interactive Governance and Social Complexity
Edited by Ash Amin and Jerzy Hausner

Employment, Technology and Economic Needs: Theory, Evidence and Public Policy
Edited by Jonathan Michie and Angelo Reati

Institutions and the Evolution of Capitalism: Implications of Evolutionary Economics
Edited by John Groenewegen and Jack Vromen

Institutions and the Evolution of Capitalism: Implications of Evolutionary Economics

Edited by

John Groenewegen

Professor of Economic Organisation and Modern Japanese Studies, Erasmus University, Rotterdam and Professor of Comparative Institutional Economics, University of Utrecht, The Netherlands

Jack Vromen

Associate Professor in the Philosophy of Economics, Erasmus University, Rotterdam, The Netherlands

Edward Elgar

Cheltenham, UK • Northampton, MA, USA

Published by
Edward Elgar Publishing Limited
The Lypiatts
15 Lansdown Road
Cheltenham
Glos GL50 2JA
UK

Edward Elgar Publishing, Inc.
William Pratt House
9 Dewey Court
Northampton
Massachusetts 01060
USA

Reprinted 2016

A catalogue record for this book is available from the British Library

Library of Congress Cataloguing in Publication Data
Institutions and the evolution of capitalism : implications of
   evolutionary economics / edited by John Groenewegen, Jack Vromen.
      "Published in association with the European Association for
   Evolutionary Political Economy."
      Includes bibliographical references and index.
      1. Evolutionary economics. 2. Institutional economics.
      3. Capitalism. I. Groenewegen, John, 1949– . II. Vromen, Jack
   J., 1958–   . III. European Association for Evolutionary Political
   Economy.
   HB97.3.I57   1999
   330—dc21   99–15584
                                                        CIP

ISBN 978 1 84064 160 8

Printed and bound in Great Britain by T.J. International Ltd, Padstow

Contents

Figures

Tables

Contributors

Laure Bazzoli, University Lumière –Lyon 2, France

Robert Boyer, CEPREMAP, Paris

Véronique Dutraive, University Lumière –Lyon 2, France

Alexander Ebner, University of Frankfurt, Germany

Sandye Gloria, University of Sient Etienne, France

John Groenewegen, Erasmus University Rotterdam and University of Utrecht, The Netherlands

Paul Krugman, MIT, Cambridge, USA

Brian Loasby, University of Stirling, USA

Jorge Niosi, Université du Quebec à Montreal, Canada

Vanessa Oltra, Université Montesquieu, France

Ernesto Screpanti, University of Siena, Italy

Wim Swaan, Hungarian Academy of Sciences, Budapest

Jack Vromen, Erasmus University Rotterdam, The Netherlands

1. Implications of Evolutionary Economics; Theory, Method and Policies

John Groenewegen and Jack Vromen

'Capitalism is change'. This famous expression of Joseph Schumpeter was not only characteristic of his days but is certainly relevant for the 1990s. The transition of East European economies, the 'Asian crisis' and the European integration all characterise the continuous change of institutions of capitalism. However, in economics the issue of change has been problematic since the equilibrium–orientated approach dominates the profession. Nowadays it is hardly questioned that evolutionary questions are of interest to economists. What is an issue of controversy, however, is the way economic evolution should be studied. Two fundamentally different approaches can be distinguished: one of the neoclassical type with maximising individuals and equilibrium as the hard core and another approach based on the neo–institutional paradigm rooted in the works of original institutionalists like John R. Commons and Thorstein Veblen.

Evolutionary economics typically aims at an understanding, explanation and prediction of changes in elements of the institutional context (norms, values, legal rules) or in institutional arrangements such as contracts, firms and labour unions. It is investigated how institutional arrangements evolve and either persist or change within a given institutional context. The possibility is not ruled out in advance, however, that changes in institutional arrangements have repercussions for changes in the institutional context.

So far evolutionary economics has mainly dealt with issues pertaining to technology and technological change (see, for example, Nelson and Winter, 1982; Dosi, Freeman, Nelson, Silverberg and Soete, 1988 and Saviotti and Metcalfe, 1991). In this volume several contributors plea for extending the scope of evolutionary economics in order to also cover changes in institutions (broadly conceived, such as in the chapter by Niosi) and technology policy (see the chapter by Oltra).

1

Thus the scope of evolutionary economics can be said to be extending. What about its 'method', the theoretical approach adopted? Here we think that what has been going on over the last decade or so is not so much a change in theoretical outlook as a sharpening of theoretical focus. Without pretending to give an exhaustive characterisation of the theoretical approach in evolutionary economics, one can say that in evolutionary processes at least two mechanisms are at work (for a more detailed discussion, see Vromen, 1997; for a related characterisation, see Marengo and Willinger, 1997).[1] One mechanism, which can be called a selection mechanism, sees to it that extant variety is reduced. This mechanism filters out materials having a performance level below some critical threshold value, preserving only the materials with a performance level exceeding this value. The other mechanism, which can be called a variety–generating (or variety–inducing) mechanism, takes care that incessantly new varieties appear in the population under study. Either (pieces of) old materials are recombined in altogether new ways, or entirely new, unprecedented materials enter the population.

Now it has been argued that if the selection mechanism were the only mechanism at work, that is if its functioning would not be perturbed by the variety–generating mechanism (or any other mechanism), then this mechanism would steer the population in the direction of some equilibrium. If we add the variety–generating mechanism, however, novelty will continuously show up disturbing the equilibrium–approximating process.

The foregoing makes it understandable why an exclusive theoretical focus on the selection mechanism is often coupled with 'end–state theorising'. Generally speaking, two pairs of distinctions can be made here. The one pair relates to the different theoretical foci just mentioned. Either an evolutionary economist focuses on the workings of the selection mechanism only, or he/she studies the joint operation of the selection and variety–generating mechanism. The other pair pertains to different theoretical orientations. Either an evolutionary theory is end–state orientated, or it is process–orientated. Whereas end–state theories pay attention only to the (purported) outcomes of evolutionary processes, process theories study the evolutionary processes themselves.

In principle these two pairs of distinctions make for four different possible combinations. Neither a theoretical focus on the selection mechanism working in isolation nor a focus on the combined workings of the selection and variety–inducing mechanisms prejudge the choice between the end–state and the process orientation. In principle, nothing prevents a theorist who wants to examine the two mechanisms working side by side from concentrating on the outcomes thereoff. In practice, however, a theoretical focus on the selection mechanism is almost invariably linked with an end–state orientation and a theoretical focus on the joint operation of the selection and variety–inducing mechanisms is almost always accompanied with a process orientation. It is easy to see why.

As already noted, it is generally acknowledged that an unperturbed operation of the selection mechanism tends to steer evolutionary processes in the direction of equilibria.[2] This makes it understandable why theorists focusing on the selection mechanism do not see a pressing need to go into the details of evolutionary processes leading to equilibria. They think they go straight to end–state equilibria while forgetting about their antecedent 'history'. This can not only be observed in economics, starting with 'classical defences' (Winter, 1987) of neoclassical equilibrium analysis by Alchian (1950) and Friedman (1953) and culminating in evolutionary game–theoretic justifications of the notion of Nash equilibrium (for an overview see Weibull, 1995). It can also be observed in proponents of the adaptationist programme in evolutionary biology (see, for example, Dawkins, 1976 and Maynard Smith, 1982; for a philosophical treatment of equilibrium explanation in evolutionary biology, see Sober, 1983). In this volume, Paul Krugman takes this stance.

If the variety–generating mechanism is not abstracted from, however, then disregarding evolutionary processes cannot be afforded, it seems, even by those who wish to consider end states only. The tendency toward equilibria brought about by the selection mechanism is then repeatedly disrupted by incessant appearances of new varieties. It is far from clear what the net result of the resulting complex interplay between the 'narrowing–down', due to the selection mechanism, and the 'widening–up', due to the variety–generating mechanism, is. This explains why a plea for paying attention to the variety–generating mechanism is so often combined with a plea for 'process theorising'.[3]

What about the relevance of the different approaches? In our opinion it is important to identify the relevant conditions as well as the relevant issues at hand. A whole array of various conditions and various issues could be distinguished here. Let it suffice to say that we think that if conditions obtain in which information is not as easily diffused, and markets are not as flexible as it is assumed in the end–state version (that is, if markets are highly institutionalised), then because of increasing variation and multiple selection mechanisms, the process version is considered to be more relevant ('different theories for different conditions', see Groenewegen and Vromen, 1996). Furthermore, when research aims at understanding the process of change so that 'how' and 'why' questions become central, then the process version seems to be more relevant then the end–state version ('different theories for different issues', see Groenewegen and Vromen, 1996).

Evolutionary economics can be said to have implications on three different levels: a theoretical, methodological and policy level. The first refers to the theoretical concepts considered relevant for analysing processes of evolution. The methodological implications deal with the question of how research in evolutionary economics should be conducted. The implication of the policy recommendations concerns the consequences for the type of recommendations evolutionary economics produces for management and government.

THEORETICAL IMPLICATION OF EVOLUTIONARY ECONOMICS

The theoretical differences between evolutionary and non–evolutionary approaches have been extensively discussed elsewhere (Delorme, 1997). In a nutshell, evolutionary approaches can be characterised in terms of the following features:

- the unit of analysis is not the isolated, atomised individual, but the individual in interaction with the environment (compare Bazzoli and Dutraive in this volume); procedural rationality replaces substantive rationality;
- the economy is basically an open system, subject to pervasive uncertainty, so that end states are hard to predict;
- institutions influence learning and selection processes in terms of initial conditions (history matters), lock–ins and trajectories;
- attention is paid to different selection mechanisms working simultaneously: efficiency and power.

Anyone acquainted with neoclassical theory will readily recognise the general tenets of the end–state variant. It is the process variant that warrants special attention. The process variant brings specific theoretical concepts with it. They can be summarised as follows:

- innovation is endogenised;
- the unit of analysis is the individual here also, but now in interaction with the environment;

- the behaviour of the individual is assumed to be procedurally rational: the individual is searching and creative. The individual can be satisfied without having maximised and creates organisational safeguards in order to cope with uncertainties;
- the coordination of the actions of individuals is taking place via institutionalised markets, where values, norms, rules and organisational structures like firms, affect expectations and offer individuals opportunities to learn.

Clearly opening the black box of the evolutionary process implies a high price in that the terms of 'the ever–present need to simplify' are not met. This is stressed by Paul Krugman in this volume.

METHODOLOGICAL IMPLICATIONS OF EVOLUTIONARY ECONOMICS

The theoretical implications have consequences also for the method of research: which method of investigation is relevant for understanding the process of evolution? Operationalisation of the concepts relevant for understanding evolutionary processes demand in each particular case a specification of the initial conditions, of the increase or decrease of variety, of the forces of selection (economic efficiency, political power), of the perception of efficiency by the principal actors, of the objectives of the actors, their power base and their interdependencies. Campbell and Lindberg (1991) offer a schema on how to structure such an analysis along several steps.

First the pressures for change that are due to alterations in the conditions should be analysed bearing on economic efficiency like changes in technology, state policies and the power of different actors in the system. These changing conditions affect the strategies of economic actors in the systems such as firms, labour unions and research institutes. At the same time policies of the state are affected by changing domestic and international political–economic conditions, such as the creation of an integrated European market, the transition of Asian economies, etc. The state, being an important actor in the evolution of governance regimes, adapts its strategies like the other actors in the economy do. The strategies selected by the different public and private actors result in a change in the varieties generated by the system.

The other mechanism of 'collective selection' consists of activities like trial and error, negotiation and bargaining and coercion. To understand what is going on in a specific situation the following constraints of this selection process should be well specified. What is the nature of the existing governance regime, for example, who are the dominant actors, what are their relationships and what is the tradition of, for instance, price behaviour? Special attention should be paid to the cultural context in which the existing governance regime operates, in which the new variety of strategies is emerging and in which the selection process takes place. The context of specific values and norms largely influences the way actors 'try and error, negotiate and bargain or coerce'.

When those elements, which in reality are interdependent, are analysed step by step, the research can result in a thorough understanding of the process of evolution.

As if this approach is not complicated enough already, Campbell (1995) concludes that the step–wise analysis described above does not really open the process box. Following Douglass North's (1990) recognition that a theory of culture and ideology should be included in order to reach an understanding of how actors interpret changing conditions and the efficiency of new strategies, John Campbell introduces the idea of 'interaction, interpretation and bricolage'. He shows a way to really open the box of the evolutionary process by stressing the importance of the type of interaction between individuals for understanding their interpretative mental frames (see also Denzau and North, 1994).

In studying the history of a country, an industry, or a firm, one gets a clear understanding of the specific interactions between the actors. In Japan, for instance, the interactions differ fundamentally from those in the US within the same industry, whereas those inside the same economy can differ markedly between industries. Within the same industry individual firms can interact differently with suppliers, buyers, competitors, local government and labor unions. Based on a detailed analysis of the differences and similarities of the interactions, one can construct the interpretative frames actors use in analysing problems and in selecting strategies. The interpretative frame of a French entrepreneur is fundamentally different from that of his Dutch colleague, while the frames of the Korean president of a industrial conglomerate like Samsung differ deeply from that of his Japanese colleague, who runs Mitsubishi Heavy Industry for example.

With respect to the first mechanism of changing variety the point Campbell makes is about alterations in patterns of interaction, causing actors to gain new perspectives leading to new interpretations of problems and solutions. Interaction changes interpretation and variety. Moreover, the ideas of interaction and interpretation are also relevant for the second mechanism, that of selection. Whether trial and error or consultation is the way to proceed in the collective selection process depends heavily on the interpretative frames of the actors, which in turn is the result of their interactions. Interpretative frames have some stability (see Boyer in this volume), but can also dramatically change due to dramatically changing interactions (see Screpanti in this volume). When the pattern of interaction is more or less stable, actors look for changes and innovations that fit into existing institutional structures. They 'bricolage' by changing the institutions through small steps, sometimes forward, sometimes backwards and sometimes sideways.

> Actors gradually craft new institutional solutions by recombining these principles through an innovative process of bricolage whereby new institutions differ from but resemble old ones (Campbell, 1997, p. 22).

Campbell makes a useful distinction between technical bricolage (a recombination of existing institutional principles solving issues of economic inefficiencies), and symbolic bricolage (new institutions take hold when they are accompanied with the relevant cultural symbols of language and rhetoric devices).

The analysis of the process of evolution suggested above results in extremely complicated multi–disciplinary research. It would however be a grave error to label this type of research as 'anything goes' where a lack of disciplining conceptualisation (in terms of rational individuals, for example) makes any kind of theorising possible. First, the integration of an interpretative analysis into the model of institutional evolution is perfectly compatible with the self–interested individual as a building block of the model. What is added to the traditional rational choice models is an analysis of how individuals weigh the relative cost and benefits and of what they perceive as costs and benefits. Acknowledging that rational self–interested behaviour is socially constructed opens the possibility that the 'how' question is answered differently in different historical periods and in different economic systems, industries and firms. When the prevailing patterns of interaction differ, then the prevailing frames of interpretation differ and then the process of bricolage differs. If one is interested in understanding those differences one should be willing to sacrifice simplicity of the analysis and to take the risk of being dragged into complexities that go well beyond the standard economic questions and analysis. Needless to say, a lot of work remains to be done here.

POLICY IMPLICATIONS OF EVOLUTIONARY ECONOMICS

The results of the research described above are not formulated in optimum end states of an evolutionary process. The results are formulated in terms of conditions under which it is likely that trajectory 'a', or 'c' will be followed instead of 'b' and 'd'. Under another set of conditions trajectory 'b' or 'd' are more likely. This holds for the level of systems (Boyer in this volume), for the level of industries and firms (Swaan in this volume), as well as for the individual level. Because the results of the process variant are formulated in terms of conditions under which it is likely that..., or in terms of scenarios, the policy recommendations for management and government are also conditional. Awareness of initial conditions, of perceptions and strategies, of lock–ins and safeguards, etc. leads to recommendations for policy makers in terms of purposefully extending the range of interaction (more windows to the outside world). This is, for instance, the case when government purposefully invites firms with different capabilities to join a specific technology programme. Then the possibility of different paths of development and of novelty in the process of 'bricolage' is intentionally kept open. Keynesian 'fine–tuning' is, for instance, not likely to be recommended by evolutionary economists because that approach presupposes that reasonably reliable detailed predictions can be given of what will happen in different policy scenarios. This does not mean that evolutionary economics is devoid of any predictive power or of policy relevance, however. Although economists may be unable to offer precise predictions, they may have something reliable to say on qualitative tendencies or trends. To borrow Hayek's phrase, they still may be able to give pattern predictions. Similarly, even though economists lack the knowledge necessary for successful fine–tuning, they may nevertheless be able to tell under what circumstances desired things are likely to happen. To follow Hayek once again, the role of the economist is better compared with that of a gardener than that of a craftsman. Like the gardener, the economist should find out under what conditions economies can be expected to flourish and prosper.

This idea can be found in several contributions to this volume. Ebner, for example, engages in developing the notions necessary to do comparative studies concerning national peculiarities that determine whether creative institutional responses are fostered with respect to changes. The rich notion of 'economic style' that he comes up with is based on the work of Schumpeter and the members of the German Historical School. Oltra defends the view that the evolution of technology policy itself is subject to similar learning and selection processes as is the evolution of technology. The two evolutionary processes co–evolve, Oltra argues.

CONTRIBUTIONS IN THIS VOLUME

This volume on the 'Institutions and the Evolution of Capitalism: Implications of Evolutionary Economics' starts with four chapters on the question of what evolutionary economics is all about.

Paul Krugman compares evolutionary theory of biologists with economic theory and comes to the conclusion that they have a lot in common. After having defined economics in terms of methodological individualism with self–interested individuals who interact, Krugman explains that evolutionary theory is similar to economics with one exception: myopia is of the essence of the evolutionist view. Referring to John Maynard Smith and William Hamilton he concludes that:

> 'In short, even though evolution is necessarily a process of small changes, evolutionary theorists normally take the shortcut of assuming that the process gets you to a maximum, and pay surprisingly little attention to the dynamics along the way' (Krugman, p. 29 in this volume).

Paul Krugman does certainly not claim that maximisation and equilibrium are to be found in reality, not at all, but these concepts of neoclassical economics are considered to be useful metaphors 'to organise one's mind'; useful fictions to understand economic reality. In practice evolutionists, like economists, ignore the processes and focus on the end result of the dynamics: an equilibrium in which individuals maximise their fitness given that which other individuals do. The reason for ignoring the analysis of the process of evolution is not that such an analysis would not be of interest, but it would make the analysis so complex that theorising would become impossible even with the modern computer technology of today.

> (...) is surely the ever–present need to simplify, to make models that are comprehensible (Krugman, p. 24 in this volume).

In the other approach to evolutionary issues the analysis of the process of dynamics is considered of crucial importance: rooted in neo–institutionalism this approach aims at opening the box of the evolutionary process in order to understand why in reality inefficient institutions and organisations survive and why efficient ones are not selected. Then path dependencies, lock–ins, power relations, the constraining and enabling role of institutions and cultural embeddedness become interdependent explanatory variables.

In orthodoxy the approach of a static comparative analysis dominates; in evolutionary theory analysis the one of a slowly evolving process. However, economic dynamics can also be of a catastrophic kind. Ernesto Screpanti discusses in this volume the idea of abrupt changes of institutional structures based on the starting point that institutions cannot be modified independently of the other elements of the system with which the institution is linked. In general, institutional structures produce satisfaction as well as frustration and when both grow, then a process of polarisation can result in an abrupt change of the system. This general model is illustrated by Screpanti with the revolutionary changes in 1989 in Eastern Europe and the come about of major innovations in clusters so well explained in the writings of Schumpeter. Screpanti observes that the question with respect to Eastern Europe really is not why the revolution took place, but more why it took so long. Already in the late 1950s the social frustration grew fast, but strong political repression helped to maintain social stability. Screpanti explains the events in terms of a more formal 'cycle in the collective will'. In the application of innovation clusters, his model is used to work out a problem posed by Schumpeter in his analysis of technological change in the long cycle: that of the reasons why great innovations which change technological systems tend to occur in bunches or, rather, in swarms that take off in the downswing of the long cycle.

A methodological implication of evolutionary economics refers to the issue of methodological individualism and collectivism. Laure Bazzoli and Véronique Dutraive outline in their contribution the disadvantages of those two methodological foundations and plea for 'a middle ground approach' of methodological institutionalism. Based on the ideas of John R. Commons they take the position that a realist analysis of human behaviour should be the grounding of evolutionary economics. Purposeful action and habitual behaviour should then be linked. Both action and the process of cognition are social; rational man becomes reasonable man. The methodological institutionalism also has consequences for the parts–whole relation: parts and the whole ought to be linked in a theory of process, a process with no beginning and no final term. It is made clear that in an approach, in which institutions are both explanatory and variables to be explained, an historical approach to evolution is necessary. Only then can one understand that parts are both cause and consequence in a process in which the units themselves, as well as the whole, are transformed and transforming.

Sandye Gloria presents an incisive analysis of 'the great divide' in the Austrian School between Kirzner and Hayek on the one hand and Lachmann on the other. Gloria provides us with a general synthetic scheme (or conceptualisation, as she calls it herself) that enables her to go right to the heart of the disagreement between the two camps. What remains somewhat obscure in the writings of the Austrians thus becomes immediately and completely transparent: whereas Kirzner and Hayek both see market participants basically as discoverers, Lachmann sees them primarily as creators of new opportunities. Lachmann puts the imaginative powers of human beings centre stage and accordingly draws our attention to disequilibrium forces in the market. Rephrased in the evolutionary jargon introduced at the beginning of this chapter, we can say that while Kirzner and Hayek stress the selection mechanism in market processes, Lachmann emphasises the variety–inducing mechanism. This leaves us with the question of why Kirzner and Hayek, despite their endorsement of subjectivism, chose to suppress the creative element in human action. In Gloria's view, Kirzner and Hayek refused to accept Lachmann's insight for the ideological reason that it would disturb their strong belief that tendencies toward equilibria inhere in markets. She also mentions the disquieting prospect of theoretical nihilism, however, that Lachmann's radical subjectivism seems to hold out. Lachmann believed that institutions serve as signposts in orienting and coordinating individual plans. But as he was unable to transform this belief into a general and unified theory of institutions, Lachmann could never dismantle the criticism of theoretical nihilism convincingly.

In the sixth chapter Brian Loasby discusses the engine of the dynamics of institutions in a capitalist society: the entrepreneur. When opening the box of the evolutionary process a deep insight into the drivers of entrepreneurs is needed. Brian Loasby discusses the impressive contributions of George Schackle to economic theory by underlining the importance of understanding the role of entrepreneurs and businessmen in the modern world. As a starting point the issue of 'selfish calculation', which Shackle considered an inadequate basis for the study of economic man, is discussed. Loasby writes about Shackle:

> But it was calculation rather than selfishness that provided the central theme of his criticism of orthodox economics; for the calculations which were required by the theories of rational choice were too often neither feasible not reasonable (Loasby, p. 95 in this volume).

Calculation of that kind requires the closure of every model with no place for the unknown and unknowable. A focus on the expectations of entrepreneurs is considered by Shackle an adequate way to grasp the process of evolution in economic reality. Brian Loasby further discusses the idea of imagination which is the basis on which entrepreneurs create their own future.

> The future is not there to be discovered, but must be created', wrote Shackle once. This does not imply that individuals construct the world at will according to their imagination, not at all: because institutions are the response to incomplete knowledge, they cannot be rationally chosen (in the technical sense used by orthodox economists) they have unexpected consequences, both beneficial and harmful, and are likely to change over time (Loasby, p. 100 in this volume).

According to Loasby then, institutional economics must be evolutionary economics and vice versa. For in a world of imperfect knowledge and of bounded rationality, processes must be structured by institutions. In the last chapters of this volume the evolution of capitalism itself is discussed.

In his contribution Jorge Niosi explores the outlines of an evolutionary analysis of the diffusion of organisational innovations. As Niosi correctly notices, evolutionary economists have so far concentrated mainly on technological issues. Organisational issues have not received much attention. Given this situation, it is only natural to ask, as Niosi does, how the spread of organisational innovations (like new Japanese management techniques) compares with what we already know about the processes in which technological innovations spread. Niosi argues that there are both analogies and disanalogies between the two processes. On the one hand, key factors determining the diffusion of technological innovations such as firm–specific, industry–specific, and nation–specific features also seem to play a major role in the diffusion of organisational innovations. On the other hand, however, there are several dimensions in which organisational diffusion is different from technological diffusion. For example, unlike technological innovators organisational innovators may only reap the full benefits of their invention by actively promoting transfer of their invention to suppliers (both domestic and foreign) and customers. Unlike technological inventions organisational inventions are not patentable. Niosi is the first to concede that a lot of work remains to be done here. What already seems clear, however, is that a sharp distinction between the creation and the diffusion of organisational novelty cannot be maintained. Because of the fact that organisational novelty involves a lot of tacit knowledge, attempts by other firms at imitating them may easily create unintended new organisational practices.

An analysis of the complexity of economic systems is central in the so–called 'French Regulation School', of which Robert Boyer is one of the founding fathers. In his contribution different models of capitalism are presented together with a theoretical framework that allows for historical, cultural and political explanations next to the economic efficiency approach. It is a mistake to assume that out of self–interested behaviour of individuals automatically efficient capitalist institutions emerge; it is equally wrong to assume that public authority can create efficient market systems by means of introducing property rights and other basic regulations. No, economic systems have to be understood as evolving complexities, of which the precise nature varies over time and of which the dynamics is the result of the behaviour of economic actors driven by efficiency, but who are embedded in and interact with a specific social–political environment. A careful analysis of the institutional specificities makes one understand the nature of capitalistic systems, their differences and dynamics. In his contribution Robert Boyer distinguishes four ideal types of capitalist systems and addresses the question of whether the Anglo–American model is becoming dominant on a world–wide scale.

Alexander Ebner synthesises different strands of theorising, bearing on the issue of which factors account for national competitiveness and innovativeness. Ebner starts his exposition with a discussion of the systems of innovation (SI) approach stressing the interrelations between institutions, organisations and technology. This discussion naturally leads him to notify Schumpeter's ideas about economic sociology. Ebner points out that in developing his ideas Schumpeter was clearly influenced by prominent members of the German Historical School, such as Schmoller, Sombart and Weber. Ebner's discussion culminates in the notion of economic style (first introduced by Spiethoff, who in turn elaborated upon Schumpeter's ideas). The notion of economic style comprises many different things, ranging from natural factors (such as population dynamics), over socio–economic structures and endogenous growth dynamics to moral attitudes and spiritual motives of economic action. It is exactly its conceptual richness and holistic (*Gestalt*) orientation, Ebner claims, that makes the notion of economic style perfectly suited to analyse differences between national innovation systems. What Ebner stresses in particular is that even on a national level an assumption of institutional homogeneity is unwarranted. Even within nations, institutional variety is the rule rather than the exception and it is the specific type (and degree) of institutional variety that determines to a large extent the capabilities of creative response in a nation and, hence, the structure and performance of its innovation system.

The issue of entrepreneurship, capabilities and the role of institutions are addressed in an empirical study of Wim Swaan. Departing from the distinction between codified and tacit knowledge, he explains that competitiveness of countries largely depends on the existence of institutions which facilitate entrepreneurs to create capabilities and to develop tacit knowledge. The character of the process of industrialisation and the nature of the organisations created and evolved in the past, can be such that the necessary capabilities and tacit knowledge do not become available. In discussing the case of Hungary the initial conditions of a centrally planned economy, as well as the nature of the reforms, are held responsible by Wim Swaan for the lack of cooperation between innovative firms necessary for developing new tacit skills. Based on data from the World Competiveness Report the position of Hungary is compared with other post–socialist countries and countries with a comparable level of development in Asia. The hypothesis that the knowledge structures are closely related to the institutions of the economic systems is confirmed by his findings. The creation of structures that favour tacit knowledge is not only an issue of investments in financial and physical capital, but first of all an issue of getting the institutions and the mentality of the entrepreneurs right.

Vanessa Oltra discusses the implications of the evolutionary approach for technology policy. Oltra first examines what policy objectives are suggested by the evolutionary approach. The evolutionary approach urges policy makers to look beyond the typical neoclassical objective of devising optimal research incentives. With its emphasis on technological trajectories and (potential) lock–in effects the evolutionary approach also draws the attention of policy makers to support innovation processes and to act upon selection mechanisms respectively. Secondly, Oltra argues that another implication of the evolutionary approach is that it implies limits to the capabilities of policy makers to attain these objectives. The notions that are central to the evolutionary approach, such as bounded rationality, (adaptive) learning and imitation, also apply to policy makers. Policy makers are themselves as much part of and subject to selection mechanisms as firms and other economic agents. This brings Oltra to her third and last point: technology, industrial structure and technology policy co–evolve. Technology policy sets the basic conditions for technological development, but is in turn itself (after some time lag) also conditioned by technological and industrial developments.

NOTES

1. In Darwin's account not two but three conditions have to be met in order for natural selection to work: variety, inheritance and selection. It can be (and has been) argued that in economics a plausible analogue of inheritance is hard to come by. Although there seems to be an increasing number of evolutionary economists backing away from searching rough–and–ready analogues,

we still believe that it is instructive to analyse work in evolutionary economics in terms of variety and selection.

2. It is also understood, however, that the equilibria evolutionary processes may converge and need not be stable, efficient or unique. Especially in the latter case (of multiple equilibria), it can be argued that attention need to be payed to the details (or 'history') of the evolutionary process even if the theoretical focus is exclusively on the operation of the selection mechanism.

3. In cultural and socio-economic evolution a complication is that the two mechanisms do not seem to operate independently from each other. Unlike Darwinian biological evolution, in which the working of the variety–generating (mutation) mechanism is believed to be unrelated to that of the selection mechanism, selection results seem to affect the emergence of new variety in socio-economic evolution.

REFERENCES

Alchian, A.A. (1950), 'Uncertainty, Evolution, and Economic Theory', *Journal of Political Economy*, 58, 211–221.

Campbell, J.L. (1995), 'Mechanisms of Evolutionary Change in Economic Governance: Interaction, Interpretation and Bricolage', in *Economics and Path Dependency*, L. Magnusson and J. Ottoson (eds.), Aldershot: Edward Elgar.

Campbell, J.L. and L.N. Lindberg, (1991), 'The Evolution of Governance Regimes', in *Governance of the American Economy*, J.L. Campbell, J. Rogers Hollingsworth and L.N. Lindberg (eds.), Cambridge: Cambridge University Press.

Dawkins, R. (1976), *The Selfish Gene*, Oxford: Oxford University Press.

Delorme, R. (1997), 'Evolution et Complexité: l'Apport de la Complexité de Second Ordre à l'Economie Évolutionnaire', in *Economie Appliqué*, no. 3, 95–120.

Denzau, A.T. and D.C. North (1994), 'Shared Mental Models: Ideologies and Institutions', *Kyklos*, 47, 3–30.

Dosi, G., C. Freeman, R.R. Nelson, G. Silverberg and L. Soete (eds.) (1988), *Technical Change and Economic Theory*, London: Pinter.

Friedman, M. (1953), *Essays in Positive Economics*, Chicago: University of Chicago Press.

Groenewegen, J. and J.J.Vromen (1996), 'A Case for Theoretical Pluralism', in *Transaction Cost Economics and Beyond*, J. Groenewegen ed., Kluwer Academic Publishers, 365–378.

Marengo, L. and M. Willinger (1997), 'Alternative Methodologies for Modelling Evolutionary Dynamics: Introduction', *Journal of Evolutionary Economics*, 7, 331–338.

Maynard Smith, J. (1982), *Evolution and the Theory of Games*, Cambridge: Cambridge University Press.

Nelson, R.R. and S.G. Winter (1982), *An Evolutionary Theory of Economic Change*, Cambridge: Belknap Press of Harvard University Press.

North, D. (1990), *Institutions, Institutional Change and Economic Performance*, Cambridge: Cambridge University Press.

Saviotti, P. and S. Metcalfe (eds.) (1991), *Evolutionary Theories of Economic and Technological Change*, Chur/Reading: Harwood Academic Publishers.

Sober, E. (1983), *The Nature of Selection*, Cambridge: MIT Press.

Vromen, J.J. (1997), 'Evolutionary Economics: Precursors, Paradigmatic, Propositions,

Puzzles and Prospects', in J. Reijnders (ed.), *Economics and Evolution*, Cheltenham: Edward Elgar.

Weibull, J. (1995), *Evolutionary Game Theory*, Cambridge: MIT Press.

Winter, S.G. (1987), 'Comments on Arrow and Lucas', in R.M. Hogarth and M.W. Reder (eds.), *Rational Choice: The Contrast Between Economics and Psychology*, Chicago: University of Chicago Press, 243–250.

2. What Economists Can Learn From Evolutionary Theorists – and Vice Versa

Paul Krugman

I am interested in issues of evolutionary economics partly because my research work has taken me to some of the edges of the neoclassical paradigm. When you are concerned, as I have been, with situations in which increasing returns are crucial, you must drop the assumption of perfect competition; you are also forced to abandon the belief that market outcomes are necessarily optimal, or indeed that the market can be said to maximise anything. You can still believe in maximising individuals and some kind of equilibrium, but the complexity of the situations in which your imaginary agents find themselves often obliges you – and presumably them – to represent their behaviour by some kind of *ad hoc* rule, rather than as the outcome of a carefully specified maximum problem. You are often driven by sheer force of modelling necessity to think of the economy as having at least vaguely 'evolutionary' dynamics, in which initial conditions and accidents along the way may determine where you end up. In working on issues of economic geography, I only found out after I had worked on the models for some time, that I was using 'replicator dynamics' to discuss the problem of economic change.

A second reason I want to contribute to a volume on evolutionary economics is that I am what we might call an 'evolution groupie'. That is, I spend a great deal of time reading what evolutionary biologists write – not only the more popular volumes but also the textbooks and, most recently, some of the professional articles. I have even tried to talk to some of the biologists, which in this age of narrow specialisation is a major effort. My interest in evolution is partly recreation; but it is also true that I find in evolutionary biology a useful vantage point from which to view my own speciality in a new perspective. The point is that both the parallels and the differences between economics and evolutionary biology help me at least to understand what I am doing when I do economics – to get, to be pompous about it, a new perspective on the epistemology of the two fields.

I am sure that I am not unique either in my interest in biology, or in my feeling that we economists have something to learn from it. Indeed, I am sure that many members of the 'European Association for Evolutionary Political Economy' (EAEPE) know far more about evolutionary theory than I do. But I may have one special distinction. Most economists who try to apply evolutionary concepts start from some deep dissatisfaction with economics as it is. I will not say that I am entirely happy with the state of economics. But let us be honest: I have done very well within the world of conventional economics. I have pushed the envelope, but not broken it, and have received very widespread acceptation for my ideas. What this means is that I may have more sympathy for standard economics than most of the members of EAEPE. My criticisms are those of someone who loves the field and has seen that affection repaid. I do not know if that makes me morally better or worse than someone who criticises from outside, but anyway it makes me different.

SISTER FIELDS

If you are familiar with economics and start reading evolutionary biology in earnest – and presumably vice versa – you quickly realise that these are sister fields. They actually have a remarkable amount in common, not only in terms of the kind of questions they ask and the methods they use, but in terms of the way they relate to and are perceived by the rest of the world.

To begin with, there is the similarity in the basic approach. Let me give you my own personal definition of the basic method of economic theory. To me, it seems that what we know as economics is the study of those phenomena that can be understood as emerging from the interactions among intelligent, self–interested individuals. Notice that there are really four parts to this definition. Let us read from right to left.

1. Economics is about what individuals do: not classes, but individual actors. This is not to deny the relevance of higher levels of analysis, but they must be grounded in individual behaviour. Methodological individualism is of the essence.

2. The individuals are self–interested.
3. The individuals are intelligent: obvious opportunities for gain are not neglected. Hundred dollar bills do not lie around in the street for very long.
4. We are concerned with the interaction of such individuals: most interesting economic theory, from supply and demand on, is about 'invisible hand' processes in which the collective outcome is not what individuals intended.

That is what economics is about. What is evolutionary theory about?

The answer basically, is that evolutionists share three of the four concerns. Their field is about the interaction of self–interested individuals – who are often thought of as organisms 'trying' to leave as many offspring as possible, but which are in some circumstances best thought of as genes trying to propagate as many copies of themselves as possible. The main difference between evolutionary theory and economics is that while economists routinely suppose that the agents in their models are very smart about finding the best strategy – and an economist is always defensive about any model in which agents are assumed to act with less than perfect rationality – evolutionists have no qualms about assuming myopic behaviour. Indeed, myopia is of the essence in their view.

My point is that because the basic methods are similar, if not identical, economics and evolutionary theory are surprisingly similar. It is often asserted that economic theory draws its inspiration from physics, and that it should become more like biology. If that is what you think, you should do two things. First, read a text on evolutionary theory, like John Maynard Smith's 'Evolutionary Genetics'. You will be startled at how much it looks like a textbook on microeconomics. Second, try to explain a simple economic concept, like supply and demand, to a physicist. You will discover that our whole style of theorising, of building up aggregative stories from individual decisions, is not at all the way they think.

So there is a close affinity in method and indeed of style between economics and evolution. But there is another interesting parallel: both economics and evolution are model–oriented, algebra–heavy subjects that are the subject of intense interest from people who cannot stand algebra. As a result in each case it is very important to distinguish between the field as it is perceived by outsiders (and portrayed in popular books) and what it is really like. We all know that economics is a field in which the most famous authors are often people who are regarded, with good reason, as not even worth arguing with by almost everyone in the profession.   Do you remember that global best–seller The Coming Great Depression of 1990 by Ravi Batra? And I guess it is no secret that even John Kenneth Galbraith, the public's idea of a great economist, looks to most serious economists like an intellectual dilettante. Well, the same is true in evolution.

I am not sure how well this is known. I have read some evolutionary economics and was particularly curious about what biologists people reference. What I encountered were quite a few references to Stephen Jay Gould, hardly any to other evolutionary theorists. Now it is not very hard to find out, if you spend a little while reading in evolution, that Gould is the John Kenneth Galbraith of his subject. That is, he is a wonderful writer who is beloved by literary intellectuals and lionised by the media because he does not use algebra or difficult jargon. Unfortunately, it appears that he avoids these sins not because he has transcended his colleagues, but because he does not seem to understand what they have to say. His own descriptions of what the field is about – not just the answers, but even the questions – are consistently misleading. His impressive literary and historical erudition makes his work seem profound to most readers, but informed readers may even conclude that there is nothing there. (Yes, there is some resentment of his fame: in the field the unjustly famous theory of 'punctuated equilibrium', in which Gould and Niles Eldredge asserted that evolution proceeds not steadily but in short bursts of rapid change, is known as 'evolution by jerks'.)

What is rare in the evolutionary economics literature, at least as far as I can tell, is references to the theorists the practitioners themselves regard as great men – to people like George Williams, William Hamilton, or John Maynard Smith. This is serious, because if you think that Gould's ideas represent the cutting edge of evolutionary theory (as I myself did until about a year and a half ago), you have an almost completely misguided view of where the field is and even of what the issues are.

This is important, because it is at least my impression that what economists who like to use 'evolutionary' concepts expect from evolution is often based on what they imagine evolutionary theory to be like, not on what it is actually like. Conversely, you learn a lot about why conventional economics looks the way it does by seeing how evolutionary theorists have been driven to some of the same positions.

To explain these rather cryptic remarks, let me briefly say what – it seems to me, but I am happy to be corrected – economists think an evolutionary approach can give us, then about what evolutionists seem to be saying in practice.

What do evolutionary economists want? I do not think that there are many economists, even among the unconventionally minded, who would quarrel seriously with my basic definition of economics as concerning the interactions among intelligent, self–interested individuals. I guess a Marxist would have problems with the whole idea of methodological individualism, and a Galbraithian would have problems with the idea that self–interest can be used without taking into account the ability of advertisers and so forth to shape preferences. But such quarrels apart, I would guess that we do not have much difference with the basic statement.

Where the dissatisfaction sets in is with how we implement the first two terms in my four–part program. Yes, of course economics is about interaction, and the agents are intelligent; but exactly how intelligent are they, and what is the nature of the their interaction?

For there is no question that conventional economics has gone beyond the general ideas of intelligence and interaction to a much harder–edged, extreme formulation. At least since Paul Samuelson published his 'Foundations of Economic Analysis' in 1947, the overwhelming thrust of conventional theory has been to say that agents are not only intelligent, but they maximise – that is, they chose the best of all feasible alternatives. When they interact, we assume that what they do is achieve an equilibrium, in which each individual is doing the best he can given that which all the others are doing.

Now anyone who looks at the world knows that these are extreme and unrealistic assumptions. Markets are generally not in equilibrium. So can't we get away from the maximisation–and–equilibrium approach to something more realistic?

Well, as I understand it, that is what evolutionary economies is all about. In particular, evolution–minded economists seem to want the following:

1. They want to get away from the idea that individuals maximise. Instead, they want to represent decisions as the result of some process of groping through alternatives, a process in which it may take a long time to get to a maximum – and in which the maximum you find may well be local rather than global.

2. They want to get away from the notion of equilibrium. In particular they want to have an approach in which things are always in disequilibrium, in which the economy is always evolving. Latterly there have also been

some economists who want to merge evolutionary ideas with the Schumpeterian notion that the economy proceeds via waves of 'creative destruction'.

Now as I understand it, evolutionary economists basically believe that an evolutionary approach will satisfy these desires. After all, real organisms often look to the discerning eye like works in progress – they are full of features that fall short of that which would adapt them perfectly to their environment, that is, they have not really maximised their fitness. They also often seem to be stuck on local maxima: dolphins may look like fish, but they still need to surface for air. Meanwhile, what is evolution but a process of continual change, which has taken us from microbes to man? And if you are a reader of Gould and his acolytes, you have the sense that evolution proceeds through spasms of sudden change that seem positively Schumpeterian in their drama.

So the attractiveness of an evolutionary metaphor – especially if you believe that economics has got off on the wrong track by basing itself on physics – is understandable. But before we get too carried away with the prospects for an evolutionary revolution, we had better look at what the evolutionists themselves really do.

WHAT EVOLUTIONARY THEORY IS REALLY LIKE

To read the real thing in evolution – to read, say, John Maynard Smith's 'Evolution and the Theory of Games', or William Hamilton's new book of collected papers 'Narrow Roads in Gene Land', is a startling experience to someone whose previous idea of evolution comes from magazine articles and popular books. The field does not look at all like the stories. What it does look like, to a remarkable degree, is neoclassical economics. It offers very little comfort to those who want a refuge from the harsh discipline of maximisation and equilibrium.

Consider first the question of maximisation. Clearly it is a crucial point about evolution that it must proceed by small steps, which imply that maxima must be approached only gradually and that you could easily be trapped on a merely local maximum. But do these observations actually play a large role in evolutionary theory? No, not really.

Look, for example, at William Hamilton's deeply influential paper 'The genetical evolution of social behaviour'. In the first part of that paper he introduces a model of population dynamics and shows that a gene will tend to spread if it enhances not an organism's individual fitness, but its 'inclusive fitness': a weighted sum of the fitness of all the individual's relatives, with the weights proportional to their closeness of relationships (an alternative way to think of this is to think of the gene spreading if it is good for its own fitness, never mind the organisms it lives in; this is the theme of Richard Dawkins's book 'The Selfish Gene'). Now Hamilton's derivation concerns process – it is a dynamic story about in which direction the next small step will proceed. But when it comes to the second part, in which he uses the idea to discuss the real world – why birds expose themselves to predators by warning their neighbours, why insects have such massively organised societies – he simply assumes that what we actually see can be viewed as the culmination of that process, that the creatures we see have already maximised. In short, even though evolution is necessarily a process of small changes, evolutionary theorists normally take the shortcut of assuming that the process gets you to the maximum, and pay surprisingly little attention to the dynamics along the way.

What about the possibility of being trapped in local maxima? Well, this is a big concern for some theorists, like the Santa Fe Institute's Stuart Kauffman – but Kauffman is not a central player in the field. The general attitude of evolutionary theorists seems to be that Nature can often find surprising pathways to places you would have thought unreachable by small steps; that over a few hundred thousand generations a slightly light–sensitive patch of skin can become an eye that appears to be perfectly designed, or a jaw–bone can migrate around and become a piece of exquisitively sensitive sound–detection equipment. This is the theme of Richard Dawkins' new book 'Climbing Mount Improbable'. It is also, if I understand it, the point of what philosopher Daniel Dennet calls 'Leslie Gelb's Second Law: Evolution is smarter than you are' (alternative version, according to Dennett: 'Evolution is smarter than Leslie Gelb').

In practice, then, evolutionary theorists generally end up assuming that organisms (or genes, when that is the more useful perspective) do maximise; the process, the necessary caveat that they must get wherever they are going by small steps, gets put to one side.

What about equilibrium? To outsiders it appears that evolutionary theory must be a theory of continuing, progressive change. In Stephen Jay Gould's latest book is an argument against the supposed orthodoxy that evolution must be a matter of continuing progress toward ever–higher levels of complexity. But who defends that orthodoxy? The really amazing thing I have found when reading evolutionary theory is how little they talk about evolution as an ongoing process. Instead, they tend to try to explain what we see as the result of a finished process, in which each species has adapted fully to its environment – an environment that includes both other members of its own species and members of other species. It is revealing that the title of the classic book by George Williams – which is often credited with a seminal role in modern evolutionary theory – a book that essentially established the principle that social behaviour should be explained in terms of the self–interest of genes – is 'Adaptation and Natural Selection'. 'Evolution' isn't in the title, and certainly not in the text if it is taken to mean some kind of inexorable drive toward greater perfection. The working assumption of Williams and most other evolutionary theorists, at least as far as I can tell, is that we should model the natural world not as being on the way, but as being already there.

The most telling example of this preference is the widespread use of John Maynard Smith's concept of 'evolutionary stable strategies' (ESS). An ESS is first best strategy for an organism to follow given the strategies that all others are following – the strategy that maximises fitness given that everyone else is maximising fitness, with each taking the others' strategies into account. Does this sound familiar? It should: the concept of an ESS is virtually indistinguishable from an economist's concept of equilibrium.

By the way: Maynard Smith's textbook is explicitly sceptical of claims that evolution is necessarily an ongoing process, let alone that it need have any particular direction. Not only do the models normally settle down to an equilibrium, so do experiments, for example with DNA evolution. Any evolutionist has got to be aware that life appears to have stayed happily single–celled for several billion years before something led to the next big step.

Now one can understand why I say that a textbook in evolution reads so much like a textbook in microeconomics. At a deep level, they share the same method: explain behaviour in terms of an equilibrium among maximising individuals.

But why does evolutionary theory in practice fail to take advantage, if we can call it that, either of the myopia or of the dynamics inherent in every evolutionary story?

WHY EVOLUTIONISTS DO NOT DO EVOLUTION

What I have argued to this point is that even though evolution is a theory of gradual change, of myopic dynamics, in practice most evolutionary theory focuses on the presumed end result of such dynamics: an equilibrium in which individuals maximise their fitness given what other individuals do. Why should the theory have taken this turn?

The answer is surely the ever–present need to simplify, to make models that are comprehensible. The fact is that maximisation and equilibrium are astonishingly powerful ways to cut through what might otherwise be forbidding complexity – and evolutionary theorists have, entirely correctly, been willing to adopt the useful fiction that individuals are at their maximum and that the system is in equilibrium.

An example. One of William Hamilton's papers, an attempt to explain why some animals form vast herds, imagines a group of frogs sitting at the edge of a circular pond, from which a snake may emerge – and he supposes that the snake will grab and eat the nearest frog. Where will the frogs sit? To compress his argument, Hamilton points out that if there are two groups of frogs around the pool, each group has an equal chance of being targeted, and so does each frog within each group – which means that the chance of being eaten is less if you are a frog in the larger group. Thus if you are a frog trying to maximise your chance of survival, you will want to be part of the larger group, and the equilibrium must involve clumping of all the frogs as close together as possible.

Notice what is missing from this analysis. Hamilton does not talk about the evolutionary dynamics by which frogs might acquire a sit–with–the–other–frogs instinct; he does not take us through the intermediate steps along the evolutionary path in which frogs had not yet completely 'realised' that they should stay with the herd. Why not? Because to do so would involve him in enormous complications that are basically irrelevant to his point, whereas leapfrogging straight over these difficulties to look at the equilibrium, in which frogs maximise their chances given what the other frogs do, is a very parsimonious, sharp–edged way of gaining insight.

Some people would say that this kind of creation of useful fictions is a thing of the past because now we can study complex dynamics using computer simulation. But anyone who has tried that sort of thing – and I have at great length – eventually realises just what a wonderful tool paper–and–pencil analysis based on maximalisation and equilibrium really is.

By all means let us use simulation to push out the boundaries of our understanding, but just running a lot of simulations and seeing what happens is a frustrating and fully unproductive exercise unless you can somehow create a 'model of the model' that lets you understand what is going on.

I could multiply examples here, but I think the point is clear. Evolutionary theorists, even though they have a framework that fundamentally tells them that you cannot safely assume maximisation–and–equilibrium, make use of maximisation and equilibrium as modelling devices – as useful fictions about the world that allow them to cut through the complexities. Evolutionists have found these fictions so useful that they dominate analysis in evolution almost as completely as the same fictions dominate economic theory.

I just said that these fictions dominate economics. But the question in economics is whether we understand that they are fictions, rather than deep–seated truths.   For there, perhaps, is where economists have something to learn from evolutionists.

In economics we often use the term 'neoclassical' either as a way to praise or to damn our opponents.   Personally, I consider myself a proud neoclassicist.   By this I clearly do not mean that I believe in perfect competition all the way. What I mean is that I prefer, when I can, to make sense of the world using models in which individuals maximise and the interaction of these individuals can be summarised by some concept of equilibrium. The reason I like that kind of model is not that I believe it to be literally true, but that I am intensely aware of the power of maximisation–and–equilibrium to organise one's thinking and I have seen the propensity of those who try to do economics, without those organising devices, to produce sheer nonsense when they imagine they themselves are free from some confining orthodoxy.

That said, there are indeed economists who regard maximisation and equilibrium as more than useful fictions. They regard them either as literal truths – which I find a bit hard to understand given the reality of daily experience – or as principles so central to economics that one dare not bend them even a little, no matter how useful it might seem to do so.

To be fair, there is some justification in the insistence of some economists on pushing very hard on the principles of equilibrium and in particular of maximisation. After all, people are smarter than genes. If I offer a model in which people seem to be passing up some opportunity for gain, you may justifiably ask me why they do not just take it. Unlike the case of genes, the argument that the alternative is quite different from what my imagined agent is currently doing is not necessarily a very good one: in the real world people do sometimes respond to opportunities by changing their behaviour drastically. In biology purely local change is a sacred principle. In economics it has no comparable justification.

And yet I think that despite the differences, it would be better if economists were more self–aware, if they understood that their use of maximisation–and– equilibrium, like that of evolutionary biologists is an useful fiction rather than a principle to be defended at all costs. If we were more modest about what we think our modelling strategy is doing, we might free ourselves to accommodate more of the world in our analysis.

Let me conclude by giving two examples of how a more relaxed, 'evolution'– style approach to economics might help us out.

TWO ECONOMIC EXAMPLES

One of my areas of research has been the study of economic geography. Perhaps the most basic insight in these models has been the possibility of a cumulative process of agglomeration. Suppose there are two regions, and one region starts with a slightly larger concentration of industry. This concentration of industry will provide larger markets and better sources of supply for producers than in the other region, perhaps inducing more producers to locate, in that region, further reinforcing its advantage, and so on. It is a good story, and I am quite sure that in some sense it is correct. Yet when I and my students try to present this work, we often run into a surprising difficulty: theorists get very upset about the dynamics.

Why, they ask, don't individuals correctly anticipate the future location of industry? How can you have such a model without forward–looking agents and rational expectations?

Now the fact is that when you try to do rational expectations in such models they become vastly more difficult, and the basic point becomes obscured. In short, here is a situation in which going all the way to full maximising behaviour – and trying to avoid the disequilibrium, evolutionary dynamics I assume – makes life harder, not easier. It seems to me, at least, that this is a situation where economists would do a better job if they understood that maximisation is a metaphor to be used only to the extent that it helps understanding.

When I run into this sort of critique I am envious of evolutionary theorists who create models like, say, the Fisher theory of runaway sexual selection, and can use myopic, disequilibrium dynamics without apology. (If you don't know that model, it works like this: suppose that there is one gene that makes female peacocks like males with big tails, and another that causes males to have big tails. If there is a preponderance of females that carry this gene, then males with big tails will have more offspring even if they have less chance of surviving because of their visibility to predators. But because a male with a big tail is likely to be the son of a female who likes big tails, this success will also tend to spread the gene for big–tail preference .... The resemblance to agglomeration is obvious.)

Another issue. Consider the question of whether and how monetary policy has real effects. In the end this comes down to whether prices are sticky in nominal terms. In my view there is overwhelming evidence that they are, but many economists reject such evidence on principle: a rational price–setter ought not to have money illusion, therefore it is bad economics to assume that they do. If neo–Keynesians like me suggest that a bit of bounded rationality would do the trick, the answer is that bounded rationality is too open–ended a concept, and can be used to rationalise too many different behaviours.

Yet in evolution the idea that there are limits to the precision of maximisation is adopted cheerfully. When a bird sees a predator, it issues a warning cry that puts itself at risk but may save its neighbours. The reason this behaviour 'works', we believe, is that many of those neighbours are likely to be relatives, and thus the bird may enhance its 'inclusive fitness'. But why doesn't the bird issue a warning only its relatives can hear? Well, we just suppose that is not possible.

In short, I believe that economics would be a more productive field if we learned something important from evolutionists: that models are metaphors, and that we should use them, not the other way around.

REFERENCES

Batra, R. (1987), *The Coming Great Depression of 1990*, New York: Simon and Schuster.

Dawkins, R. (1976), *The Selfish Gene*, Oxford: Oxford University Press.

Eldredge, N. (1989), *Life Pulse: Episodes from the Story of the Fossil Record*, Harmondsworth: Penquin Books.

Gould, S.J. (1998), *The Fractious of Life*, New York: Academy of Sciences.

Hamilton, W.D. (1964), 'The Genetical Evolution of Social Behaviour, I and II', *Journal of Theoretical Biology* 7: 1–32.

Maynard Smith, J. (1982), *Evolution and the Theory of Games*, Cambridge: Cambridge University Press.

————(1989), *Evolutionary Genetics*, Oxford: Oxford University Press.

Williams, G. (1974), *Adaptation and Natural Selection: A Critique of Some Current Evolutionary Thought*, Princeton/London: Princeton University Press.

3. Discontinuous Changes in Institutional Systems

Ernesto Screpanti[*]

INTRODUCTION

Often the evolution of institutions does not occur smoothly. Sometimes change is dramatic and abrupt. When this happens, many institutions are abandoned all together and substituted by new sets of rules and habits, thus giving rise to morphogenetic processes. In this chapter a model of catastrophic change is developed which seems suitable for application to different cases of social morphogenesis.

First an evolutionary theory of institutions is summarily presented. Reference is made to an approach which is now becoming a tradition, although it grew as a heterodox flight from neoclassical institutionalism, and whose theoretical foundations have been laid down by Simon (1955, 1957), Loasby (1976), Earl (1983), Heiner (1983), Hodgson (1988), Hargreaves Heap (1989), Sjöstrand (1992), Tool (1995), to mention just a few.

The schematic rundown follows, where the bare bones of a theory of institutional change are displayed. In the next paragraph the notion of 'institutional system' is introduced as defining a set of closely knit institutions. Then it is argued that institutional systems pose a fundamental problem to the theory of change, namely that of the impossibility of modifying an institution independently of the others which are structurally linked to it. After that catastrophe theory is used to construct a model of morphogenesis of institutional systems.[1] The model is very general and is

---

[*] Without bearing any responsibility, Bruno Dallago, Shaun Hargreaves Heap, Marc Tool and an anonymous referee deserve my warmest thanks for their comments on an earlier draft of this chapter.

developed without referring it to any particular application. In subsequent paragraphs, however, two examples are offered of how the model can be applied. The first deals with the 'revolution of 1989' in Eastern Europe, the second with the Schumpeterian account of the tendency of major technological innovations to occur in clusters. Finally the conclusions suggest some ways in which this model of the modality of change can be completed to explain the causes too.

A RUNDOWN OF THE THEORY OF INSTITUTIONS AND INDIVIDUAL BEHAVIOUR

The theory of institutions followed in this chapter[2] aims at explaining both the role of institutions in constraining individual behaviour and that of individual action in sustaining the process of institutional evolution. It is based on the argument that individual behaviour can be accounted for on the ground of three behavioural criteria.

The first is the criterion of institutional compliance. In conditions of bounded rationality and incomplete information the individuals, in order to simplify decisions, conform to existing institutions. Individual awareness is not required: agents are not assumed to apply a rational calculus any time they comply with an institution. However, to avoid the risk of annihilation of the individual as a rational agent, 'the principle of institutional incompleteness' is assumed, which states that no institution is able completely to determine behaviour. Institutions only play the role of narrowing the field of options among which individuals can take decisions.

Therefore with the decision–maker who complies with an institution there always remains some, though simplified, problem–solving activity to carry out. This result necessitates a second behavioural criterion, called 'conditional improvement'. It states that, within the field of action left open by an institution, individuals undertake some problem–solving activity in the attempt to improve their situation or at least not worsen it. It is assumed that all individuals are endowed with subjective evaluators (Egidi, 1992) by means of which they assess an improvement. Evaluators are subjective in the sense that they can be different in different individuals, and are firmly ingrained in the individuals' knowledge. The criterion of conditional improvement does not necessarily lead the decision–makers to the best solution for any given problem, either on the basis of an abstract principle of evaluation such as for example the maximisation principle, or on the basis of the very evaluators adopted by the decision–makers themselves. In fact the criterion states only that the decision–makers will put an end to the problem solving activity when a solution has been found that makes them feel better. This happens because the problem solving activity, although simplified by institutions, remains a time consuming one. The criterion of conditional improvement restores the individual to his position of an agent endowed with rationality, although a limited one.

Many students acknowledge that institutions, not only directly affect individual behaviour, but also produce deeper influences on cultural endowments and therefore on the formation of preferences and cognitive maps (Hodgson, 1988) – a fact that could lead to embarrassing results and to the adoption of too weak an ontology of the social being as a subject deprived of all autonomy of decision and ability of purposeful action. The risk of many contemporary approaches to institutions is that of jumping out of the frying pan of individualist reductionism into the fire of holistic metaphysics. This can be avoided, though, by resorting to a hypothesis put forward by Hodgson (1984, 1988) and known as the principle of impurity or institutional plurality. The idea is that in any given historical context many alternative institutions exist which are capable of satisfying a specific institutional need. Therefore the influence of institutions on cultural endowments is not univocal, so that human preferences are not totally prescribed by the institutional environment. The individual has some possibility of choice in the determination of preferences. Obviously it is a limited autonomy, for it is defined as relative to the historical and institutional context in which the individual lives. But it is sufficient to prevent social atoms from becoming cogs in a machine. If individuals can choose goals and subjective evaluators, albeit from a narrow range of possibilities, the actions they perform through their compliance with institutions could turn out to be truly purposeful.

These considerations lead us to formulate a third behavioural criterion, called 'institutional revision': when the compliance with a given institution produces a worsening of the situation, the individual is induced to abandon the old institution and to conform to another one or to follow a non–institutionalised behaviour.

HOW DOES AN INSTITUTION CHANGE?

Behaviour constrained by institutional compliance is of the precautionary kind. The definition of tolerance or reservation thresholds is always associated with it. The thresholds can take the form of reservation prices or premiums, and can be adopted even unwittingly. In fact the individuals may be unaware of a tolerance threshold, as long as an institution works, i.e. as long as the problem–solving activity allowed by the institution enables them at least not to feel worse off. However, when such worsening occurs the threshold may become evident. The magnitude of a tolerance threshold represents a sort of minimum level of satisfaction and is an increasing function of the goals or aspirations an individual associates with an institution complied with.

Reservation thresholds and aspirations are social variables, in the sense that they depend strongly on social conventions. At the same time, however, they are behavioural properties that vary among individuals. This is not a contradiction. In fact what happens in reality is that different individuals who comply with a given institution might have different aspirations and reservation thresholds; but, due to the social character of those benchmarks, that variability is never so wide. Furthermore the aspirations of many interacting individuals, and therefore their reservation thresholds, usually tend to vary in the same direction.

The trespassing of a reservation threshold brings about the conditions for institutional revision, but may be insufficient to actually prompt the change. Besides the dissatisfaction caused by trespassing the threshold, the perception of the costs of change also affect the decision to revise an institution. Many such costs are psychological in nature, like risk aversion or the fear of a punitive reaction of the social environment. Other kinds of costs may have a more tangible economic nature. Just consider the cost of the investment necessary to set going an institutional innovation, or the losses associated with sunk costs.[3]

Also with the costs of change it is not necessary for their perception to be completely mindful, at least until the decision to change is knowingly pondered, nor is it necessary for costs to be obtained as the result of a precise cost-benefit calculation. However, once the possibility of changing is examined, individuals tend to take on a more calculating attitude.

The satisfaction of an individual with respect to a given institution is measured as the difference between the real achievements obtained through that institution and the reservation threshold associated with it.

Dissatisfaction occurs when that difference is negative. It can be measured as the modulus of the difference. When there is dissatisfaction, individuals start considering the possibility of institutional revision. They decide to carry on with the revision when the degree of dissatisfaction is over and above the cost of change. Frustration is defined as the difference between dissatisfaction and the cost of change. It does not depend only on dissatisfaction. It is also affected by the perception of the ability or possibility to overcome dissatisfaction, that is to say by the perceived costs of change. The higher these costs, given the degree of dissatisfaction, the more resigned will an individual be – and the more resigned the less frustrated. The term 'frustration' is here used to define a psychological experience that predisposes an individual to take on a more innovative or revolutionary mood, a mental feeling which is abated by the perception of a high cost of change.[4] An institution is actually abandoned when the degree of frustration is positive.

The simple abandonment of an old institution on the part of an individual and the adoption of a new form of behaviour does not necessarily imply institutional change. In fact, if the new kind of behaviour is an innovation, it is not a form of institutionalised behaviour by definition. However, if it produces satisfaction, it could be imitated by other individuals. In this way a diffusion process is set in motion that could result in the creation of a new institution when the new kind of behaviour has become habitual for a sizeable mass of individuals. It need not be the totality, nor even the majority, of the members of a given social system. It may happen that two or more alternative kinds of behaviour are adopted by different masses of individuals. In this case a certain behavioural sphere is characterised by institutional plurality. This process of institutional change is called 'change by diffusion'. It involves prevalently habits, or institutions in the sense of Veblen.

On the other hand, a different process of change applies to rules, or institutions in the sense of Commons, a process which is called 'change by deliberation'. A rule that binds all the individuals belonging to a social system can only be modified or abolished by deliberation, and this requires the formation of a collective will. When a rule is abolished, it automatically ceases to bind, so that it is not possible for two or more alternative rules to regulate a social relation in a given institutional sphere. There cannot be institutional plurality with social rules in a given system.

The link between satisfaction or frustration and behavioural change is not so direct as it might seem at first sight; for the former are mental feelings whilst the latter is an act; and an act implies the formation of a 'will'. That link is normally mediated by 'moods'. These are the attitudes individuals entertain toward the existing institutions and take the form of propensities to stick to them or to change them. Moods can appear in various degrees of intensity, but, since the problem is whether to change or not, they can be divided into two opposing kinds, namely 'conservative' and 'revolutionary' moods. Although the relationship that links them to the degree of satisfaction or frustration is difficult to define with any precision, it seems sensible to assume it is a homeomorphism.[5] In other words, moods tend to become conservative when satisfaction prevails, and the more intensely so the higher the degree of satisfaction, whilst they tend to become revolutionary when frustration prevails. Then it could be said that the will to change is itself a homeomorphism of moods: individuals decide to change when the existing situation gives rise to a degree of frustration that induces the formation of revolutionary moods.

If both the relationship between the will and the moods and that between the moods and the degrees of satisfaction or frustration are homeomorphisms, any consideration about the formation of the will and the moods becomes redundant from an analytical point of view, and one could legitimately jump from the degree of satisfaction to the act change. However this kind of shortcut is only allowed in the analysis of the change of a single institution, when it is reasonable to assume an individual can not feel simultaneously satisfied and frustrated. As it will be shown below, the possibility that satisfaction and frustration are felt simultaneously can no longer be excluded when sets of institutions, instead of single institutions, are considered. In this case the relationship between moods, satisfaction and frustration becomes somewhat blurred and can not be reduced to a trivial homeomorphism, so that due attention must be paid to the processes of formation of moods and collective wills.

INSTITUTIONAL SYSTEMS

An institutional system is a set of institutions structured in such a way that it is not possible, at least for a subset of them, to change one without changing many others. Let us call this subset 'institutional core', 'fundamental' or 'core institutions' those belonging to it and 'subsidiary institutions' those that can be changed without altering the core. Most institutions in modern societies are structured in system form. Organisations are institutional systems, political parties, firms, states etc. are all institutional systems, if production routines are considered as special forms of 'local' institutions, even a technology is an institutional system.

Institutional systems pose a fundamental problem to the theory of change: when some fundamental institutions produce frustration it is not possible to change them without changing the entire system. But if other institutions produce satisfaction the decision–makers confront a situation of decision conflict. An individual can obtain simultaneously satisfaction from some institutions and frustration from others. Which criterion will then be adopted to decide whether it is worthwhile changing the system? One might think that the impulse to change is sparked when the overall degree of frustration overcomes the overall degree of satisfaction. But things are not that easy in reality. First of all, it is unlikely that frustration and satisfaction carry the same weight for all individuals in prompting their willingness to change. Secondly, since it is social behaviour that is concerned, the formation of a collective will is required. And it is not to be expected that all individuals carry the same weight in the formation of the collective will.

An institutional system is associated with a set of individual aspirations and goals. To say it in a traditional way: any individual associates a preference set with a given institutional system; therefore a systemic change implies a metapreference choice (Frankfurt, 1971; Jeffrey, 1974; Sen, 1974, 1977; Hirschman, 1982). It is not necessary to assume that the metapreference set completely accounts for the change. In reality, individuals often change by abandoning routinised or habitual behaviour and adopting innovations; or they may abandon an institution or an institutional system without necessarily conforming to another institution or institutional system which is already known. Often the abandonment of old institutions sets off a process of search, innovation and diffusion of new forms of behaviour which may possibly and only slowly lead to the formation of new institutions. In other words it is possible that change occurs blindly or almost so. On the other hand, it is plausible that things happen in this way, if it is true that the proneness to change is mainly affected by push factors, i.e. by the degrees of frustration and satisfaction produced by the old institutions. Therefore the metapreference set may be incomplete to the point of admitting, *ex ante*, only the institutions complied with. All this does not pose problems though, since analysis is limited to the modality of change and not to its content.

THE MODEL

Let F represent 'systemic frustration' and S 'systemic satisfaction'. M measures 'moods', i.e. the individuals' inclination to systemic change. Moods govern the metapreference choices. If M0 defines 'neutral moods', $M > M0$ represents 'revolutionary moods' and $M < M0$ 'conservative moods'. Since this analysis is focused on the modalities of change rather than on its causes or contents, the terms 'conservative' and 'revolutionary', as they are used here, are devoid of any political implication: they just define an attitude or proneness to stick to the existing institutional system or to abandon it. Frustration and satisfaction are conflicting behavioural factors, which means that, given the degree of satisfaction, M increases with frustration, and, given the degree of frustration, M increases when satisfaction diminishes.

However frustration and satisfaction affect moods in different ways with different individuals. Let V (M;F,S) = VF,S (M) be a frequency distribution of moods. V is a collective moods function[6] parametrised on F and S. A family of such functions is represented in Figure 3.1. Consider the VF1,S1 distribution. It reveals how individuals are distributed over all values of moods when frustration and satisfaction are F1 and S1. It reaches a maximum at M1. This means that M1 represents the moods shared by the largest group of individuals, not necessarily the majority. If M0 represents neutral moods, VF1,S1 shows a collective distribution of sentiments in which conservative moods prevail. VF4,S4 on the contrary, exhibits a situation in which revolutionary moods prevail.

Figure 3.1 Change in collective sentiments

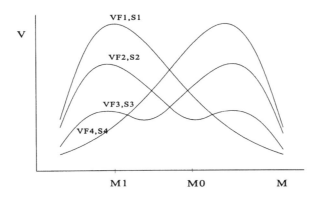

By applying a classification theorem of Thom (1969, 1972) and Mather (1969), we know that, if only two parameters exist, the V function cannot that public sentiments are divided, in the sense that public opinion is split into two consistent groups. One of them may be dominated by conservative moods and the other by revolutionary moods.

When F and S vary, the distribution of moods changes. Imagine a social dynamics in which, following a smooth variation of frustration and satisfaction, collective sentiments change wave–like, for example from VF1,S1 to VF4,S4 through VF2,S2 and VF3,S3 in Figure 3.1. In this example a conservative public opinion has gradually changed, first splitting into two opposing groups with a conservative prevalence (VF2,S2), then into two opposing groups with a revolutionary prevalence (VF3,S3) and finally unifying into a revolutionary attitude (VF4,S4).

The distribution of collective sentiments constitutes the motivational substratum that can lead to compliance with an institutional system or its change. An institutional change can take the form of a deliberate collective decision, such as when an election is required in order to change a constitution. But it can also take the form of a convergence of a mass of people on the adoption of a particular behavioural institution, such as when the establishment of a fashion leads to the diffusion of a social habit. For the moment it is not necessary to know whether the formation of a formal majority of consensuses is required. What is important to know is that a collective change presupposes the formation of a collective will. Since the choice consists in the decision to change or not, in order to obtain a clear expression of collective will it is necessary that a unique aggregation of moods be formed. In other words, the prevailing will must be unique and must be yes or no, even when moods are split into two great opposing aggregates. One of the two aggregates must succumb.

It is assumed that an aggregation 'force' is at work in public opinion that pushes individuals to adapt their will to one which gathers high support, i.e. the will of the modal individual. One could think, for example, that the tendency of some individuals to conform to the ideas of others with which they have similar sentiments, thereby producing a collective will that obtains the highest possible consensus. In this way a process of reciprocal influence would be at work in which individuals are induced to modify their opinions slightly as a consequence of the contacts they have with other individuals with similar opinions. There will then be a tendency for wills to aggregate around the moods that warrant the greatest number of contacts, i.e. the ones with the highest frequencies.[7]

To use an expressive mathematical locution, one could say that a 'force' is at work through the 'potential' of collective moods which leads to the formation of a collective will. The latter corresponds to the individual mood located at a maximum of the potential. In other words collective will, $\mathfrak{M}$, is governed by the gradient[8] of V. The collective wills corresponding to the different values of F and S are represented as manifold μ in Figure 3.2.

Figure 3.2 Formation of a collective will

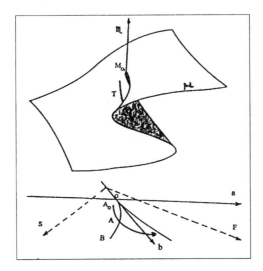

The points in which manifold μ folds down and up is the fold curve, whose projection onto the F–S plane is the 'cusp bifurcation set', B. Line b, which divides the F–S surface into two areas, is the 'Maxwell bifurcation set'. Finally line A represents an example of how behavioural factors F and S can change. T, its projection on manifold μ, identifies a trajectory of the collective will.

Let us observe what happens in this example. At time 0 the degrees of satisfaction and frustration are located by point A_0. The distribution of moods is unimodal and has a maximum at a level of moods lower than M_0. Collective will is dominated by conservative moods. With the passing of time both frustration and satisfaction increase along line A. At first, it is the rise in satisfaction that governs the formation of collective will in spite of an increase in frustration, a situation that persists as long as A remains outside the cusp bifurcation set, B. The increase in satisfaction overrules that of frustration and public opinion becomes more and more conservative. However when line A crosses the left arm of the cusp bifurcation set a relevant aggregate of revolutionary individuals appears on the stage. To these actors the effects of frustration surmount those of satisfaction. The distribution of moods becomes bimodal and public opinion splits into two prominent opposing parties. At any rate, as long as A remains on the left of set b the absolute maximum belongs to conservative moods, $\mathfrak{M} < M_0$. Then, when line b is crossed revolutionary moods prevail. Finally, when the right arm of set B is crossed, public opinion is again unified around a unique maximum, in which however $\mathfrak{M} > M_0$

Let us recall that manifold μ contains attractors and repulsors of the public opinion aggregation process. Attractors, which correspond to the maxima of the distribution function, are located in the blank sheets of the manifold; whilst repulsors, which correspond to the minima, are located in the shadowed sheet inside the fold curve.

The gradient that describes the process of formation of public opinion determines a fast dynamic process. Thus one could figure out the occurrence of rapid oscillations of collective moods that might be both deterministic and stochastic. There is no need to know anything more precise about these oscillations. Suffice it to know that outside the cusp bifurcation set they converge to manifold μ. This means that the sentiments dominating public opinion have a strength of attraction sufficient to overcome any disturbing event. Within the cusp bifurcation set, however, it is possible for a stochastic shock, even a small one, to succeed in dramatically displacing public opinion, since people are divided into two sizeable opposing parties. Graphically, an exogenous shock may move the value of $\mathfrak{M}$ from a point in the bottom blank sheet ($\mathfrak{M} < M_0$) of manifold μ to a point in the shadowed sheet. Since this contains the repulsors of the dynamics, it might rapidly push $\mathfrak{M}$ toward new attractors in the upper blank sheet ($\mathfrak{M} > M_0$). In other words, all the points in the bifurcation set B are points of potential catastrophe. It must be noted that on the right arm of the cusp bifurcation set change is catastrophic even independently of the existence of any exogenous shock, since outside the bifurcation set the distribution function again becomes unimodal.

To sum up, a small increase in frustration may in general be sufficient to trigger off a revolutionary change in the institutional system, even if satisfaction is still increasing. An institutional system can simultaneously generate frustration and satisfaction for the simple reason that the unsatisfying institutions cannot be modified without changing the entire system and resistance to systemic change can arise when some other institutions are considered satisfying. In these cases public opinion tends to split into two opposing parties, so that even a small increase in frustration can displace predominance from the conservative to the revolutionary party.

AN APPLICATION: THE REVOLUTION OF 1989

The formal difference between the cusp and the Maxwell bifurcation sets, B and b, has interesting political implications. Let us consider two different kinds of collective will formation processes, democratic and hegemonic.

In the former, the collective will changes when the majority changes. Collective moods can be so distributed to give rise to two big parties. As long as the majority of individuals are dominated by conservative moods the conservative party prevails. Institutional change occurs when the majority of individuals become revolutionary, and is catastrophic when the median individual, if he/she does not abstain, changes his/her mind.[9] Graphically this happens when line A crosses set b from the left. This is called the 'Maxwell rule'.

More interesting is the other kind of process. The process is hegemonic when social groups exist who are able to affect the formation of either the moods or the will of the collectivity, or both. In the first case there are attempts at raising the frequency of a reference group exhibiting the desired moods and at extending its influence to other individuals. This occurs with advertising and propaganda, for instance. In the second case the distribution of moods is left unaltered, but action is exerted on its influence on the formation of the collective will.

A hegemonic process attacking directly the formation of collective will can be effective only when behavioural factors are located within the cusp bifurcation set. In the distribution of moods is unimodal, so that the only way to affect the collective will is to change moods. On the other hand, even a small shock can set off a catastrophe within the cusp bifurcation set; thus minority groups may succeed in imposing their will on the majority, expediting or delaying the expected change.

In the points between set b and the left arm of set B (call it 'the area of revolutionary violence') the majority of people is conservative. If the evolution represented by line A were to continue to approach the right arm of set B, a revolutionary change would have to take place sooner or later. A revolutionary minority could attempt to precipitate it, for example, by destabilising the system. In fact a shock that strikes the fast dynamics of M in that area could push it on the set of repulsors of manifold μ, thus triggering off the revolutionary catastrophe before the revolutionary party obtains the majority of consensuses. On the other hand, at the points between b and the right arm of B ('the area of conservative violence') there is a revolutionary majority. If the conservative party has power, it may try to delay the change. This can be done through two kinds of policy. First, by abolishing the democratic rule, thus making set b irrelevant. Secondly, by stabilising moods, so as to prevent the possibility of shocks in the fast dynamics triggering a revolution. The use of power and the control of state organisations, then, could be aimed at preventing the collective will from adapting to the change in moods.

However, if the fundamental factors of change, frustration and satisfaction, go on moving toward the right arm of the cusp catastrophe, sooner or later revolutionary change will take place. In order to prevent this possibility, more radical and structural methods have to be used. One of these is to sustain an increase in achievements, thus feeding satisfaction. Economic growth and the extension of social welfare are the main road to political stability.

Another such method is to depress aspirations and reservation thresholds. If individuals do not expect too much, it is sufficient to give them only a little to make them satisfied. And the main road to the depression of aspirations is ideology. Notice that the depression of the reservation thresholds produces a twofold effect. It serves, not only to raise the satisfaction brought about by the satisfying institutions when achievements are low, but also to reduce frustration brought about by the unsatisfying ones. This kind of action is therefore doubly effective, which explains the importance assigned to ideological control in conservative regimes.

There is, finally, another effective method: the reduction of frustration through an increase in the costs of change. Due to lack of space, the exercise of singling out the various techniques for raising these costs is left to the reader. But a word will be spent to recall one of the most powerful tools: fear. Uncertainty and the fear of change are perhaps the instruments of conservation most widely employed by the power élites.

If this model is applied to the revolution that has recently broken out in Eastern Europe[10], it is easy to understand that what really deserves to be explained is not the revolution itself but the reasons why it took place so late. In fact conditions were already ripe for it in the late 1950s – early 1960s (Chattopadhyay, 1994). This was true especially in the Middle–European countries, in which social frustration grew fast among the working classes in that decade. Comparisons with Western societies let aspirations rapidly swell, especially in terms of freedom, work conditions and social welfare, and only a strong political repression helped maintain social stability. Repression, however, went hand in hand with political and economic centralisation, thus fuelling a slowing down of economic achievements. A political–economic cycle (Nuti, 1985; Screpanti, 1986) was set in motion, most notably in Poland, East Germany, Hungary and Czechoslovakia. Attempts at economic reformation and political decentralisation fuelled social unrest by reducing repression and the perception of the cost of change; but social disorder induced attempts to restore political repression and economic centralisation, thus paving the way for a slowing down in economic performance. This process can be formalised in terms of a cycle in the collective will in which the latter repeatedly jumps up and down the fold curve without being able to stabilize on the acceptance of a given institutional system. The reason why no such a cycle could be observed in Russia must be found mainly in two conditions: firstly, the greater power that the Bolshevik and nationalist ideologies had maintained over the mind of the Russian working class and people at large, and secondly the greater efficacy that fear and political repression must have had in Stalin's country. However the great depression of the 1970s and the 1980s brought about some dramatic changes in the evolution of social behaviour factors. Comparisons with the economic, social and political conditions prevailing in Western Europe and, especially, the attraction of the American way of life, fuelled the aspirations of the Eastern working classes. At the same time economic depression contributed to worsen economic achievements. Finally the advent of Gorbachev brought about a slackening of political and military repression both inside the Soviet Union and in the satellite countries, so that fear and the cost of change declined considerably. Social frustration grew very fast in all those countries in the 1970s and the 1980s, in some of which they began to prove able to set off a revolution. In many countries moods had already entered deeply into the area of conservative violence, in which the imminence of a revolution is perceived by everybody, and went on approaching the cusp bifurcation set. In these conditions a small stochastic shock was sufficient to trigger off the catastrophe.

ANOTHER APPLICATION: INNOVATION CLUSTERS IN SCHUMPETERIAN THEORY

I have indulged in an application to political systems mainly because this is the best way to show the influence that the processes of collective will formation may exert on the way change occurs in bifurcation situations. It goes without saying, however, that this model of discontinuous change is suitable for many other applications. Since there is not sufficient space for a convincing argument on this proposition, least of all for setting down all the possible applications, I will use this section to sketch just another case.

It concerns technological systems. These look like, if not can be completely reduced to, institutional systems. In fact a technology can be defined on the ground of the routines with which it moulds labour activity (Nelson and Winter, 1982) and routines are a kind of behavioural institution. A technological system can be treated as an institutional system insofar as it consists of a set of routines. In a technological system it is possible to distinguish fundamental or core techniques, which make up the 'core subsystem' (Tushman and Rosenkopf, 1992, p. 331), from subsidiary techniques.

The model developed in this chapter could be used to work out a problem posed by Schumpeter in his analysis of technological change in the long cycle: that of concerning the reasons why great innovations which change technological systems tend to occur in bunches or, rather, in swarms that take off in the downswing of the long cycle (Mensch, 1979; van Duijn, 1983).

In applying the model to this case, 'satisfaction' measures profits and 'dissatisfaction' losses (including the profits foregone by postponing innovative investments). Among the costs of change, particularly important are the investment costs for introducing innovations, the opportunity costs linked to sunk funds and, most of all, the uncertainty about the change towards a productive system with unknown user costs and demand conditions. In the downswing of the long cycle, collective satisfaction, i.e. the amount of profits of profitable processes, shrinks. On the other hand frustration rises because of the increase in losses of unprofitable processes, the increase of forgone profits due to the postponement of innovative investments and, especially, because of the reduction in opportunity costs linked to sunk funds. The latter reduction is caused by the fact that prolonged depression leads to permanent excess capacity, whilst, at the same time, by slowing down the investment process and the replacement of equipment, it accelerates depreciation and obsolescence.

It must be added that the costs of change, especially the psychological costs that depend on the state of confidence, the degree of risk aversion and the perception of uncertainty, are affected by mental habits and social beliefs that are moulded by social institutions and culture. Long depressions are likely to lead to the substitution of the social institutions that might have obstructed the diffusion of innovations, and to the establishment of new sets of institutions that might encourage technical change.[11] For example, although the Fordist paradigm was available long time before, the Fordist boom of the Golden Age (1950–70) was prepared by the dramatic institutional changes that occurred during the long crisis of 1929–45.

The process that brings to a technological revolution is illustrated graphically by the tendency of trajectory T in Figure 3.2 to bend toward the bifurcation sets. Once the trajectory has entered the cusp, an exogenous shock, such as a deep crisis, a big labour dispute, a generational change, a political, social or cultural change, could be sufficient to trigger off the technological catastrophe. In fact, when trajectory T has entered the cusp, a sizeable number of inventions have cumulated and a considerable number of entrepreneurs are waiting for better times. In these conditions a small change in frustration could have trigger effects and spark off the catastrophe. The collective will in this application coincides with 'animal spirits', social attitudes that tend to form in an epidemic way, through imitation, collectively determined expectations, social influence, etc. It is in the formation of the collective will that the 'swarm' develops.

In the case of technological systems the Maxwell set is irrelevant because entrepreneurs do not wait for a majority resolution to decide investments. On the other hand it is probable that the left arm of the cusp set is also fairly irrelevant, since entrepreneurs could try to delay as long as possible disinvestment of existing capital equipment in a situation of strong uncertainty. However, the longer the lapse of time in which innovative investments are delayed, the more frustration cumulates and the more dramatic will be the revolution when it breaks out. This is why it is important to apply the theory to a long cycle context. Two or three year recessions, followed by strong recoveries lasting five or six years, are unable to sustain the piling up of frustration and unexploited inventions necessary for catastrophic changes to occur. But a period characterised by long and deep recessions followed by short and weak recoveries, as takes place in a long downswing, is indeed able to do just that. In fact great technological revolutions tend to occur toward the end of long depressions and prepare the technical conditions for epochal upturns.

SUMMARY AND CONCLUSIONS

An explanation has been offered as to why many phenomena of institutional change occur in the form of catastrophic processes. The basic reason must be found in the fact that institutions are often organised in systems, so that it is impossible to change the fundamental ones without changing the whole system. This implies that an institutional system can survive for a long time even if it produces dissatisfaction and frustration in the individuals who abide with it. It is unlikely that an institutional system be considered fully satisfying by all individuals. Normally there are institutions that are complied with by many individuals who would abandon them if it were possible, but cannot do so because they are interlocked with other institutions which work well. Who likes paying taxes? However they must be paid if an efficient national health service is desired.

Thus any institutional system produces both satisfaction and frustration, two conflicting factors of behaviour. By using catastrophe theory it has been shown in quite a general way that a situation in which satisfaction and frustration both grow could give rise to polarisation processes in collective moods which would lead, after long periods of latency, to abrupt changes in the institutional system.

This is a theory of the modalities of institutional change, not yet of its causes. To account for the latter, it is necessary to explain the evolution of the two behavioural factors, the degrees of satisfaction and frustration, which so far have been treated as parameters. A theory of modalities however must not be underrated. In fact there is a scarcity of theories in this field that does not stand comparison with the richness, if not the embarras de richesse, in the field of the theories of causes.

There is no intention to enter this new field here, but it might be stimulating to single out, among the theories of the causes of change, some which seem congruous with the model presented here. Particularly interesting are those theories in which satisfaction and frustration are functionally linked – interesting because they lend themselves to an account of change as an endogenous process. It is worthwhile mentioning four of them which appear to suit the theory of catastrophic change very well.

The first has been elaborated by myself (Screpanti, 1984). It refers to industrial relation systems. The basic idea is that economic growth feeds the workers' achievements and that, as a consequence, their aspirations and reservation thresholds also rise. Thus frustration rises too. In other words frustration is an increasing function of satisfaction. Sooner or later the growth of the two contrasting behavioural factors will cause social disorder and catastrophic changes in the industrial relations set–up. The cycle will tend to be repeated in the long period.

A second example is offered by Boudon (1986) in a model that develops a finding of Stouffer (1949). The degree of frustration produced in a competitive process depends on the proportion of losers in the population. It is proved that frustration rises, not only when the winners' reward increases and the stake in the game diminishes, but also, paradoxically, when the proportion of winners rises. This is a very simple model, but seems suitable for application in a number of fields, like market competition, investment in R&D, career opportunities in an organisation, etc.

Hargreaves Heap (1989) has improved on this model by disaggregating the players in two social strata, called 'dominant' and 'subordinate' groups, and by assuming the number of winners in both groups to be an increasing function of the number of competitors. He shows that frustration tends to be higher in the dominant group, mainly because the reward of competition and the proportion of winners are higher, but also because risk aversion is lower in this group. Another interesting result is that a redistribution of wealth from the rich to the poor, not only reduces inequality, but also modifies the degree of frustration in both groups, raising that of the poor and lowering that of the rich.

Boudon's and Hargreaves Heap's models do not show how changes in frustration and satisfaction affect moods and produce institutional change, but it would not be difficult to reformulate them to fit the model of change developed in this chapter.

Finally, another theory that lends itself to formalisation on the ground of the model developed here was elaborated by Leblebici, Salancik, Copay and King (1991), who hypothesize that the progressing of institutionalisation processes cause scarcity of the resources required by conformity. In this case one could assume that growing institutionalisation is linked to an increase in the satisfaction bought about by institutions. The sting of scarcity could be formalised in terms of a tendency of frustration to increase too. The tension between these two opposing processes, according to Leblebici, Salancik, Copay and King, stimulates institutional innovations and subsequently the overcoming of the old institutions. Then with the diffusion of the new institutions a new institutionalisation process is set in motion, and the cycle of change is perpetuated.

These four examples have been offered, not with the intention of completing the theory of the modality of change with a theory of the causes, but only to show the versatility of the model here proposed.

NOTES

1. In order to avoid boring technicalities, analytical considerations are reduced to a minimum and confined to footnotes. The reader interested in the mathematical background is addressed to Zeeman (1977, chapter 10) and Gilmore (1981, chapter 6).

2. Here I follow my personal understanding (Screpanti, 1995) of the evolutionary theory of institutions.

3. According to Dallago (1996) the economic costs of institutional change can be reduced to four types: a) additional learning and measurement costs, associated with the need to collect information and measure the advantages of the new institutions, b) additional enforcement costs, associated with the need to enforce the agreements generated by the new institutions, c) adaptation costs, caused by the necessity to develop new routines, d) transition costs, depending both on the investment required by the new institutions and the losses caused by abandonment of the old.

4. This might seem to put some strain on the usual meaning of the word 'frustration', but it is a matter of sheer convention. The reader who prefers to preserve the usual meaning of the term 'frustration' and make it to coincide with that of 'dissatisfaction', could adopt a different convention, for example to add the cost of change, C, to the degree of satisfaction, S, instead of subtracting it from the degree of dissatisfaction, D. In either cases a high cost of change would produce the effect of abating the proneness to change. The equivalence of the two conventions can be better appreciated in the case in which satisfaction and dissatisfaction are felt simultaneously, as it will be shown in section 5: their analytical implications would be the same, because the condition $S+C>D$ is identical to the condition $S>D-C$.

5. It is even possible to envisage a neutral mood, defined as the attitude prevailing when an individual is indifferent or uncertain toward change.

6. V is assumed to be a potential. Its universal unfolding is

$$V(M; a, b) = \frac{M^4}{4} - \frac{M^2}{2} - aM$$

where $a=F-S$ and $b=F+S-Z$, Z a constant.

7. In reality a perfect correspondence between the collective will and the modal mood is not required. It is sufficient for the former to be an increasing monotonic transformation of the latter. One such transformation is provided by the median voter theorem (Downs, 1957). In fact, whenever the distribution is unimodal, the median individual is near the modal one and typically changes in the same direction of it. A problem with this theorem is that it does not necessarily hold when the possibility is admitted that tail individuals, i.e. those located at the extreme left and the extreme right of the moods distribution, tend to abstain. If this possibility is considered, a criterion of collective will formation could be envisaged according to which a value of moods near to a modal value, M_m, is chosen that maximises the area over $\delta_2 (M_m) + \delta_1 (M_m)$, as shown in Figure 3.3.

Figure 3.3 Collective will near a model value

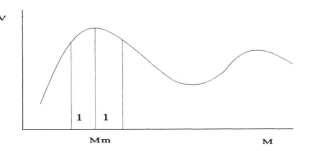

where $\delta_2 (M_m)$ and $\delta_1(M_m)$ are the highest differences of moods tolerated by the individuals who do not abstain, whilst $M_m + \delta_2 (M_m)$ and $M_m - \delta_1 (M_m)$ are abstention thresholds. Notice that values of $\delta_2 (M_m)$ and $\delta_1 (M_m)$ can be defined which ensure that M_m is an increasing monotonic transformation of a modal mood – a sort of a 'modal voter theorem' – even when the distribution is bimodal. Notice also that in this case it is not the collective will that is attracted by the median individual. Quite the contrary, it is the latter who is attracted by the modal collective will, if she does not abstain.

8. The gradient is

$$\frac{dM}{dt} = \frac{\partial V(M; a, b)}{\partial M} = M^3 - bM - a$$

The maxima of the potential, $\mathfrak{m}$, represent attractors of the collective will, the minima repulsors. These points are determined by the condition:

$$\mathfrak{m}^3 - b\mathfrak{m} - a = 0$$

which is the equation of manifold μ.

9. Remember that, as it was argued in note 5, the median voter theorem does not hold when the moods distribution function is bimodal and collective will is attracted by the modal individual.

10. A more complex application of catastrophe theory to the problem of institutional change in Eastern Europe can be found in Eger and Weise (1992).

11. The idea that a mismatch between social and technological systems can obstruct technical advance, as well as the hypothesis that long downswings can help overcoming such a mismatch, has been developed by many students in different approaches, e.g. the French Regulation School, the approach of the Social Structure of Accumulation, the Science Policy Research Unit. See Tylecote (1992) for an insightful and comprehensive analysis.

REFERENCES

Boudon, R. (1986), 'The Logic of Relative Frustration', in J. Elster (ed.), *Rational Choice*, Oxford: Basil Blackwell.

Chattopadhyay, P. (1994), *The Marxian Concept of Capital and the Soviet Experience: Essay in the Critique of Political Economy*, New York: Praeger.

Dallago, B. (1996), 'Investment, Systemic Efficiency and Distribution', *Kyklos*, 49, 615–41.

Downs, A. (1957), *An Economic Theory of Democracy*, New York: Harper & Row.

Duijn, J. J. van, (1983), *The Long Wave in Economic Life*, London: Allen & Unwin.

Earl, P.E. (1983), *The Economic Imagination: Toward a Behavioural Analysis of Choice*, Brighton: Wheatsheaf.

Eger, T. and P. Weise (1992), 'Economic Transformation Processes: Political Possibilities and Social Limitations', in H.–J. Wagener (ed.), *On the Theory and Policy of Systemic Change*, Berlin: Physica, 51–65.

Egidi, M. (1992), 'Organisational Learning and the Division of Labour', in M. Egidi, and R. Marris (eds.), *Economics, Bounded Rationality and the Cognitive Revolution*, Aldershot: Edward Elgar, 148–173.

Frankfurt, H.G. (1971), 'Freedom of the Will and the Concept of a Person', *Journal of Philosophy*, 68, 5–20.

Gilmore, R. (1981), *Catastrophe Theory for Scientists and Engineers*, New York: Wiley.

Hargreaves Heap, S. (1989), *Rationality in Economics*, Oxford: Basil Blackwell.

Heiner, R.A. (1983), 'The Origin of Predictable Behaviour', *American Economic Review*, 560–95.

Hirschman, A.O. (1982), *Shifting Involvements: Private Interest and Public Action*, Princeton: Princeton University Press.

Hodgson, G.M. (1984), *The Democratic Economy: A New Look at Planning, Markets and Power*, Harmondsworth: Penguin.

———— (1988), *Economics and Institutions*, Cambridge: Polity Press.

Jeffrey, R. (1974), 'Preferences among Preferences', *Journal of Philosophy*, 71, 377–92.

Leblebici, H., G.R. Salancik, A. Copay and T. King (1991), 'Institutional Change and the Transformation of Interorganisational Fields: An Organisational History of the U.S. Radio Broadcasting Industry', *Administrative Science Quarterly*, 333–63.

Loasby, B.J. (1976), *Choice, Complexity and Ignorance: An Inquiry into Economic Theory and Practice of Decision Making*, Cambridge: Cambridge University Press.

Mather, J. (1969), *Right Equivalence*, Pre-print, University of Warwick.

Mensch, G. (1979), *Stalemate in Technology: Innovations Overcome the Depression*, Cambridge: Ballinger.

Nelson, R.R. and S.G. Winter (1982), *An Evolutionary Theory of Economic Change*, Cambridge: Harvard University Press.

Nuti, D.M. (1985), 'Political and Economic Fluctuations in Socialist Systems', European University Institute, *Working Papers* No. 156.

Screpanti, E. (1984), 'Long Economic Cycles and Recurring Proletarian Insurgencies', *Review of the Fernand Braudel Center*, 7, 509–48.

———— (1986), 'A Model of the Political–Economic Cycle in Centrally Planned Economies, European University Institute' (*Working Papers* No. 201. Also published in L. Marcolungo, M. Pugno and F. Targetti (eds.) *L'Economia Mondiale in Trasformazione*, Milan: Angeli, 1988.

———— (1995), 'Relative Rationality, Institutions and Precautionary Behaviour', in J. Groenewegen, C. Pitelis and S.–E. Sjöstrand (eds.), *On Economic Institutions: Theory and Applications*, Aldershot: Edward Elgar, 63–84.

Sen, A. (1974), 'Choice, Ordering, and Morality', in S. Körner (ed.), *Practical Reason*, Oxford: Basil Blackwell, 54–67.

———— (1977), 'Rational Fools: A Critique of the Behavioural Foundations of Economic Theory', *Philosophy and Public Affairs*, 6, 317–44.

Simon, H.A. (1955), 'A Behavioural Model of Rational Choice', *Quarterly Journal of Economics*, 69, 99–118.

———— (1957), *Models of Man: Social and Rational*, New York: Wiley.

Sjöstrand, S.-E. (1992), 'On the Rationale Behind Irrational Institutions', *Journal of Economic Issues*, 26, 1007–40.

Stouffer, S.A. *et al.* (1949), 'The American Soldier', Princeton: Princeton University Press.

Thom, R. (1969), 'Topological Models in Biology', *Topology*, 313–35.

———— (1972), *Stabilité Structurelle et Morphogénèse*, New York: Benjamin.

Tool, M. (1995), *Pricing, Valuation and Systems: Essays in Neo Institutional Economics*, Aldershot: Edward Elgar.

Tushman, M.L. and Rosenkopf, (1992), 'Organizational Determinants of Technological Change: Toward a Sociology of Technological Evolution' in B. Shaw and L.L. Cummings (eds.), *Research in Organizational Behaviour*, London: JAI Press.

Tylecote, A. (1992), *The Long Wave in the World Economy: The Current Crisis in Historical Perspective*, London: Routledge.

Zeeman, E.C. (1977), *Catastrophe Theory: Selected Papers 1972–1977*, Reading: Addison Wesley.

4. The Legacy of J.R. Commons' Conception of Economics as a Science of Behaviour

Laure Bazzoli and Véronique Dutraive

American Institutionalism appears as an important school of thought if one wants to develop today an evolutionary analysis in economics concerned with the analysis of processes in historical time (Delorme, 1994) and which considers reality as creative and transmutable (Davidson, 1996). Notably, one of the theoretical fundamentals of the so–called old institutional economics[1] lies in its criticism of the standard conception of economic behaviour and rationality for the purpose of working out a realistic understanding of economic phenomena. Considering that the central problem of social sciences is the problem of formation and evolution of social order and that this supposes to place human agency at the core of the analysis, the special feature of the institutionalist research program was to put to the forefront the necessity of a profound reconstruction of the theory of behaviour presented as an alternative to the mainstream conception of rational choice and broadly developed in interaction with other social sciences, especially psychological sciences. This reconstruction was seen as the central element for the viability of this program: if one wants to theorise the institutional foundations of the economic system and their dynamic properties, one cannot start with an atomistic and purely rational individual whose behaviour is given. Starting with this critical view, institutionalists have developed an alternative conception of action and rationality.[2] It seems now clear that this program has anticipated a major trend of contemporary economic analysis: explicitly or not, the limits of the rational choice framework appear in many of the works in the mainstream tradition; as Denzau and North (1994) say, it is necessary to 'open up the black box of rationality' and this has notably opened the way to a recognition of the role of habits and institutions in human action and of the necessity to break with the strict separation between economics and psychology (Fusfeld, 1989). Then 'the return of institutionalism' (Hodgson, 1994) is founded on the fact that it is the research program which represents the most direct and enduring challenge to the assumption of pure rational behaviour, which was replaced by another behavioural hypothesis leading to a reformulation of the concept of rationality itself.

We want to stress here the specific legacy of the conceptual framework developed by J.R. Commons – one of the leading figures of the institutionalist movement who has been relatively neglected until recently (Ramstad, 1996b) – for the drawing up of an institutionalist theory of human agency. We will argue that this author, by adopting the pragmatist philosophy of Peirce and Dewey about the process of thought, has founded a framework of analysis focused on the concept of transaction which links the theory of action (individual behaviour) and the theory of institutions (collective action). In order to elaborate a realist theory of behaviour this author has stressed the necessity to articulate the individual and collective dimensions of behaviour through the study of its cognitive and institutional basis. Two major lessons for contemporary analysis derive from this conception. First, transforming the behavioural foundations of economic analysis supposes to integrate psychological hypothesis (e.g. to integrate the study of motivations and preferences in economic analysis) and this leads to recognise the crucial role of socio–institutional factors in the shaping of human agency (Lewin, 1996). Second, this framework, which offers an institutional theory of human behaviour in transactional settings, explicitly leads to a *via media* between individualism and holism. In other words, Commons shows that building an alternative conception of economic action requires the study of the interactions between individuals and institutions (the part–whole relations) and to take into account the logics of mediation, that is to say breaking with reductionism in economics. This was a prerequisite of an institutionalist evolutionary analysis, and Commons, as Rutherford (1994) has stressed, is the institutionalist who has pioneered the elaboration of this *via media*.

We will first underline the philosophical orientations which found the institutionalist attitude toward the theory of human agency. Then we will develop Commons' analysis of behaviour and explain the concepts he has proposed to make economics a transactional and evolutionary theory which recognises the essential role of institutions in economic action. We will finally show that this conception leads to the defense of a new principle in economics that can be called 'methodological institutionalism'.

PRAGMATIST PHILOSOPHY: FOUNDATION OF THE INSTITUTIONALIST VISION OF ECONOMICS AS SCIENCE OF BEHAVIOUR

If mainstream economics tends to deny the links between economics and philosophy, institutionalists have always stressed the great significance of the philosophical 'preconceptions' (as Veblen said) of economic analysis in terms of ontological and methodological choices.[3] Their own research program, especially in the case of Commons, is an offspring of the pragmatist philosophy. This approach appears in opposition with the philosophical tradition which has founded neoclassical economics: the cartesian tradition as basis of the atomist and mechanist thought that has characterised modernist science.[4] We will not discuss here all the consequences of the adoption by institutionalists of this philosophical worldview; we want to stress that the pragmatist theory of knowledge implies a philosophical realism in terms of method that leads to a new conception of reason, forming the essential characteristics of Commons' vision of economics as a science of behaviour.

Pragmatism as Method

C.S. Peirce has explicitly presented the pragmatist philosophy as the defense of realism against the nominalist position which has dominated, in his viewpoint, philosophy since the time of Descartes and which seemed to him inconsistent with the development of the experimental method in sciences. Realism is against 'the "cult" of the foundational individual element' that characterises nominalism (Tiercelin, 1993), because it considers that there are no such things as isolated essences, and that thought can only experience 'existents in interrelation'. Furthermore the 'real' exists outside individual thought although its apprehension is always mediated by signs. The problem for the realist is therefore to exercise his/her thought on real objects and not on a hypothetical world which can not be controlled by experience. Peircian realism points to the fact that pragmatism is an alternative to both rationalism and empiricism (Mirowski, 1987), which appear as the two faces of nominalism in modernist science (Hodgson, 1993). It is on this basis that pragmatism is a criticism of the famous epistemological opposition between induction and deduction. For Peirce the logics of experimental science is the logics of abduction as an hermeneutic process of formulating hypothesis about the real. Peirce is a central author in the foundation of realism because he has shown that the essential moment of a realist analysis is not induction nor deduction but abduction, 'the movement from a conceptualisation of some manifest phenomenon to an hypothesis about the possible structures which give rise to or govern it' (Lawson, 1989, p.68).

Following this new epistemology, Commons (1934) rejected the formalism and *a priori* method of pure economics (where 'things work out mathematically to an inevitable conclusion', he said). But he was not an empirist. He considered that theory had to be a 'realist abstraction' (a mental tool) useful to study a reality that cannot be seen as predeterminable and immutable.[5] From this point of view, economic analysis is concerned, as Max Weber have defended it, with the *understanding* of human conducts in economic activities; and for Commons this cannot be achieved through an axiomatisation of choices but through a concrete study of human behaviours. The principle of rationality in mainstream economics has an instrumental role – it is an essential axiom in order to construct determinist and predictable models of economic laws – and this explains the split between economics and other social sciences; all the elements of choice (and in the first place, preferences) are given. As Mirowski shows, the assumption of rational economic man puts the analysis of cognitive processes outside the scope of economics and leads to separate the context of socialisation from the context of choice. Then the conflict between institutionalism and neoclassical economics appears as a 'battle between realism and nominalism': for the former, human beings 'are part of the natural world and hence *experience* life from their particular matrix of space and time', while for the latter they 'stand outside life and reexamine (...) the totality of their consumption set in light of changes of circumstances' (Khalil, 1994, p. 262). From the institutionalist viewpoint, this conception, which has been justified by the 'as if' epistemology of M. Friedman, is not relevant for building a realistic theory of human behaviour. Adopting a position that is also defended by Herman Simon (1959, 1979, 1992) who underlines the fallacy of Friedman's argument, institutionalists have considered the necessity to articulate economics and psychology in order to base economic analysis on relevant assumptions about human action. That is to say, to elaborate a realist abstraction and not a fiction.[6] The principle of mechanical, impersonal and pure rationality reveals not only a preference for simplicity over complexity (for purpose of mathematical tractability), but carries implicitly strong assumptions about human nature, that have been undermined and invalidated by the developments in psychological sciences.[7] For Commons, the point is to articulate representation (mental patterns) and action, and to mobilise the results about a cognitive basis of action to understand human economic behaviour. Institutionalists were the first to defend the fact that we need a descriptive theory of the process of action (empirical assumptions) to incorporate behavioural hypothesis as explanatory variables in economic theory.[8] Furthermore, the influence between economics and psychology runs both ways because the essential point for institutionalists is to understand the factors shaping economic behaviour and this supposes to place human agency in its social realm.[9]

A New Conception of Reason

For this purpose, the pragmatism of Peirce, Dewey and James is essential because it is a theory of the process of thought that is based on a new conception of reason which breaks away from the cartesian dualism of mind and body and which puts to the forefront the fact that thought is a process of learning mediated by prior knowledge and grounded in habits (Waller, 1988). Peirce, as Commons (1934, p. 150) said, 'dissolved Hume's skepticism by creating the concept of active mind' on the basis of experimental psychology, whereas the cartesian tradition rests on a concept of the mind as a passive receptacle of sense impressions. For Peirce, thought is a creative activity of giving meaning to things, and this requires a conception of the mind as the whole body in action in a world of uncertain change. For Peirce (1878, 1879) the 'law of the mind' lies in the propensity to form habits. Because intellectual activity is directed at removing the discomfort associated with doubt, thought is a process of formation of beliefs and the logic of beliefs rests on fixing in our mind a rule of conduct, that is, for Peirce, a habit. A habit is a general rule that guides our conduct and the process of learning is a process of formation and transformation of habits in light of experience, as the manifestation of human intelligence and the basis of all intellectual activity.[10] James underlined that this human propensity to form habits is a type of economisation of our cognitive ressources. Dewey also stated that habit means the very exercise of the will in so far as it is an acquired predisposition to modes of response, types of action (and not to a specific action) evaluated by its consequences (Jensen, 1987). Furthermore, Dewey (1922) stressed that the understanding of habits is the key to social psychology. Dewey developed an organic conception of human action. For him, 'unceasing activity is the natural state of human existence (...). Habits, physical *and mental*, are the means by which the innate impulse for activity is given direction' (C. Ramstad, 1996a, p. 417). Individual cognitive processes are formed by acquired habits. The mind must be analysed as a system of habits constructed in the interaction between the natural world and the social world; it is shaped by the participation of the individual in a community of experiences where habits are learned and spread. Each human conduct is a *transaction*, that is to say an interaction between the individual and his natural and social environment. Human action and cognition are then inherently social. Their formation and evolution derive from the conflicts of established habits with new experiences where habitual behaviour fails. This process can be analysed as a process of abduction, that is the creation of new insights which resolve problems and impulse change in habits and beliefs and their associated modes of conduct. But this process is not a smooth one because habits are durable, past–oriented, and as such resist to change. As Waller (1988) underlines, pragmatism puts to the forefront the duality of habits and the fact that human nature cannot be considered as given – it evolves with its environment and changes it.

So, in this conception, mind is an active organ of adaptation to an uncertain and changing environment, and human reason lies in its capacity to form and adjust habits of conduct in the context of social interactions. As Putnam (1992) and Shalin (1992) notice, pragmatism offers a procedural conception of rationality as a reasonable disposition embodied in the community. It stresses the role of collective cognitive patterns of action formed by interaction (Renault, 1995, 1996). It is this conception, which reveals an organicist ontology as it will be specified later, that J.R. Commons has developed as behavioural foundation of institutional economics. We will now expose what system of analytical concepts he proposed to analyse economic behaviour.

INSTITUTIONAL ANALYSIS OF HUMAN ACTION IN COMMONS' TRANSACTIONAL ECONOMICS

It is Veblen who first underlined the paradox of conventional economics: individuals are the cornerstone of the analysis but their behaviour is determined by exogenous individual variables. Evolutionary analysis supposes on the contrary to break away from this determinist conception in order to study what shapes economic behaviour and its evolution. He then introduced an analytical tradition which showed the impossibility of limiting economic behaviour to rational choice (where every action is regulated by conscious rational calculation and individuals are utility–maximising agents) and the necessity to stress the crucial role of habits and institutions in human agency.

The Transactional Viewpoint of Commons

The originality of the work of Commons lies in the fact that he considered interactions between individuals – that is, transactions – inserted in going concerns – that is to say, in durable institutions – to be the units of analysis of economic behaviour.[11] For him, the general problem of economics is to understand how order is generated in a world where individuals are both in conflicts and in cooperation. To understand the problem of human activity in society, one cannot consider society as 'a sum of isolated individuals' and start with individuals as atoms: we have to theorise economic behaviour in transactional settings. The individual is always at the core of the theory of social phenomena, not as an 'object of nature' with a fixed make up, but as part of an ongoing social process, as a participant in 'transactions' or joint actions where individual wills meet and where collective action (institution) controls individual action.

The point here is that a transaction is a part–whole relation (Ramstad, 1986; Renault, 1995). As a part, a transaction is limited by existing working rules (economic as well as ethical and legal) that define authorized transactions and bring order out of conflicts. As Commons says, the scope of private interests becomes the scope of rights, duties, liberties and exposures to others liberties. At the level of transactions, one can analyse the effects of collective action on inter–individual interactions as an essential condition of the social link because it prevents that conflict of interests degenerating into a Hobbesian war of all against all. In fact, collective action through working rules sets limits to individual action and at the same time is, 'by the act of control (...) a liberation of individual action from coercion, duress, discrimination, or unfair competition, by means of restraints placed on other individuals' (Commons, 1934, p.73). As a whole, a transaction is a situation of negotiation between individuals where the rules themselves are interpreted and adjusted and where individual preferences and wills are altered. Then individuals and rules are social constructs that are continually modified in the process of interaction. This conception of transaction is a processual and organicist conception (Hodgson, 1994) borrowing directly from Dewey: the unit of analysis is that of the activity of individuals in their social environment with a process of permanent adaptation between the two.

From this transactional point of view, the implicit psychological assumptions of neoclassical economics are not relevant, because they do not apprehend cognitive processes which precede action in transactional settings that articulate conflicts, dependance and order. Putting to the forefront social interactions and their collective patterns implies for

Commons a new conception of human psychology (Biddle, 1990; Ramstad, 1990). He used the term 'negotiational psychology' as the behavioural foundation of his institutional economics, this foundation being for him essential to understand economic transactions.[12] This negotiational psychology, grounded in pragmatist philosophy and its image of people as 'pragmatic human beings', has two main characteristics. It is a 'volitional psychology': it takes into account the very specificity of social sciences which deal with human purposes and wills in a context of radical uncertainty. It is also a 'social psychology' because individuals are social beings and their actions are always transactions with others. Therefore Commons' conception of the process of human action articulates its individual and social dimensions: the point is to take into account the mental processes at work and the institutional forces 'which operate through and interact with' those processes (Samuels, 1990, p. 223). This conception of human agency leads, as we will show, to a new vision on rationality that has anticipated present analyses in terms of procedural and contextual rationality.

A 'Volitional Psychology': the Role of Habits

For Commons, 'the peculiar quality of the human will in all its activities, distinguishing economics from the physical sciences, is that of choosing between alternatives (...) the choice is the whole mind and body in action' (Commons, 1931, p. 654). For institutionalists, classical rationality, which portrays a mechanical maximising individual determined by its exogenous preferences, is inconsistent with the active and purposeful dimension of man; furthermore, because mainstream economics is not transactional, it cannot integrate the mental processes of people as they engage in transactions as active interaction between human wills in conflict (Biddle, 1990). Borrowing from the pragmatist analysis of the process of thought, Commons considers the mind as 'a creative agency looking toward the future and manipulating the external world and other people in view of expected consequences' (Commons, 1934, p. 17). The purpose of all human action is to control or influence future events and others' behaviour. The will is a choice of a degree of power over things and human beings, grounded in expectations of consequences. Then, the fundamental 'law of human nature' is, for Commons as for Dewey, the search for security of expectations, as a condition for man to live on a day–to–day basis in society. Following pragmatists, Commons considers that this security is the product of habits acquired in the past experiences of individuals in transactions. Indeed most transactions are rather 'simple affairs' because individuals follow habitual modes of conduct which form shared expectations and are a means of coping with the complexity and the uncertainty that human brain cannot face.[13] These habits found what Commons calls 'routine transaction'. Their specificity is that they do not imply a conscious deliberation, a constant attention. Habits are a form of non–reflective behaviour that arises with repeated experiences and that is perdurable. The crucial point then is that the existence of routine transactions is the condition for the active exercise of thought. As Dewey has shown, 'the mind is consciously employed only when habitual behaviour fails to maintain "adjustment" between organism and environment' (Ramstad, 1996a, p. 417). For Commons, human will has this particular ability to focus on a single factor in order to bring about the intented result; it is the case in 'strategic transactions', that is, situations which are new (or which reveal new opportunities) and where past habits become inappropriate.[14]

The volitional side of negotiational psychology reveals two essential dimensions of the institutional theory of human agency. First, as Fusfeld (1989) underlines, it defends that individual action is made in real time; present action is a result of expectations about the future and of a process of learning from past experience which transform sense–data into information and knowledge (process of cognition) and shape individual choice. In a context of radical uncertainty perfect knowledge of consequences of actions and of possible alternatives is impossible; 'the will is a process of repeatedly choosing and acting upon the best alternative actually accessible at the time' (Commons, 1934, p. 19). Then, secondly, this conception of action offers a vision of human rationality radically different from the standard conception which associates it with optimisation and continuous deliberation. Most transactions are treated as routine ones because 'the human mind would be overwhelmed if it had to subject each transaction to the detailed scrutin that a strategic transaction demanded' (Biddle, 1990, p. 6). As Hodgson (1996) says, institutional analysis shows that there is an ontological primacy of habits in human agency because they are the very condition of higher–level thinking to emerge. But we cannot consider that habits themselves are the product of optimisation, as neoclassical analyses argument leads to a *reducio ad absurbum* and because rationality itself is a product of habit. In this conception, the link between rationality and optimisation is broken and replaced by a link between purposeful action and habitual behaviour. Habits are the condition for dealing with cognitive limits in face of uncertainty and complexity; they are the basis of a process of learning that can lead to new behaviour; they are the condition of the creative activity of the individual mind which concentrates on strategic transactions and innovation. As Tugwell (1922) noticed, 'reflection is a modifier, an adjuster, not an originator of conduct'. Human reason lies as well in the ability to apprehend strategic opportunities (rational action) as in the fact to follow routine transactions (habitual action).[15] Habits and rationality are two twin forms of the expression of human intelligence that cannot be opposed nor assimilated. These two forms express the fact that human behaviour is motivated by satisfying and not by optimisating (Ramstad, 1990, 1996a). Besides, (Simon, 1979; March & Simon, 1991) recognises the great insight Commons has brought to a realistic analysis of human agency. Notably, he has shown that rational behaviour lies in the ability of the mind to focus on 'limiting factors' and therefore to adapt to a situation (procedural rationality) and to result in a satisfying solution (in Commons' terms: a relative control of the future). Then strategic transactions are at the core of the adaptation of habits and of the creation of new rules of conduct. But Hodgson (1985) underlined that institutionalists went further than Simon: to put the stress on the positive role of habitual behaviour is to recognise that all behaviour is not in the same way conscious and reflective, but that there exists a hierarchy in cognitive and decision–making processes.[16] The distinction that Commons made between routine and strategic transactions seems for us totally validated by the present results of cognitive psychology which show that 'it is precisely the routinisation of the cognitive processes and the lack of full awareness that makes complex "calculations" possible' (Hodgson, 1985, p. 74).[17]

A Social Psychology: the Role of Institutions

For Commons, as for all institutionalists, this routinisation cannot be apprehended through individualistic psychology, but through social psychology that Dewey have developed and for which 'the external environment that give our actions their meanings and to which we adjust our behaviour is mainly a social one' (Biddle, 1990, p. 12). Individuals are embedded in the social realm that endow them with conventions, rights and duties. Then, elements of their behaviour and choices (preferences, acquisition of information and knowledge, conceptual apparatus, representations, perception and categorisation) are learned: they are socially shaped and affected by the behaviour of others (they are not only internal to the individual) because they 'involve continuous interaction between the individual and others in the context of changing social institutions and values' (Fusfeld, 1989, p. 363). This statement leads to recognise the role of institutions and their rules in the formation of individual habits of conduct (that is, their role on cognitive processes) and in what shapes individual action. It defends the fact that agency and institutions have to be closely articulated: there is no exteriority between the two (Hodgson, 1996). Institutions are, as Veblen taught, 'settled habits of thought common to the generality of men' that are the locus of the process of socialisation of individuals and of internalisation of social norms enforced by social sanctions. For institutionalists, it is what differentiates habits and institutions (Rutherford, 1994). Social psychology shows, as Commons said, that 'the human will is not a lawless capricious force but that it operates within certain limits'.

From an epistemological point of view, the search for uniformities in human behaviour is for Commons an essential condition of its scientific study. But he thought that the principle of pure rationality is not satisfying in order to standardise behaviour because it is inconsistent with purposefulness, diversity of individuals and 'active mind'. For him, uniformities derive from experiences of repeated transactions. He then considered that it is institutions that delimit and give meaning to individual actions and habits. Following the contextual theory of meaning proposed by pragmatism (meaning is given by signs), Commons has considered that the analysis of institutions (that is collective action from customs to going concerns) is the very condition of knowledge in social sciences. As Mirowski expresses it: 'because there exist no innate rules of rational economic behaviour, the only gauge of such behaviour resides in the particular economic community (...). The appropriate epistemological unit is the institution (...) that endows individual economic actors with the ability to cope with interpretations of action and with change' (Mirowski, 1987, p. 1020).[18]

From an analytical point of view, the rational man of conventional economics is supplanted, if economics want to be a social science, by what Commons calls the 'institutionalised man' and (as he preferred) the 'institutionalised mind'[19] means that 'individuals begin as babies' and learn by their participation in transactions the customs of their community, the customs 'of subordination to the working rules of the many concerns of which they are members' (Commons, 1934, p. 74), process of socialisation by which they become real individuals. Then individual habits are bent and moulded by the individual's participation in activities of society. 'Thus, Commons perceives an individual's concrete "economic" aspirations and habitual ways of responding to "economic" stimuli to be a consequence of his participation in the community's economic activities, not the reverse' (Ramstad, 1996a, p. 418). For him, habitual and rational action derives from what he calls 'habitual assumptions', that is mental representations and models that shape individuals' perception; these habitual assumptions are socially formed by customary assumptions, that is, 'collective opinion in control of individual opinion (...) to which individual habit must conform if individuals are to work together' (Commons, 1934, p. 698). Then it is these 'collective opinions' that produce shared mental models and rules of conduct which lead to the internalisation of social rules. Institutions have the essential role to regulate individual behaviour and to inject order in transactions, because through their working rules that determine what individuals can, may, or must do or not do in their transactions, they provide the security of expectations without which individuals will not be willing to enter into transactions on a day–to–day basis (Biddle, 1990; Ramstad, 1990).[20]

Hodgson (1985, 1988, 1996) shows that current cognitive sciences put to the forefront the social dimension of the process of cognition – that is the social nature of individual action – that old institutionalists considered as essential for the theory of human agency[21] institutions are indeed a crucial part of the cognitive processes through which sense–data are perceived and made meaningful by agents, knowledge is acquired and preferences are shaped (Hodgson, 1996). In order to study a purposeful human agent which actively seeks to change his existing situation, and not a 'goal directed machine', the institutionalist thesis clearly defended by Commons is that we have to explore the social construction of reality, and therefore the institutional influences on individuals, because it is on the basis of past habits and in a framework of socially defined possibilities that voluntary action takes place.[22] In this perspective, social influence doesn't mean social determinism. In other words, institutions are at the same time constraints *and* enabling frameworks for individual action that shape it without predetermine it. Institutions give consistency and stability to human activity by producing and reproducing habits of thought and action, by defining stable rules of the game of conflicting transactions.

Then two main cornerstones of Commons' institutional theory of behaviour exist.

1. The social dimension must not be a parameter but the core of the analysis of individual action. The point is to explain the conditions of individual behaviour (Boland, 1979) as a product of a social process of learning that moulds and transforms expectations, preferences, goals (the bounds of 'bounded rationality', as Hodgson says), and to understand the process of creation by institutionalised men of their environment which is not given. This conception also leads to cast people in their social roles (Atkinson and Reed, 1992) that shape and differentiate their habitual assumptions.[23] Furthermore, this offers a picture of the

individual as not only self–interested, but also as a creature searching for security, equity and cooperation (what Commons called an 'instinct of justice', see Ramstad, 1990). Then the rational man becomes a reasonable man embedded in a community that constraints and liberates him. The logics of reasonability is simply that individual action is mediated by the necessity to deal with others.

2. Determinants of behaviour are not given. We cannot begin, as Commons said, with 'an eternal reason binding upon men henceforth without change' as a basis for a positive and evolutionary theory of institutions (Rutherford, 1994). We have to study the process of adaptation of habits and institutions that change individuals themselves. This process is a long one and puts to the forefront the role of strategic transactions. Individuals are not passive, they are rational in the very sense that they act on the existing situation when it becomes a limiting factor for the pursuit of their interests.

On this basis, Commons defended a new methodological position in economics by stating that 'social science investigates habitual and customary assumptions (that is institutions and their working rules) as an explanation of transactions' (Commons, 1934, p. 698). This position leads to the rejection of methodological individualism and is based upon a reconsideration of the problem of the relation of parts and wholes.

COMMONS' INSTITUTIONALISM AS A METHODOLOGICAL MIDDLE GROUND

Commons defended that an institutionalist reconstruction of the theory of behaviour is an essential step for changing the foundations of economic theory, that is, building an institutional economics. For him, the meaning of this project of refoundation is to elaborate an alternative both to 'individualism and collectivism'. This has to be understood at two levels: at the ontological level (the conception of the nature of reality, of the individual and society) and at the methodological level (the mode of theoretical explanations considered as scientifically relevant); these two levels are linked because the methodological precepts are not independent from the vision of the reality to be explained and the model of man adopted (Rutherford, 1994). Notably, conventional economic theory of human behaviour depends logically on an atomist ontology that leads to a reductionist version of methodological individualism which itself is an offspring of nominalist philosophy (for which only individual entities exist) (Hodgson, 1993; Brochier, 1994). On the contrary, the pragmatist philosophy implies an organicist or holistic ontology and leads to the rejection of any form of reductionism, especially because of its opposition to the belief of the possibility to obtain some absolute and immutable foundations for knowledge (Lawson, 1989). On this basis, Commons' institutionalism leads to an original methodological middle ground.

From ontology to methodology: some limits of methodological individualism

Let us first consider the ontological opposition. The key distinction between atomism and organicism is that the former assumes that the relations between entities (ultimate components of reality) are external (that is, atomic entities exist and have qualities independently of their relations with other entities), whereas the latter assumes that these relations are internal, that is, as Dewey said, that entities are parts of transactions with their environment, their qualities are the very outcomes of their interrelations and then one cannot study parts without studying wholes and conversely (Hodgson, 1993, 1994; Winslow, 1994).[24] Then, if human agency has a causal power, 'social structures (...) exist prior to any individual act (at a given point in time and place) and govern it (...) by providing limiting and enabling conditions (they are necessary for action to take place). In this sense social structures have causal powers' (Lawson, 1989, p. 64). If 'organicism is perfectly compatible with the existence of real agency (...) [the] point is that, where relations are internal, maintenance of the requisite degree of self–identity cannot be taken for granted' (Winslow, 1994, p. 13, 15). In other words, organicist ontology is not opposed to individualism in the very sense that social theory is concerned with human action. However, it denies that only individuals exist and claims that social wholes exist (they are, for the individual, objective structures 'out there' and are more than the sum of their parts; it also denies that individual behaviour can be taken as given because 'they are not only socially formed but subject to ongoing modification in the process of social interaction' (Hodgson, 1994, p. 61). All this leads to stress the reductionist fallacy of methodological individualism 'that postulates autonomous self–subsistent individuals' (Samuels, 1994, p. 143) and to 'question (...) the legitimacy of stopping short at the individual in the process of explanation' (Hodgson, 1994, p. 62). Then, we see that the ontological position of institutionalism is the basis of its behavioural assumptions and implies therefore at the methodological level a criticism of individualism.

The principle of methodological individualism 'affirms that the most productive way of pursuing knowledge of human beings and society is to study individuals *qua* individuals' (Samuels, 1994, p. 142) 'by reference to a model of rational individual behaviour (that is, freely choosing self–interested individuals unconstrained by social norms), tracing out the unintended consequences in terms of human interactions (...), taking individuals as given (...) (and assuming) an initial institution free "state of nature"' (Hodgson, 1996, p. 11). Field (1979, 1984) has clearly expressed what a lot of authors sometimes call the 'logical impossibility of methodological individualism' (Brochier, 1994; Elster, 1989; Hodgson, 1994, 1996; Rutherford, 1994). The point is that individual rationality is in itself not sufficient to generate order *if* certain conditions exterior to individuals, that is, collective rules and norms prior to, and necessary for, inter–individual exchanges, do not exist. In other words, the fundamental limit of methodological individualism is that it implies 'assumptions which implicitly include methodologically collectivist considerations' (Samuels, 1994, p. 143); it implicitly demonstrates the logical necessity for holistic or social conditions (Brochier, 1994). The modern neoclassical analysis searching to elaborate a new institutional economics, fails at the same level.[25] Trying 'to carry this process of explanation to its conclusion', 'it attempts to eliminate rule structures as an exogenous category by explaining them as resulting from some prior process of short–term maximisation. Unfortunately, such attempts invariably flounder on the necesssity on (...) adducing a set of rules for making rules. This does not eliminate the category of rules as something separable and not derivable from maximising behaviour' (Field, 1979, p. 55). Then rational choice models cannot avoid to posit logically anterior rules or norms that define the constraints and the arena within which these behaviours take place, that is some rule structure 'not ultimately reducible to the individual interests of the agents involved (...), not ultimately explainable as resulting from the aggregation of their choices' (*ibid.* p. 58). As Hodgson expresses it: 'what is forgotten is that in the (...) hypothetical 'state of nature' from which institutions are seen to have emerged, a number of weighty rules, institutions and cultural and social norms have already been presumed. Arguably, these original institutions (...) are unavoidable' (Hodgson, 1996, p. 12). The point is that reductionism leads to an infinite regress that appears unsuccesful to eliminate statements about institutions from explanation. Methodology is then a major point of departure.

Toward a Methodological Middle Ground

The great improbability of succesfully completing the reductionist program (the problem of infinite regress) is the consequence of the impossibility of using given individuals unconstrained by institutions as the starting point of the analysis of social phenomena.[26] This problem is now recognised, especially since Agassi's work. If, as Hodgson (1994, 1996) underlines, we take seriously into account the question of infinite regress, then neither individual nor social factors have legitimate explanatory primacy (reductionism is unfounded), and 'why aren't we equally methodological institutionalists' as Robert Nozick has asked (1977, p. 359). It is precisely this position that, in our viewpoint, Commons has defended, as an alternative to all type of reductionism, alternative that integrates both individuals and institutions on the basis of new behavioural assumptions. The interest to present his methodological conception lies not only in its clarification in modern terms; the point is also to underline the originality of the institutionalist interpretation of the nature of the methodological middle ground which appears today for a large number of authors as the only solution to the limits of reductionism and as necessary to build an economics of institutions (Rutherford, 1994).

Commons considered that social science has two great specificities. First, its object is human action in its diversity and purposefulness. Second, social science is concerned with the study of part–whole relations, that is, with the understanding of the processes of social interactions in which individuals are products and active parts. This very understanding of the nature of social science explains not only that Commons' institutionalism is opposed to individualist reductionism (for reason of oversimplification about human nature and social interactions), but also that it cannot be interpreted as a crude methodological holism (for reason of oversocialised view of human behaviour and determinism of social wholes). Indeed, Commons has pioneered the way to a real *via media* (Bazzoli, 1994). If the problem is to transcend the opposition between the primacy of the individual and the primacy of the whole, we have to consider the dialectical interaction between the individual and the collective level as the centre of the analysis (Delorme, 1994). From that point of view, Commons' conception of parts–wholes relations is fruitful: at its conerstone lies the defense of the necessity of a dual stress on agency and structure (Hodgson, 1996) for understanding social phenomena, dual stress which underlines the difference of logical level between parts and wholes, and which breaks away from what Commons refered as 'the historic fallacy of Inverted Sequence'. Three points specify his conception.[27]

1. The part in Commons' organicist analysis cannot be the individual; it has to be the transaction as a social construct entwining individual agency and institutional structure (see *supra*). As Samuels emphasises, 'it is the cognition by the individual and the actions of individuals *vis–à–vis* institutions that counts, but it is a socialised and individualised individual, laden with both habit and purpose, who counts' (Commons, 1990, p. 221). We must replace the individual *qua* the individual as unit of analysis by transactions where individuals and social patterns are mutually formed through interaction.

2. Institutions are then essential units of analysis because they mediate between parts and wholes and serve as transmission mechanisms for forces at both levels (Samuels, 1994). In this conception, rules and institutions are analytically prior to the individual (Ramstad, 1990) because they are 'socially constructed invariant' (Mirowski, 1987). Institutionalism bases economic analysis on institutional specifics and relative invariants rather than as historical universals (Hodgson, 1994), considering institutions as the central explanatory variable in social science.[28] The point is that this conception, based on the analysis of 'interactive agents mutually entwined in durable and self–reinforcing institutions', 'provides a quite different way of approaching the problem of theorising the relationship between actor and structure' (...): 'the concept of institution (...) points not to a spurious supra–individual objectivity, nor to the uniformity of individual agents, but to the concept of socio–economic order arising not despite but because of the variety at the micro–level'. Thus, this concept connects 'the micro–economic world' of transactions and 'the macroeconomic sphere of seemingly (...) impersonal structures' (Hodgson, 1996, p. 22–23). As Commons said, starting with individuals rather than 'working rules of going concerns' reverses both the historical and the causal sequence.

3. What is crucial indeed is a theory of process in order to understand the formation of parts and wholes, and to go beyond reductionism and infinite regress. For Commons, the pragmatists philosophers have drawn the conclusion from evolutionism by putting to the forefront the notion of process with no beginning and no final term. Then, one cannot understand social interactions and society by starting with a 'state of nature'. Institutions are both explanatory variables and variables to be explained (institutional change) and this supposes to have an historical approach to evolution. This means that present situation and institutions are the product of the transactions of institutionalised human beings in a past situation with different institutions (one cannot explain institutions without reference to other prior institutions) and that this process will

produce a new situation. The stake of transactional analysis lies precisely in the understanding of 'parts as both cause and consequence in a process in which the units are themselves both transformed and transforming and in which the whole is itself also both transformed and transforming' (Samuels, 1994, p. 145).[29] Evolutionary processes are about the simultaneous and cumulative development of parts and wholes, where institutions play a selective role and human agency plays a creative one, through a tension between existing institutions and strategic transactions, a process which has no ending and no efficiency function. This ruins the rationalist analysis of the genesis of rules (Rutherford, 1994).[30]

From our point of view, the methodological middle ground that appears in Commons' work cannot be assimilated to Agassi's institutional individualism. Their project has undoubtedly some similarity: the purpose is to explain institutions and their evolution in reference to human agency and at the same time to take into account the influence of institutions on individuals.[31] What we would call 'methodological institutionalism' (to express the specificity of the institutionalist research program) differs at least on two crucial points: the vision of the individual and the status of history. On the first point, Agassi tends to maintain as starting point of the analysis the abstract individual (perfectly free and rational) of methodological individualism and this makes impossible the apprehension of the complex dialectics between the individual and the collective, of the opacity of social wholes for individuals and the effects of collective dimensions of individual conducts. The institutionalist theory of human agency, that acknowledges the role of habitual behaviour and of social rules (especially their consequences in terms of power structures and social places, see O'Neill, 1973), is a fatal blow to the assumption of rationality (Waller, 1988) and to the vision of human beings as independent individuals. Then, on the second point, taking into account the historical dimension of society and of its rule structures is also incompatible with the abstract individual as the conerstone of the analysis. One have to start with an 'institutional state of society' that forms the behaviour of human beings who will change it through a long process of mutual adaptation between individuals and institutions. As Brochier (1994) underlines, if one is interested with the historical and dynamic dimensions of the economy, then we cannot consider individual variables as the only explanatory ones.

Thus methodological institutionalism demands a really new conception of the individual and of its behaviour and underlines the necessity to study the historical evolution of the social patterns of action. On these two points, the concepts of transaction and institution as units of analysis are the means to an alternative to individualism (without leading to collectivism), alternative which defends a multilevelled analysis and implies a profound transformation of the vision of the individual on which economic theory is founded.

CONCLUSION

To study the thoughts of an 'old institutionalist' such as J.R. Commons is not only an intellectual exercise in the history of economic thought. It has a very actual meaning in so far as we must be conscious 'that much we want to say has already been said before' (Hodgson, 1996, p. 26). More and more, leading figures in economic science (such as Arrow, Hahn or North) recognise that it is time to deconstruct the standard image of rationality and of the economic actor, in order to explain economic phenomena and especially to integrate the role of institutions. Then, like Hodgson we think that 'modern economics cannot reasonably avoid key themes established by "old" institutionalists' – notably a multifacetted and general analysis of behaviour stressing the articulation of cognition and institutions through habits, the specificity of human reason, and the role of changing collective patterns – , nor the original method they have defended to make economics an evolutionary and realist science. But this supposes a reformulation of economics at the philosophical, ontological and methodological levels – pragmatism is incompatible with nominalism – and a rejection of the division between economics and the other social sciences (division that was essential to sustain the rationalist conception of action, Hodgson, 1985). This certainly explains the difficulties of institutionalism in our discipline. Anyway the task today for institutionalists is to develop and elaborate a general theory grounded in the great insights of the old founders. We have here underlined some legacies of Commons' transactional analysis of part–whole relations to the understanding of human action and interactions. His thought seems for us important to develop today a theory of the economic life process stressing the complex interaction between individuals and institutions.[32] We consider as Field that in so far as new institutionalists 'have made their peace with Commons on the appropriate scope of economic inquiry, it is time that peace be made as well on the issue of method' (Field, 1979, p. 67). This is a crucial issue for the purpose of building a modern institutional economics.

NOTES

1. There are today two traditions in the economics of institutions. The so–called 'old institutionalism' American tradition which spread at the beginning of the century, around the work of T.Veblen, J.R.Commons, J.M.Clark and W.C.Mitchell and which represents the first school putting institutional issues at the core of economics; althought this school has known a relative decay in popularity, the tradition has continued through the famous works of Ayres, Myrdal and Galbraith, and today is developed by such authors as Hodgson, Samuels, Dugger, Rutherford or Ramstad (often called neo institutionalists). The main characteristics of this school of thought are its critical appraisal of the mainstream tradition in economics and its purpose to build a theory of the social embeddedness and evolutionary dynamics of economic phenomena. The second tradition, the so–called 'new institutional economics', is more recent and is distinguishable from the 'old' one by the attempt to integrate institutional elements in neoclassical and Austrian thought; this school covers such different works as the property rights approach (Demsetz, Posner), the agency theory (Jensen, Meckling), the transaction cost economics (Coase, Williamson, North), game theory applied to institutions (Shubik, Schotter), and Austrian approaches (Langlois). Its main characteritic is to try to explain institutions in the framework of methodological individualism. As Field (1979) properly remarks, the new institutionalist program represents a profound evolution of the economic theory: whereas the development of neoclassical economics has been synonymous with the interpretation of the analysis of institutions as beyond the scope of economic inquiry (which has at the same time put institutionalists out of the profession), it is now recognised that economists have a responsibility to investigate institutions; then today the conflict is less about the appropriate scope of economics than about the appropriate methodology of institutional analysis. The third part of this chapter will develop this statement.
2. In other words, the revision of the theory of behaviour was for institutionalists central to construct a coherent alternative to neoclassical economics. As Mitchell affirmed long ago, it is not so the analysis of evolution of institutions that distinguishes institutional economics than the application to this problem of a new conception of human nature and conduct (Mitchell, 1935).
3. That is to say, in terms of the conception of what is to be explained (vision of the ultimate nature of reality) and how to explain it (vision of the method to obtain knowledge about the object); cf. *infra*.
4. For developments about the crucial links between institutionalism and pragmatism, see notably Dufourt (1995) and Mirowski (1987); more precisely about the great influence of pragmatism on Commons, see Bazzoli (1994) and Ramstad (1986). It must be noticed that this philosophical foundation explains not only the originality of the institutionalist tradition, but also its failure to be recognised in economics where logical positivism has been the dominant conception. On the contrary, the revival of institutionalism today can be linked to, and is reinforced by, the revival of pragmatism in American philosophy and the challenge contemporary epistemology poses to cartesianism and positivism.
5. It is then a persistent error to affirm that institutional economics is 'anti–theoretical'. On the contrary, this tradition is distinguished by a reflection on the type and the degree of abstraction necessary to the understanding of complex evolving phenomena (Rutherford, 1994; Ramstad, 1986).
6. Simon makes exactly the same point when he considers economists have forgotten, as Marshall and Commons have stressed, that economics is a behavioral science which supposes a strong link with psychology: 'the normative microeconomist 'obviously' doesn't need a theory of behaviour : he wants to know how people ought to behave, not how they do behave. On the other hand, the macroeconomist's lack of concern with individual behaviour stems from different considerations. First, he assumes that the economic actor is rational, and

hence he makes hard predictions about human behaviour without performing the hard work of observing people. Second, he often assumes competition, which carries with the implication that only the rational survives. Thus, the classical economic theory of the markets with perfect competition and rational agents is deductive theory that requires almost no contact with empirical data once its assumptions are accepted' (Simon, 1959, p. 252–254).

7.   As Ayres (1936) said, 'economics absorbed a great deal of psychology in the eighteenth century but has learned nothing since'. The judgments professed by institutionalists at the beginning of the century (Tugwell, 1922; Mitchell, 1914; Commons, 1934; Ayres, 1936) about the lessons of experimental psychology which spread at that time, have been validated by the contemporary developments of these sciences, and notably cognitive sciences (Fusfeld, 1989; Hodgson, 1985, 1988; Samuels, 1990). With Samuels (1990), we must underline that the work of Hodgson is a major contribution to the institutional theory of human agency for he integrates modern findings in these areas.

8.   The epistemological position common to institutionalists and behaviourists like Simon is then that the assumption of rationality is more an article of faith 'out of place in the real world' than an empirically verifiable foundation for a scientific discipline (Fusfeld, 1989).

9.   This articulation was clearly expressed by Mitchell: 'A slight but significant change seems to be taking place in the attitude of economic theorists towards psychology. Most of the older writers made no overt reference to psychology, but tacitly imputed to the men whose behaviour they were analysing certain traits consistent with common sense and convenient as a basis for theorising. By recent writers, on the contrary, no intercourse with psychology, long practised in silence, is explicitly proclaimed to be the proper policy'. It may even be that economists will find themselves not only borrowing from but also contributing to psychology. For if that science is ever to give a competent account of human behaviour it seems necessary that economists should do a part of the work. Human nature is in large measure a social product, and among the social activities that shape it the most foundamental is the particular set of activities with which economists deal' (Mitchell, 1914). Simon also follows this point of view: 'Recent years have seen important new explorations along the boundaries between economics and psychology. For the economist, the immediate question about these developments is whether they include new advances in psychology that can fruitfully be applied to economics. But the psychologist will also raise the converse question – whether there are developments in economic theory and observation that have implications for the central core of psychology. If economics is able to find verifiable and verified generalisations about human economic behaviour, then these generalisations must have a place in the more general theories of human behaviour to which psychology and sociology aspire. Influence will run both ways' (Simon, 1959, p. 253).

10. 'Intellectual power is nothing but facility in taking habits and in following them in cases essentially analogous to, but in non–essentials widely remote from, the normal cases of connections of feelings under which those habits are formed' (Peirce quoted by Waller, 1988, p. 114).

11. Long before Williamson, Commons has shown that economics has to take the transaction as the unit of analysis. But whereas Williamson analyses transaction as a contract defined by opportunistic individuals to entail the transference of a good or service, Commons considers that transaction is a unit of economic activity involving transfer of legal control and regulated by collective action (Dutraive, 1993; Hodgson, 1994; Ramstad, 1996a).

12. Biddle notes that we cannot find in Commons' theoretical works 'a well developed theory of negotiational psychology. I think that Commons was aware of this, and that he saw the development of negotiational psychology as a project for his successors' (Biddle, 1990, p. 96). Therefore, what we suggest here is an interpretation to specify Commons' thought.

13. As Commons says, 'within this changing complexity and uncertain futurity (participants in transactions) must act *now*' (Commons, 1934, p. 683).

14. Commons' theory is well summed up by Biddle: 'Commons believed that (...) the continuing task of the individual was to identify each new transaction as a member of some class of

transactions experienced in the past. When this classification seems obvious little deliberation was required prior to action, for the individual could rely on habitual forms of behaviour that had proven themselves in the past. (...) When an individual sensed a transaction was different in some important way from past transactions, and saw in it an important opportunity to advance his purposes, it became for him a strategic transaction. Rather than falling back on habit, he would *think*, and he would respond creatively to the situation as he assessed it' (Commons, 1990, p. 5).

15. Irrationality, says Biddle (1990), lies in the fact of maintaining routines that have failed. For Commons, this is a fundamental characteristic of human behaviour; he spoke of man as a being of ignorance, passion and stupidity to refer 'to this tendency to cling to habits that were generating unwanted consequences'.

16. 'Simon recognises the existence and function of unconscious habit in human action (...). But it is difficult to see how habit (...) can play a prominent part in the formal behaviouralist theory that is based on some type of ('bounded') rational decision making' (Hodgson, 1985, p. 72).

17. This opens the way to the integration of intuition and emotion in the analysis of rationality, as Peirce long ago insisted upon. Moreover, Samuels (1990) underlines that the institutionalist conception of habitual behaviour as a condition of the exercise of 'the human–will–in–action', conception which implies the integration of cognitive phenomena in economics, is crucial to go beyond the usual dichotomies in economics, especially two false dichotomies: the one between rationality and non–rationality, and the one between individual and society (see *infra*).

18. Mirowski underlines a very interesting point that should be developed: institutional economics is 'a theory of the semiotics of trade, production and consumption, which serves to explain how actors interpret the significance of transactions' (*ibid.*); 'Commons's theory of transactions follows directly from his embrace of what we have called Peircian hermeneutics, as it attemps to supply a theory of semiotics to explain the actors' interpretations of the meanings of legitimate transactions' (Mirowski, 1981, p. 1027).

19. As Ramstad (1996a) underlines, this notion reflects exactly Dewey's idea that people *are* habits.

20. Considering that collective control is the dominant principle of economic life (in order for individuals to maintain the material basis of their biological and social existence, see Ramstad, 1990), Commons analysed two types of collective action: unorganised institutions (like customs), and organised institutions (what he called 'going concerns'). Customs are noncodified behavioural patterns to which individual adherence is more or less compulsory, and they are for Commons the most general principle of collective control. The specific role of organised institutions (with explicit working rules as codified customs) is to impose sanctions which are those collective inducements that require individuals to conform their behaviour to that of others; they are the 'objective structures out there' (Hodgson, 1996) that regulate more directly individual behaviours and social interactions.

21. This is the major point of departure between institutionalism and Austrian economics (on the psychological foundation of this school, see Garrouste, 1996; Rizzello, 1996). For institutionalists, if 'cognitive theory *does* show that human knowledge has a subjective character', this 'does not mean that the *process* of cognition is entirely subjective (...). Emphatically, cognitive theory does not lead to the exclusion of the social dimension but to its reinforcement' (Hodgson, 1985, p. 83). It is why the study of cognitive processes cannot lead to subjectivism but to the study of cognitive and practical functions of institutions.

22. For Ramstad (1990), the crucial point in Commons' vision is that 'as customs are internalised as habits, individuals come to "voluntarily" behave in a mutually consistent – or "orderly" – fashion (...). As behavioral patterns are repeated (...) (individual action) although performed "voluntarily" and subjectively experienced as "free choice", actually may be little more than a manifestation of working rules' (p. 67).

23. For Commons, the foundation of shared customary assumptions was 'similarity of interests and similarity of transactions engaged in'. He also showed that negotiational psychology is conditional upon the type of transactions where actors are in distinct social positions: bargaining transactions rely on persuasions and coercions, managerial transactions on commands and obedience, rationing transactions on arguments and pleadings (Biddle, 1990).

24. If it is difficult to definitively classify theories from this point of view, Winslow underlines the fact that mainstream economics has always been atomistic because it wholly derives from the rational choice axiom that assumes 'to universally characterise individual behaviour' and that treats all the elements of individual choice 'as invariant with time and place hence as atomic'. This attitude is incompatible with the organicism that Commons explicitly embraced. He refered to pragmatist philosophy (for which the mind – internal world – apprehends objects in the same part–whole relation that characterises reality – external world –) and to Whitehead's organicist conception of physics which defended a multilevelled ontological hierarchy (Hodgson, 1993).

25. New institutional economics is not an homogeneous school of thought; if it cannot be reduced to the neoclassical tradition, it seems to us that the common feature of all the works lies in the defense of methodological individualism (even in a revised version) and its assumption of rationality.

26. Field (1984) and Rutherford (1994) have particulary shown that game theory is a perfect example of this impossibility; the state of nature, as an analytical device necessary to the reductionist program, does not avoid to presuppose the arena in which players compete or cooperate, that is, some specific institutions and basic norms of behaviours, and at the first place a shared language and nonbetrayal norms.

27. Notice that this conception of social science is incompatible with traditional formal modelling. It is why Commons defended the Weberian method of 'ideal–types' as a process of abstraction which takes into account the dimensions of purposefulness and historicity that specify social data and that can lead to the understanding of parts–wholes relations (Bazzoli, 1994; Ramstad, 1986).

28. And not only as one of the parameters of the context in which the individual makes an uncaused, unmoulded or unconstrained choice. This conception is in opposition both to individualism and subjectivism by defending that purposes, preferences *and* social influences on them can and have to be studied (Hodgson, 1993).

29. Stressing that individuals and institutions are both causes and effects leads to recognise that the individual and the social levels have a relative autonomy.

30. That is why Field defends that 'the hope that rule structures can, in principle, be made totally endogenous using economic models, thus avoiding the sort of research which Commons and his students undertook, is a chimera' (Field, 1979, p. 67).

31. Rutherford (1994) notices that if the necessity of this attitude is more and more acknowledged, this leaves open the nature of the *via media*; we think that the debate about this question is essential.

32. Biddle (1990) thinks that 'the tools of game theory have provided a means of analysing many ot the more complicated transactional situations that interested Commons' *if* 'the determinate solutions generated by its rigidly stylised models (...) were regarded not as ends in themselves, but as suggestive guides for the investigator studying the economic life process' (p. 24). We are more doubious about this subject. The problem concerns the very apprehension of interactions; game theory supposes that interactions can be analysed as a process of individual choice (it is a branch of decision theory); it doesn't integrate historical time nor the conditions of participation to a game, and doesn't discuss the stakes of interactions.

REFERENCES

Agassi, J. (1987), 'Methodological Individualism and Institutional Individualism', in Agassi, J., Jarvie, I.C. (eds.) *Rationality: the Critical View*, Martinus Nijhoff Publishers.

Atkinson, G. and M. Reed (1992), 'The Individual in a Going Concern'. *Journal of Economic Issues*, 2, June.

Ayres, C.E. (1936), 'Fifty Years' Developments in Ideas of Human Nature and Motivation', *American Economic Review* (Supplement), March.

Bazzoli, L. (1994), *Action Collective, Travail, Dynamique du Capitalisme: Fondements et Actualité de l'Économie Institutionnaliste de J.R. Commons*, (Ph.D Thesis), Université Lyon 2, à paraître (forthcoming) Édition L'Harmattan.

Biddle, J.E. (1990), 'The Role of Negotiational Psychology in J.R. Commons's Proposed Reconstruction of Political Economy', *Review of Political Economy*, 2, March.

Boland, L.A. (1979), 'Knowledge and the Role of Institutions in Economic Theory', *Journal of Economic Issues*, 4 (13).

Brochier, H. (1994), 'A Propos de l'Individualisme Méthodologique: l'Ouverture d'un Débat', *Revue d'Economie Politique*, 104 (1).

Commons, J.R. (1931), 'Institutional Economics', *American Economic Review*, December.

———— (1934), *Institutional Economics. Its Place in Political Economy*, New York: The Macmillan Company, reprint 1990, New Brunswick: Transaction Publishers.

Davidson, P. (1996), 'Reality and Economic Theory', *Journal of Post–Keynesian Economics*, 4 (18).

Delorme, R. (1994), 'Economic Diversity as Cement and as a Challenge to Evolutionary Perspectives', in R. Delorme and K. Dopfer (edS.), *The Political Economy of Diversity*, Edward Elgar Publishing Ltd.

Denzau, A.T. and D.C. North (1994), 'Shared Mental Models: Ideologies and Institutions', *Kyklos*, Vol. 47.

Dewey, J. (1922), *Human Nature and Conduct: an Introduction to Social Psychology*, Henry Holt and Company.

Dufourt, D. (1995), 'Conclusion' in COREI, *L'Economie Institutionnaliste. Les Fondateurs*, Economica, Collection Économie Poche.

Dutraive, V. (1993), 'La Firme entre Transaction et Contrat : Williamson, Épigone ou Dissident de la Pensée Institutionnaliste?', *Revue d'Economie Politique*, 103 (1).

Elster, J. (1989), *Solomonic Judgements,* Cambridge: Cambridge University Press.

Field, A.J. (1979), 'On the Explanation of Rules Using Rational Choice Models', *Journal of Economic Issues*, 1(13), reprinted in G.M. Hodgson (1993) (ed.) *The Economics of Institutions*, Edward Elgar Publishing Limited.

———— (1984), 'Microeconomics, Norms, and Rationality', *Economic Development and Cultural Change*, 4 (32), reprinted in G.M. Hodgson (1993) (ed.) *The Economics of Institutions*, Edward Elgar Publishing Limited.

Fusfeld, D.R. (1989), 'Toward a Revision of the Economic Theory of Individual Behaviour', *Journal of Economic Issues*, June.

Garrouste, P. (1996), 'The Problem of the Coherence of the Hayekian Evolutionism', Communication au Colloque 'L'Évolutionnisme, Fondements, Perspectives et Réalisations', Paris, La Sorbonne, 19 and 20 Septembre.

Hodgson, G.M. (1985), 'The Rationalist Conception of Action', *Journal of Economic Issues*, December, reprinted in M. Tool and W.J. Samuels (eds.) *The Methodology of Economic Thought*, Transaction Publishers, 1989.

———— (1988), *Economics and Institutions. A Manifesto for a Modern Institutional Economics*, Oxford: Polity Press.

———— (1993), *Economics and Evolution*, Oxford Polity Press.

———— (1994), 'The Return of Institutional Economics', in N.J. Srelser and R. Swedberg (eds.) *The Handbook of Economic Sociology*, Princeton University Press, Russel Sage Foundation.

———— (1996), 'The Viability of Institutional Economics', *Journal of Economic Literature*, forthcoming.

Jensen, H.E. (1987), 'The Theory of Human Nature', *Journal of Economic Issues*, 3 (21), September.

Khalil E.L. (1994), 'Rules', in G.M. Hodgson, M. Tool and W.J. Samuels (eds.) *The Elgar Companion to Institutional and Evolutionary Economics*, Edward Elgar Publishing.

Lawson, T. (1989), 'Abstraction, Tendencies and Stylised Facts: a Realist Approach to Economic Analysis', *Cambridge Journal of Economics*, Vol. 13.

Lewin, S.B. (1996), 'Economics and Psychology: Lessons for our Own Day from the Early Twentieth Century', *Journal of Economic Literature*, Vol. 34, September.

March, J.G. and H.A. Simon (1991), *Les Organisations*, Traduction Française, Dunod, (Édition Originale 1958).

Mirowski, P. (1981), 'Is There a Mathematical Neo Institutional Economics?', *Journal of Economic Issues*, 3 (15).

———— (1987), 'The Philosophical Basis of Institutional Economics', *Journal of Economic Issues*, 3 (21), September.

Mitchell, W.C. (1914), 'Human Behaviour and Economics: a Survey of Recent Literature', *Quarterly Journal of Economics*, Vol. XXIX, November.

———— (1935), 'Commons on Institutional Economics', *American Economic Review*, 4 (25).

Nozick, R. (1977), 'On Austrian Methodology', *Synthese*, No. 36.

O'Neill, J. (1973), 'Scientism, Historicism and the Problem of Rationality', in J. O'Neill (ed.) *Modes of Individualism and Collectivism*, New York : St Martin's Press.

Padioleau, J.G. (1992), 'Individualismes et Institutionnalismes Méthodologiques', *Analyses de la S.E.D.E.I.S.*, No. 90, Novembre.

Peirce, C.S. (1878), 'La Logique de la Science – Première partie: Comment se Fixe la Croyance', *Revue Philosophique*, VI, (1879), 'La Logique de la science –Deuxième partie : Comment rendre nos idées claires', *Revue Philosophique*, VII.

———— (1984), *Textes Aanticartésiens*, Présentation et Traduction de J.Chenu, Aubier.

Putnam, H. (1992), *Définitions. Pourquoi ne peut–on pas 'Naturaliser' la raison?*, Traduction, Présentation et Entretien par C. Bouchindhomme, Editions de l'Éclat.

Ramstad, Y. (1986), 'A Pragmatist's Quest for Holistic Knowledge: the Scientific Methodology of J.R. Commons', *Journal of Economic Issues*, 4 (20).

———— (1990), 'The Institutionalism of J.R. Commons: Theoretical Foundations of a Volitional Economics', *Research in the History of Economic Thought and Methodology*, Vol 8.

———— (1996a), 'Is a Transaction a Transaction?', *Journal of Economic Issues*, 2 (30).

———— (1996b), 'John R.Commons's Puzzling Inconsequentiality as an Economic Theorist', *Journal of Economic Issues*, 4 (29).

Renault, M. (1995), 'Communication, Interaction et Coordination des Comportements. Une Approche Pragmatique–Institutionnaliste', Communication au Colloque 'La Connaissance dans la Dynamique des Organisations Productives', Aix–en–Provence, 14–15 Septembre.

———— (1996), 'L'Évolutionnisme Institutionnaliste Américain: Nature, Culture et Connaissance', Communication au Colloque 'L'Évolutionisme–Fondements, Perspectives, Réalisations', Paris, 19 and 20 Septembre.

Rizzello, S. (1996), 'Economic Change, Subjective Perception and Institutional Evolution', *Quaderni di Ricerca QR 91 N.01*, Universita Degli Studi di Torino.

Rutherford, M. (1994), *Institutions in Economics. Old and New Institutionalism*, Cambridge: Cambridge University Press.

Samuels, W.J. (1989) (ed.) 'Austrian and Institutional Economics', *Research in the History of Economic Thought and Methodology. A Research Annual*, Vol. 6.

———— (1990), 'Institutional Economics and the Theory of Cognition', *Cambridge Journal of Economics*, No. 2.

———— (1994), 'Part–Whole Relationships', in G.M. Hodgson, M. Tool and W.J. Samuels (ed.) *The Elgar Companion to Institutional and Evolutionary Economics*, Edward Elgar Publishing.

Shalin, D.N. (1992), 'Critical Theory and the Pragmatist Challenge', *American Journal of Sociology*, 2 (98), September.

Simon, H.A. (1954), *Administrative Behaviour*, New York: The Macmillan Company.

———— (1959), 'Theories of Decision–Making in Economics and Behavioural Sciences', *American Economic Review*, 3 (49), June.

———— (1979), 'Rational Decision Making in Business Organisations', *American Economic Review*.

———— (1992), 'Methodological Foundations of Economics', in J.L. Auspitz et al. *Praxeologies and the Phylosophy of Economics*, Transaction Publishers.

Tiercelin, C. (1993), *C.S. Peirce et le pragmatisme*, Paris: PUF.

Tugwell, R.G. (1922), 'Human Nature and Economic Theory', *The Journal of Political Economy*, 3 (30).

Veblen, T. (1919), 'The Limitation of Marginal Utility', in W.C. Mitchell, A. Mackelley (eds.), *The Writings of Thorstein Veblen*, New York: 1964.

Waller, W.T. (1988), 'The Concept of Habit in Economic Analysis', *Journal of Economic Issues*, 1 (22).

Winslow, T. (1994), 'Atomism and Organicism', in G.M. Hodgson, M. Tool and W.J. Samuels (eds.), *The Elgar Companion to Institutional and Evolutionary Economics*, Aldershot: Edward Elgar Publishing.

5. Discovery Versus Creation: Implications of the Austrian View of the Market Process

Sandye Gloria

The Austrian tradition can hardly be described as a unified paradigm. The divergences between the foremost exponents are striking. Consider for instance the following controversies: Menger explicitly rejects the Böhmian theory of capital and interest; Wieser develops interventionist advice that contrasts with the liberal ideology of the whole tradition; Hayek refuses the Misesian apriorism; Lachmann and Kirzner sharply disagree on the role of the equilibrium concept in economic analysis.

Nevertheless, there seems to be a ground upon which Modern Austrians (from Hayek (1937) onwards) are relatively unified: the view of the market as a process.[1]

In this chapter, we will stress in a first step that beyond this apparent agreement, there is no unity at all. Indeed, it is possible to define two distinct conceptions of the market process within the realm of the Austrian tradition itself, namely the one of Hayek–Kirzner and that of Lachmann. We will in a second step investigate the origins of this divide. We will show that the cleavage lies in the exclusion of the creative dimension of the human mind from the Kirzner–Hayek conception: by contrast with Lachmann's view, agents are limited to discovery, discovery of profit opportunities and discovery of knowledge.

The distinction between discovery and creation implies much more than a mere intellectual curiosity about historical and analytical linkages between authors. More precisely, one of the issue at stake concerns the normative level: an analysis limited to discovery can attempt to prove the efficiency of unhampered markets, whereas the introduction of creation leads to the recognition of the coexistence of equilibrium and disequilibrium market forces.

A SYNTHETIC REPRESENTATION OF THE AUSTRIAN MARKET PROCESS

Within the Austrian logic, the market is viewed as a process; its thrust results from the interaction between individual plans. Agents are conceived as dynamic actors by contrast with the orthodox definition of Homo Economicus, a mere reactor to external stimuli. The market process is more precisely the outcome of the succession of three sequences:

- confrontation of individual plans: the market configuration is the result of the confrontation of the effective individual actions that took place in the past;
- revision of plans: if inconsistencies between plans occur, i.e. if plans are not well coordinated, it means that some individuals failed to reach their objectives; they will be lead to modify their original plans;
- consequences of the adjustments: the interaction of the new plans leads to a new market configuration.

From this very general framework, it is possible to distinguish between three distinct views of the market process within the Austrian tradition itself: the views of Kirzner, Hayek and Lachmann. In order to delineate the specificities of each one, we propose the following conceptualisation (see Figure 5.1).

This diagram is useful for two reasons. First, it provides a synthetic overview in which it is possible to position, despite their diversity, the three authors and their conception of the market process. Second, starting from this framework, we can determine precisely what are the splitting points between the authors.

THE KIRZNERIAN MARKET PROCESS

The Kirznerian view of the market process flows from the theory of entrepreneurship. Kirzner introduces a new dimension in the concept of human action inherited by Mises: entrepreneurship. Entrepreneurship expresses itself through the quality of alertness. An alert individual is able to find out unexploited profit opportunities. Profit opportunities consist in price discrepancies between sellers and buyers in a same market and reflect

Figure 5.1 A general representation of the Austrian market process

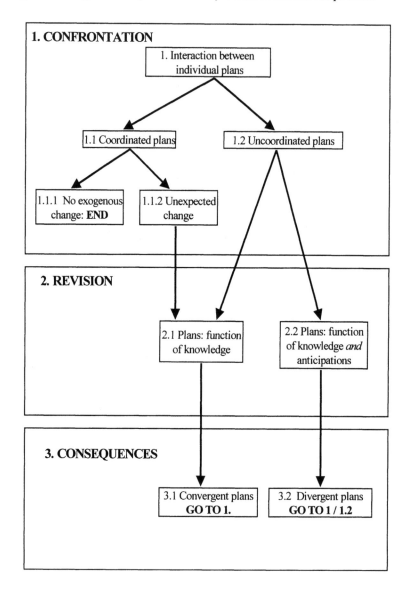

the imperfection of the economic configuration: in a perfectly coordinated world, all profit opportunities have been exploited and there is no room for entrepreneurship; in a disequilibrium world, discoordination is the consequence of imperfect knowledge, and imperfect knowledge is precisely the source for profit opportunities. The alert agent is not an individual possessing more knowledge than the others but an individual whose incentive is, through the existence of profit opportunities, to drive out new knowledge. Entrepreneurship consists in the exploitation of the profit opportunities discovered through alertness. This category of action has an equilibrating effect on the economic configuration: entrepreneurs contribute to the diffusion of the new knowledge their alertness allows them to discover. The exploitation of a profit opportunity renders available for all agents the existence of a punctual disadjustment on the market. They can revise their plan on the basis of this new knowledge. The degree of coordination depends precisely on the amount of knowledge available to agents. From that perspective, entrepreneurship is considered to be the propeller of the adjustment toward equilibrium. The role of the entrepreneur is to reduce the initial ignorance of the economy through the discovery and diffusion of new knowledge that is revealed by the exploitation of profit opportunities.

> For me the changes the entrepreneur initiates are always toward the hypothetical state of equilibrium; they are changes brought about in response to existing pattern of mistaken decisions, a pattern characterised by missed opportunities. The entrepreneur, in my view, brings into mutual adjustment those discordant elements which resulted from prior market ignorance (Kirzner, 1973, p.73).

The Kirznerian market process stemming from entrepreneurship theory is given the following conceptualisation.

Suppose that the initial market configuration is one of ignorance, i.e. a situation in which individual plans are not coordinated (1.2); discoordination means existence of unexploited profit opportunities. Alert entrepreneurs notice these possibilities and take advantage from profitable arbitrages between price discrepancies on markets. This kind of action conduces to reduce ignorance in the decision–making environment (2.1).

The process converges toward equilibrium as profit opportunities are found out and exploited (3.1). The equilibrium configuration is reached when the whole set of knowledge which defines the economic configuration is made available to individuals, through entrepreneurship $(1 \rightarrow 1.1 \rightarrow 1.1.1)$. Such an adjustment mechanism is based on the implicit assumption of the existence of an underlying reality to be discovered. Equilibrium is only when the set of knowledge is fully made explicit for agents; entrepreneurship is the element of change from ignorance to perfect knowledge of the data that defined the given and stable economic configuration.

Figure 5.2 The Kirznerian view on the market process

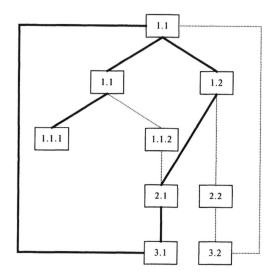

THE HAYEKIAN MARKET PROCESS

The Kirznerian conception represents a specific instance of the Hayekian market process. The specificity stems from two circumstances:

1. On the one hand, Hayek does not rely on the assumption of an immutable reality that is out–there and waiting to be discovered once for all. His world is one of continual change. Unexpected change results from changes in exogenous variables; consequently and unlike Kirzner, Hayek sees no use in focusing (...) on a long–term equilibrium which in an ever changing world can never be reached (Hayek, 1946 (1949), p. 101). The set of knowledge to be discovered throught competition is not immutable and plans have to continuously adapt to this circumstance. Nevertheless, both of the authors have the same objective: to stress the efficiency of the market process, defined as a coordinating device.

2. On the other hand, the argumentation provided by Hayek is much more general than the theory of entrepreneurship: the author develops a conception of competition as a discovery procedure. The price system resulting from individual confrontations in an unhampered market provides relevant signals for agents to adjust their plans. These prices are not equilibrium prices (in an ever changing world) but the market order is built precisely from the negative feed–backs that agents extract from them.[2] Discoordination stems from the diffuse nature of knowledge upon which agents rely to form their plan; competition, through the role of the price system, is a procedure of discovery and diffusion of knowledge and thus plays a coordinating function. According to Hayek, competition represents the most efficient procedure for knowledge discovery. This assertion is indeed a strong hypothesis. The author justifies the existence of a tendency toward equilibrium on the basis of empirical evidence:

> It is only with this assertion (the supposed existence of a tendency towards equilibrium) that economics ceases to be an exercise of pure logic and becomes an empirical science; (...) In the light of our analysis of the meaning of a state of equilibrium it should be easy to say what is the real content of the assertion that a tendency towards equilibrium exists. It can hardly mean anything but that under certain conditions the knowledge and intentions of the different members of society are supposed to come more and more into agreement (...). In this form the assertion of the existence of a tendency towards equilibrium is clearly an empirical proposition, that is, an assertion about what happens in the real world which ought, at least in principle, to be capable of verification. (Hayek, 1937, p. 44)

The Hayekian procedure thus unrolls as follows (cf. Figure 5.3).

In an inefficient configuration (1.2), market prices act as signposts for agents, providing knew knowledge about the direction in which plans have to be modified (2.1). In that perspective, competition is by assumption an efficient device of knowledge discovery and entails the convergence of plans (3.1). The occurrence of unexpected change prevents the economy from reaching a long term equilibrium (1.1.2). Competition permits the adaptation to the new configuration via its capacity to diffuse the new relevant knowledge (2.1 and so on...).

THE LACHMANNIAN MARKET PROCESS

The logical founding of Lachmann's view of the market process is similar in all points but one with the Kirzner–Hayek conception. The splitting point concerns precisely the definition of individual plans. According to Hayek,

Figure 5.3 The Hayekian conception of the market process

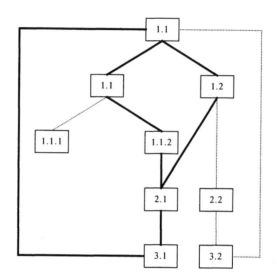

plans are conceived on the basis of subjective interpretation of past experience. Lachmann introduces a second dimension, plans are the outcome of the interaction of two elements:

- knowledge as Hayek puts it, that is a diagnostic of the economic situation understood as interpretation of experience;
- anticipations, that is an interpretation of the future situation, understood as imagination.

> (...) plans are products of mental activity which is oriented no less to an imagined future than to an experienced past (Lachmann, 1969, p. 95)

Given this enlargement of the concept of plan, the resulting view of the market process sharply contrasts with the traditional one – a true butterfly effect![3] Market is described as a continuous process, characterised by unexpected change and inconsistency of plans. This later feature is the direct consequence of the introduction of subjective anticipations. Plans are divergent because subjective anticipations are based on the image agents form about an 'unknown though not unimaginable' future.[4] Competition could conduce to the diffusion of relevant knowledge, but good anticipations cannot be diffused by any ways, for once they revealed themselves relevant they are already obsolete and need to be revised; no *ex ante* criterion of success exists. Inconsistency of plans challenges the traditional view of a tendency toward equilibrium. Market is an undetermined process governed by the interaction of equilibrium and disequilibrium forces.

The representation of the Lachmannian market process concerns only the right branch of our diagram (cf. Figure 5.4).

Figure 5.4 The Lachmannian view on the market process

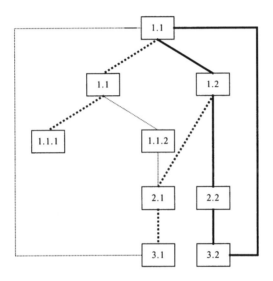

Inconsistency of plans is the rule and reflects the fact that plans are built up not only from subjective knowledge but also from subjective anticipations (2.2 → 3.2). As a result, the economic configuration emerging from the interaction of individual plans is definitely one of discoordination (3.2 → 1. → 1.2). In that perspective, there is no more reason to emphasise the equilibrating function of the market. Divergence of plans is the consequence of the extension of the subjective dimension to anticipations and represents, within the Lachmannian view, the propeller of change.

> The market process consists of a sequence of individual interactions, each denoting the encounter (and sometimes collision) of a number of plans, which, while coherent individually and reflecting the individual equilibrium, are incoherent as a group. The process would not go otherwise (Lachmann, 1976b, p.131).

DISCOVERY VERSUS CREATION

The cleavage between the traditional and the Lachmannian views of the market process proceeds from a different conception of the individual agent. Both lines consider the agent as an actor, in continuity with Mises' developments on Human Action (Mises, 1949). However, the subjective dimension of the human mind is extended to creativity within Lachmann's view, as opposed to the Hayek–Kirzner one, which limits itself to discovery. The creative agent builds plans upon his/her imagination of the future whereas the discoverer elaborates plans exclusively on the basis of the knowledge at his/her disposal. In that perspective, the degree of coordination of individual plans, that is the degree of efficiency of the market process, depends on the stock of knowledge it allows agents to discover and to use. Competition is analysed as an efficient – the most efficient – discovery procedure and the role of the entrepreneur consists in finding out unnoticed profit opportunities and diffusing the knowledge they reveal through their exploitation.

The sharp distinction between discovery and creation is never made explicit by the authors concerned. Nevertheless, no doubt that the thoroughgoing choice in the words of Hayek gives evidence to a conscious recognition of the existence of an issue ; the term 'creation' is carefully avoided. Maybe Kirzner makes it more explicit when he recognises the relevance of the critics addressed to his theory of entrepreneurship:

> My theory of entrepreneurship has sometimes been criticised as viewing the future as a kind of tapestry waiting to be unfolded: it is already there. It is simply behind the screen; it only has to be unrolled and when the future will come into the field of vision, whereas the truth surely is, the critics point out, that the future does not 'exist' in any philosophically valid sense. It must be created so that the notion of alertness in the sense of seing what is out of there in the future is a mistaken notion. I recognise the philosophical validity of this kind of criticism (interviewed by Boehm, 1992).

Beyond the conflict under analysis, the distinction between discovery and creativity appears also to contribute to a large extent to the tensions characterising the odd relationships between traditional Austrians and Schumpeter.

Consider first of all their opposition regarding the theory of the trade cycle and the role of credit: according to Hayek, economic fluctuations are initiated by the reduction of the monetary rate of interest below its natural rate, through credit creation; such a reduction is analysed as an erroneous signal provided by the banks, without real counterpart (increase in monetary savings). This signal acts as an incentive to investment for entrepreneurs. Crisis is precisely the consequence of the lengthening of production period in a context where intertemporal preferences stay the same. In this analysis, banks appear to deteriorate the ability of free market to provide the good signals for investment. In the Schumpeter perspective, the role of credit is exactly drawn the other way round: credit represents a necessary condition for the system to evolve from one configuration to another. The impulsion of change comes from the creative behaviour of entrepreneurs who, instead of being limited to the discovery and interpretation of the relevant market signals, introduce innovations in the system: new ways of doing things and new things. Entrepreneur is a disrupter of stability and the credit system is indispensable for the viability of the transition he initiated.

This consideration leads to a second circumstance in which traditional Austrians stand in stark opposition with Schumpeter: precisely the role of the entrepreneur. According to Kirzner, the entrepreneur fills an equilibrating function through the discovery of unnoticed profit opportunities, bringing the economy from ignorance toward equilibrium, i.e. a configuration in which all profit opportunities have been discovered and where the whole stock of knowledge is available to agents. In the Schumpeterian analysis, the well–known expression of creative destruction synthesises the extent of the gap: the entrepreneur is the agent of change and disequilibrium. Creativity means the break in continuity towards a disequilibrium dynamic. The contrast between the Kirzner–Hayek view and that of Schumpeter is perfectly well drawn by Kirzner himself:

> For Schumpeter the essence of entrepreneurship is the ability to break away from routine, to destroy existing structures, to move the system away from the even, circular flow of equilibrium. For us, on the other hand, the crucial element in entrepreneurship is the ability to see unexploited opportunities whose prior existence meant that the initial evenness of the circular flow was illusory – that, far from being a state of equilibrium, it represented a situation of disequilibrium inevitably destined to be disrupted. For Schumpeter the entrepreneur is the disruptive, disequilibrating force that dislodges the market from the somnolence of equilibrium; for us the entrepreneur is the equilibrating force whose activity responds to the existing tensions and provides those corrections for which the unexploited opportunities have been crying out (Kirzner, 1973, p.127).

The Schumpeterian actor creates profit opportunities whereas the Kirznerian entrepreneur is limited to the discovery of existing opportunities.

Harking back to the present issue, a set of questions arises: why do not traditional Austrians follow Lachmann in his extension of the subjectivist dimension to anticipations? Why is the Austrian theory of the trade cycle based on an implicit assumption of perfectly elastic anticipations and why do not Mises and his followers deepen the implications of the speculative dimension inherent of every human action? All these questions are the symptom of the same phenomenon and call for the same answer: the rejection of the creative dimension of the human mind from the analysis.

According to us, Lachmann does not go far enough in his analysis. More precisely, he wonders why,

> Austrians fail to grasp with both hands this golden opportunity to enlarge the basis of their approach and, by and large, treated the subject (of subjective expectations) rather gingerly? (Lachmann, 1976a, p. 58).

However, the author does not come to grips with the problem. He dodges the question simply saying that at this point, there seems to be a real conundrum, or referring in his deepest argument to the strict adherence of Mises to a neo–Kantian rationalism that impeded him from taking into account the full consequences of the very idea of time. In that perspective, Lachmann quotes Shackle, according to who 'time is the denial of the omnipotence of reason' (Shackle, 1972, p. 27); Mises deals with the dimension of time and more precisely with a Bergsonian conception of time; he therefore acknowledges the speculative aspect inherent to every human action but never went further in this recognition, for instance through the development of an analysis of the subjective nature of anticipations. No reason is given for Hayek's limitation to knowledge discovery, despite the fact that the adherence of the author to the subjectivist paradigm is by and large recognised. The following well known quotation appears numerous times in both Kirzner's and Lachmann's works:

> It is probably no exaggeration to say that every important advance in economic theory during the last hundred years was a further step in the consistent application of subjectivism (Hayek, 1952, p. 31).

Why then, are traditional Austrians reluctant to extend the subjectivism of tastes and preferences to anticipations? This attitude may appear curious given that their adherence to the subjectivist paradigm is beyond doubt and the introduction of the creative dimension of the human mind through imagination seems to follow the natural course of progress described by Hayek in the foregoing quotation.

There seems to be no logical reason for this neglect. Moreover, the limitation of human action to discovery contradicts the emphasis Austrians put on time and its implications, namely incertitude and error.

Ultimately, there seems to be only one reason that justifies such disregard. We are here referring to an ideological reason; the fact is that the introduction of imagination, i.e. of the creative dimension, would have overwhelming consequences on the representation of the market process. Consider precisely the results reached by Lachmann: we stressed above that the definition of plans in terms of knowledge – discovery dimension- and anticipations – creative dimension – leads to the recognition of the influence of both equilibrating and disequilibrating forces. The existence of a tendency toward equilibrium brought about by competition and market activities is theoretically questioned; theory can do no more but describing the market as an indeterministic process, the efficiency of which (in terms of plans coordination) can no longer be established.

This result stands in sharp conflict with the normative objectives of traditional Austrians, oriented toward an unconditional defense of laisser–faire and free–markets. In that perspective, Oakeshott (1962, p. 21) characterises in one expression the unifying feature of Hayek's works: it is 'a plan to resist all planning'. This applies to the whole Austrian tradition ... except Lachmann.

The attitude of traditional Austrians toward Lachmann is rather ambivalent. This stems from the fact that the results of his analysis, quite embarrassing for anti–interventionist supporters, are built upon a deductive framework the foundations of which are the expression of the purest Austrian essence: the enlargement of the subjectivist dimension cannot be criticised for it represents an improvement in Hayek's sense, toward a deeper understanding of complex socio–economic phenomena and the introduction of anticipations in the definition of plan do nothing more than making explicit Mises' assertion of the speculative dimension inherent to every human action. As a result, what is criticised is not the issue of subjective anticipations, i.e. the full recognition of freedom of choice, but its logical implications, namely the view of market as a non–convergent process. More precisely, critics typically accuse Lachmann of theoretical nihilism. Traditional Austrians underline the indeterminist result of his approach: the market is the outcome of a constellation of divergent forces and this is strictly speaking all that can be theoretically deduced from the analysis.

However, such critics ignore the endeavour of the author to show that the alternative does not stand between determinism and chaos. The strict indeterminacy of market process is evidence of the limits of pure abstraction. However, the task of the theoretician does not finish at this point. The pure theory of the market process as we presented it in Figure 5.1 cannot go beyond the relatively general assertion of indeterminacy, unless the decision–making environment is specified. According to Lachmann, economists should aim at providing not an abstract and general theory of the market process but different theories of market processes.[5] The author refers to an ideal-typical method of analysis as it is advocated in the works of Max Weber. More precisely, the general framework of Figure 5.1 should be enriched through the specification of the institutional set–up that characterises the typical process under analysis. Our framework thus needs to be completed by a general theory of institutions. Such a theory should make the level two of our general diagram precise. More precisely, Lachmann's theory of institutions as he developed it in his 1970 book, is an attempt to investigate the role of institutions in the formation and revision of individual plans. Institutions, described as reference points in a world of radical uncertainty, serve as benchmarks, guides to the elaboration of plans.

> An institution provides means of orientation to a large number of actors. It enables them to coordinate their actions by means of orientation to a common signpost. (...) (Institutions) enable us to rely on the actions of thousands of anonymous others about whose individual purposes and plans we can know nothing. They are nodal points of society, coordinating the actions of millions whom they relieve of the need to acquire and digest detailed knowledge about others and form detailed expectations about their future action (Lachmann, 1970, p. 49–50).

The theory of institutions fills a different part in Lachmann's approach of the market process compared with the Hayekian logic. Hayek's theories of cultural evolution and spontaneous order are oriented toward a different end, namely the establishment of the superior efficiency of organic (spontaneous) phenomena upon pragmatic ones (planned). The Hayekian theory of institutions constitutes another argument for justifying the assumption of existence of a market tendency towards equilibrium. On the contrary, Lachmann's theory of institutions constitutes more than an implicit assumption that underlines the view of the market process.

We reach here the real limit of Lachmann's developments: he lacks a general and unified theory of institutions to complete the exposition of the market process and without such a theory, his view of the market process is indeed subject to the criticism of theoretical nihilism. Nevertheless, the orientation is given and maybe we could find here the ground for a fruitful cooperation with the Institutionalist logic.

NOTES

1. Cf. Dolan (1976, ed.), especially the articles from Lachmann (1976b), 'On the central concept of Austrian Economics: Market Process' and Kirzner (1976), 'Equilibrium Versus Market Process'.
2. Cf. Hayek , p. 184.
3. From now on, the term 'traditional', when employed to characterise an Austrian proposition, will refer to the Kirzner–Hayek view of the market process.
4. Lachmann, (1976a), p. 59.
5. Cf. Lachmann, 1986, Chapter 6.

REFERENCES

Boehm, S. (1992),'Austrian Economics and the Theory of Entrepreneurship: I.M. Kirzner interviewed by Stephan Boehm on 2 May 1989', *Review of Political Economy*, 4.1.

Hayek, F.A. (1937), 'Economics and Knowledge', *Economica,* Vol 4, No.13.

—— (1946), *The Meaning of Competition*, Conference, Princeton University, 20 Mai, published in Hayek (1949, 92–106).

—— (1949), *Individualism and Economic Order,* London: Routledge and Kegan Paul.

Lachmann, L. (1970), *The Legacy of Max Weber,* London: Heinemann.

—— 1969), Methodological Individualism and the Market Process, in Streissler (1969, ed.), *Roads to Freedom,* Essays in Honour of Friedrich A. von Hayek. London: The Free Press of Glencoe.

—— (1976a), 'From Mises to Shackle: An Essay on Austrian Economics and the Kaleidic Society', *Journal of Economic Literature*, 14.

—— (1976b), 'On the Central Concept of Austrian Economics: Market Process', in *The Foundations of Modern Austrian Economics*, E .Dolan ed..

—— (1986), *The Market as an Economic Process,* Oxford: Basil Blackwell.

Mises, L. von (1949), *Human Action, a Treatise on Economics,* London: William Hodge and Company Limited.

Oakeshott, M. (1962), *Rationalism in Politics and Others Essays,*London: Methuen.

Shackle, G.L.S. (1972), *Epistemics and Economics, A Critique of Economic Doctrines,* Cambridge: Cambridge University Press.

6. Uncertainty,[1] Intelligence and Imagination: George Shackle's Guide to Human Progress

Brian Loasby

HUMAN KNOWLEDGE

George Shackle's work as an economist is distinguished by its combination of commitment, scholarship, and enjoyment. He believed that economic problems were of great practical importance and offered profound intellectual challenges; they demanded an active engagement with ideas and with the human condition, careful thought, and a clear understanding of what any analytical method could achieve and what it could not; but an honest and open–minded response to these challenges brought pleasure in the achievements of others – and, occasionally, one's own. Shackle was deeply appreciative of his predecessors and contemporaries; he valued economic theory highly, and sought to communicate its value, and its fascination, in his writing. His treatment of all those who had struggled with the major issues of economics is consistently marked by scrupulous argument and perfect courtesy, based on a sympathetic understanding of the reasons which had led each of them to use the assumptions and methods which had shaped their conclusions. He knew that theorists must simplify, modify, and distort, and demurred only when they sought to apply their results with inadequate attention to their range of applicability.

In an article first published in 1964, Shackle (1966a, p. 30) adopted Sir Isaiah Berlin's distinction between two kinds of scientist, epitomised by a line from Archilochus – 'The fox knows many things, but the hedgehog knows one big thing'. Shackle argued, there and in other places, that the time for hedgehog economists, who could expound a single core of arrange our partial theories according to the assumptions on which they depended, 'some assuming perfect knowledge, some acknowledging uncertainty, some concerned with progressive, irreversible evolution, some with mechanical, insulated, deterministic repetition: an outfit of tools, not an ultimate philosophy' (Shackle, 1966a, p. 32). Yet Shackle himself knew one big thing: that the behaviour of an economy depends on the interactions of people who are all trying to act sensibly on the basis of their limited knowledge and in the face of an unknowable future.

In *The Years of High Theory: Invention and Tradition in Economic Thought 1926–1939* (1967) Shackle offers a guide to the problems of developing a corpus of economic understanding. To provide a unifying theme for an apparently diverse range of theoretical innovations, he unconsciously reinvented Adam Smith's 'Principles which Lead and Direct Philosophical Enquiries' (1980) – a remarkable case of multiple discovery more than two centuries apart. Theories are patterns that we impose on phenomena in order to protect us from surprises, and to give comfort – which is no less real for being illusory – in the presence of a threatening unknown. When surprises nevertheless come (for theories are human inventions, not disclosures of final truth) we are pushed beyond the bounds of reason, which is where we do not like to be, and therefore struggle to extend those bounds by inventing better patterns.

Smith's account of cosmology culminates – though Smith was careful to warn us not to believe that it had concluded – in the unprecedented scope of Newton's connecting principles; Shackle provides an ironic counterpoint by showing how the search for a better set of unifying principles in economics led to the disintegration of economic theory, and to a situation in which the fox's kind of knowledge was the only kind available. The attempt to construct a new synthesis by the integration of a more elaborate model of general equilibrium and a more rigorous definition of rational choice, which attracted the most determined efforts of most leading economists for most of the post–war period, appears to lend considerable weight to Smith's and Shackle's theory of scientific development; nor was Shackle surprised by increasing signs of a second disintegration.

The neoclassical endeavour to impose order, and to extend that order into new areas, such as the law and the family, is entirely true to Shackle's view of the human condition; but much of the content of neoclassical theory is not. How can we develop a good theory of the consequences of not knowing by assuming that we do know? Closed models of rational choice, leading to well–defined equilibria of optimising agents, may meet the criteria of rigour which their candidates extol; but the resort to game theory in order to eradicate what Herbert Simon called the 'scandal' of oligopoly, in which rationality seemed unable to guarantee a rigorous answer, has raised doubts about the very meaning of that apparently precise term 'rationality', and demonstrated the relevance of Shackle's criticism. Perhaps mainstream theorists will come to join Shackle in echoing Keynes' (1937, p. 214) protest: 'we simply do not know'.

SHACKLE AND MARSHALL

Had Shackle been able to accept the place he was offered at St Catherine's College, Cambridge in 1920, he would probably have read classics or modern languages; but had he studied economics there his name might have become as closely associated with that of Alfred Marshall as it is with that of John Maynard Keynes. There could hardly be a more perceptive account of Marshall's endeavour to use the notion of equilibrium to provide a theory of economic evolution than is provided in sixteen pages of *A Scheme of Economic Theory*. 'Equilibrium is a state of adjustment to circumstances, but it is a fiction, Marshall's own and declared fiction, for it is an adjustment that *would* be attained if the very endeavour to reach it did not reveal fresh possibilities, give fresh command of resources, and prepare the way for inevitable, natural, organic further change': thus in a single sentence Shackle (1965, p. 36) recognises the scope of Marshall's ambitions, displays the ingenuity and daring of the means by which he endeavoured to realise them, and suggests how easily his successors could misunderstand both.

The ready identification of Shackle as a post–Keynesian has diverted attention from his fundamental affinity with Marshall. Both were deeply concerned with everything which might contribute to human progress, and with the obstacles to human progress that might arise from overconfidence in human rationality (against which Adam Smith also warned). Having defined economics as 'a study of mankind in the ordinary business of life', Marshall (1920, p. 1) elaborated that definition in the following words: 'Thus it is on the one side a study of wealth; and on the other, and more important side, a part of the study of man. For man's character has been moulded by his everyday work, and the material resources which he thereby procures, more than by any other influence unless it be that of his religious ideals'. The moulding of character is not much discussed in modern economics; people are construed as economic agents, who do not have character – just a consistent set of preferences (which rarely incorporate social values). But

Shackle, like Marshall, insisted on a more comprehensive view of human motivation. The guiding principle of his professional life was that economics should be true to the human condition.

Both Marshall and Shackle were particularly impressed with the importance of business as the prime source of material improvement, through the scope which it afforded for the generation, exploration, and testing of new ideas; nor did they neglect the effect of enterprise on human character. Both were keen observers of business practice, but without any desire to participate in specifically business education. Shackle recognised the importance of *Industry and Trade* (1919) in Marshall's life's work, and applauded his refusal to exclude the passage of time and the changes that it brings in perceptions and opportunities from his technical analysis. The consequences of that refusal have seriously damaged Marshall's reputation among professional economists; but Shackle shared Marshall's view – clearly expressed, but rarely acknowledged – that the problems of time and change would eventually prove fatal to the dominant position of mechanical equilibria in economics.

Marshall did not believe that the threat to mechanical models of economic coordination implied a threat to coordination itself; for he had another coordinating principle in reserve, in the multiple forms taken by the organisation of knowledge, which allowed increasing specialisation to be matched by closer integration. This principle of organisation, with its reliance on trade connections and continuing relationships of many kinds, implies that any model of atomistic competition is orthogonal to the proper explanation of coordination; but this devastating implication was never fully exploited by Shackle, probably because his experience of economic and political disorder in the 1930s had left him far less confident than Marshall had been before 1914 that disorder would be confined to temporary depressions, marked by a loss of business confidence, rather than becoming endemic.

THE INSUFFICIENCY OF CALCULATION

Shackle followed Marshall (and Adam Smith) in refusing to accept the central importance in economic theory of the equilibria of purely self–interested economic agents. Selfish calculation was an inadequate basis for the study of man. But it was calculation rather than selfishness that provided the central theme of his criticism of orthodox economics; for the calculations which were required by the theories of rational choice were too often neither feasible nor reasonable. Since he was a practising Christian, it seems appropriate to consider this issue in religious terms.

Mark Perlman (1993) has recently commented on the implications for economics of two interpretations of the Fall of Man. The more usual interpretation emphasises the necessity to work for subsistence, and is well represented by the conventional definition of economics as the study of scarcity, and the conventional focus on allocative efficiency. The other tradition, which emphasises the human consciousness of imperfect knowledge, is almost entirely ignored by economists; and it has to be ignored in order to reach clear analytical conclusions on allocative efficiency. The logic of rational choice, and the formal specification of the equilibria which such choices support, requires the closure of every model, and so there is no place for the unknown, still less for the unknowable. In his later years, Shackle often replaced 'uncertainty' with 'unknowledge', perhaps using this uncharacteristic inelegance to rebuke economists for their evasions.

Now the irony – and perhaps the tragedy – of economic development is that the triumphs of rationality (in its broader sense) that have provided the potential for alleviating scarcity through the development of evermore complex forms of the division of labour, have faced us with evermore complex problems of coordination if this potential is to be realised rather than being dissipated in unemployment; and since these are problems of imperfect knowledge, they do indeed appear to lie beyond the compass of orthodox economic theory.

There has been no shortage of technical skill and virtuosity among macroeconomic and monetary theorists in the past twenty years; yet it has produced very little useful advice on how to reduce unemployment. Indeed, the insistence on fully–specified rationality has made it difficult to interpret unemployment as anything other than voluntarily–chosen leisure; in some models that choice may be mistaken, but it is necessarily a rational choice, given the chooser's information set. Therefore the cure for unemployment must lie in better information; hence the recommendation to reduce, and preferably abolish, inflation which, it is claimed, causes people to confuse general and relative price changes.

Shackle agreed that unemployment occurred because people did not have the knowledge that is required in order to ensure the effective coordination of economic activities. But he eloquently and repeatedly defended and developed Keynes' argument that this lack of knowledge was an inherent characteristic of a world in which complete knowledge of the consequences of one's actions, even in the attenuated form of a closed set of contingencies, was unattainable. It does not seem likely that we can explain unemployment satisfactorily by pretending to knowledge that neither economists nor economic agents can ever acquire.

NIHILISM AND PRACTICAL WISDOM

Critics of Shackle's insistence on the insufficiency of knowledge have accused him of nihilism: if we have no recognised procedure for closing our models, then how can we reach any conclusions which will allow us either to make reliable predictions of the consequences of our actions or to make sensible decisions? One might respond to such criticisms by observing that such critics appear neither to understand David Hume's demonstration that there is no way of establishing the truth of anything that we usually call knowledge nor to accept Popper's warning against trying to assign a numerical probability to the truth of any hypothesis, as we are required to do by subjective expected utility theory. Is there not a certain lack of rigour in attempting to build an elaborate structure, either for forecasting or for decision, upon a falsehood? It is not only macroeconomic forecasters who are thereby exposed to the laughter of the gods.

But this charge of nihilism needs a more extensive investigation if we are properly to understand and apply Shackle's arguments. For they have substantial practical relevance. Peter Drucker, who was trained as an economist, and has an unsurpassed reputation as a perceptive analyst of management, argued in 1969 that 'the economic understanding and policy we need' required a microeconomic theory which would recognise 'the concept of knowledge as the central factor in productivity'. As the pioneer of such a theory Drucker identified Shackle, who 'attempts to base a comprehensive theory of economics on the expectations of businessmen and entrepreneurs. ..... His is the first true economics of a moving goal, the first economics based on teleological dynamics' (Drucker, 1969, pp. 207, 210).

The role of management in maintaining a 'teleological dynamics' was elaborated in a number of papers written by Henry Boettinger, who was Director of Corporate Planning at AT&T in the 1970s. Boettinger (personal communication) had been advised to read Shackle by Ronald Coase, and cited him in an article in *Harvard Business Review* (1967), which evoked a letter from Shackle; this led to an enduring friendship, including a series of conversations in which Boettinger appeared to the delighted Shackle like 'walking chapters from *Industry and Trade*'. Speaking at the Oxford Centre for Management Studies (now Templeton College) in 1973, Boettinger quoted Shackle's words to the 1966 meeting of the British Association: 'There are those who believe that life consists of a series of imposed situations to each of which there is one right response, and there are those who think that we impose upon the material chaos a psychic order of our own invention, not seeking to solve a problem but to conceive a work of art' (Shackle, 1966b, p. 755). Boettinger commented that 'management sciences necessarily adopt the first of these approaches, but the management arts can be comfortable only with the second'. The reason is simply that the future is unknowable; therefore the only way in which we can address what Drucker called 'the futurity of present decisions' is through imaginative constructions. To generate imaginative constructions, to explore their implications, and thereby to improve the quality of present decisions, was, for Boettinger, the function of a planning department.

The relevance of Shackle's work for business practice was also recognised by Charles Suckling, of I.C.I. and, more recently, the Royal Commission on Environmental Pollution. He found *Epistemics and Economics* (1972) a valuable aid in the management of innovation. (Boettinger recommended it to some of his business colleagues.) Those who have regarded that work as the supreme embodiment of Shackle's nihilism may find this hard to understand; but the issues explored by Shackle are fundamental to the intelligent use of knowledge. Suckling (personal communication) has cited Shackle's (1972, pp. 353–354) warning that 'When the compass of potential knowledge as a whole has been split up into superficially convenient sectors, there is no knowing whether each sector has a natural self–sufficiency.....Whatever theory is then devised will exist by sufferance of the things which it has excluded' and commented that '*ceteris paribus* is a linking, essential theme in all types of modelling, in science and in design, in effect in all prediction'. The neglect of this theme can tempt us to assume the self–sufficiency of the model which we are using; its acknowledgement can warn us, as Suckling argued, to enquire how susceptible are our conclusions to influences which have been consciously or unwittingly excluded from that model; we may thus enjoy the benefit of foresight, rather than the kind of hindsight which is provided by judicial enquiry after a disaster.

Thus the ground for supposing knowledge insufficient is a part of knowledge (Shackle, 1949, p. 281). Moreover, the attempt to capture all relevant aspects of a complex problem in a single measure, whether this be subjective expected utility or anything else, conceals the patterns of detail which are essential for the effective management of problems. It does not allow for investigation of the unquantifiable and the unknown, the discovery of unsuspected difficulties and opportunities, and the process of shaping plans and projects in response to such discoveries. Shackle's denial that any single objective measure is correct – which is explicitly not equivalent to a claim that any subjective measure is as valid as any other – is therefore not fatal to reason. It is, on the contrary, the beginning of managerial wisdom, and was so treated many years ago by Drucker (1969) and Ansoff (1965).

Shackle's (1949, p. 277) assertion that 'policy must legislate for uncertainty' is exemplified in the development of managerial practice within Royal Dutch–Shell, in which the preparation of central forecasts has been replaced by the creation of a range of scenarios which describe possible futures and are intended to liberate the imaginations of their managers from the pretence of knowledge which is implicit in forecasting models. This development was not directly stimulated by Shackle's work, but one of those involved, Michael Jefferson, examined the relationship between Shackle's theory and Shell's practice at the British Association meeting in 1981. Jefferson (1983, p.125) declared that 'the skein of his thoughts and words weave a manner of thinking and basis for decisions which the businessman will understand'; by contrast an exposition of Shell's use of scenarios a few years later baffled a group of economists who had attended a meeting in order to hear the latest forecasts for North Sea oil, and could not understand Shell's refusal to assign probabilities to their scenarios. But, as Jefferson (1983, p. 123) follows Shackle in arguing, with non–seriable problems 'the probabilistic approach ...... is tantamount to attaching probabilities to unknowledge'.

In the developing field of environmental economics, where inter-disciplinary cooperation is indispensable to good policy advice, and the inadequacy of knowledge is hard to evade, Shackle's views are receiving some attention. It has already been suggested that his concept of focus losses – which might be construed as worst credible cases – might be used as a criterion for deciding whether to apply a 'precautionary principle' (Perrings, 1991). Analytically, this proposal may be interpreted as an extension, to incorporate externalities, of a more detailed scheme for the use of focus losses as a guide to the management of industrial research, which was developed in the mid–1960s by a chemical engineer and used inside I.C.I. (Allen, 1968). Both schemes are devised for settings in which there are no good basis for probability distributions, but in which time may be expected to bring fresh knowledge; in such settings what is required is not the selection of an optimal plan but the choice of the next step in a continuing sequence. These are special cases of a very general class of management decisions.

In contrast to Shackle's advice on coping with uncertainty, what could be more nihilistic than the standard doctrine which proclaims as its theoretically ideal economy an equilibrium in which every future time and every future contingency is already known and provided for? To be born into such a world would be to find oneself a prisoner of time and circumstance, with no decisions to take, no schemes to plan, and the certainty of never having a single fresh idea. Can one imagine a more bleak and barren prospect? 'Conventional economics is not about choice, but about acting according to necessity. Economic man obeys the *dictates* of reason, follows the *logic of choice*' (Shackle, 1949, p. 272). For the view of the 'all is solvable and foreseeable' school is fatalism; the reverse of hope, the opposite of freedom' (Shackle, 1966a, p.133). 'When all life's questions are answered for any one of us, like will surely have ceased to hold for him any interest or purpose' (Shackle, 1953, p. 1).

IMAGINATION AND POSSIBILITY

We do not, and cannot, have the knowledge that has to be assumed by economists to construct their theories of rational choice, or their models of equilibrium. But it is precisely this double impossibility which constitutes the good news which was repeatedly proclaimed by George Shackle: the uncertainty which many economists seem to regard as a threat to economic analysis, and even to the possibility of rational behaviour, provides room for imagination, and the hope of discovering new knowledge. If the world could be accurately represented by a rational expectations general equilibrium, or indeed by fully–specified games, then economists could not possibly do what they claim to do – develop better theories.

Mark Perlman (1990, p.17) has drawn attention to Shackle's 'important, and virtually novel, emphasis on the role and uses of imagination', which takes us deeper into the foundations of choice than does its conventional resolution by economists into preferences, opportunities, and calculable consequences; for when there are many gaps, both recognised and unrecognised, in our knowledge then imagination is not only required in the act of choosing, but also in the formulation of the options between which we are to choose: 'The future is not there to be discovered, but must be created' (Shackle, 1969, p. 16). If economists really wish to understand human choice (and it is not clear that most of them do) then much more attention needs to be paid to human imagination.

To indicate how this might be done, we may turn to an economist whose work is rarely linked to Shackle's. In seeking to emphasise the exceptional character of his entrepreneurs Schumpeter (1934, p. 85) declares that the new is only the figment of our imagination. He does not tell us any more about the entrepreneur's imagination, but he does assume that what is imagined turns out to be true. Thus, once the entrepreneur has conceived a new combination, all that is required is the determination to proceed, and a stable pattern of activity which permits the calculation that it is worthwhile to proceed. We have systemic innovation in an orderly world. This is an inadequate conception of the innovative process, as many empirical studies have demonstrated. George Shackle, however, was impressed first by the coordination failures which afflicted all industrial countries in the 1930s, and then by Keynes' theory of unemployment, which, in chapter 12 of the *General Theory* and his *Quarterly Journal of Economics* article of 1937, was firmly based on the unknowability of the future. It is therefore not surprising that Schumpeter's model had no appeal for him; what he sought to provide was a theory of reasoned decision–making in a disorderly world – for that was the world in which decisions had to be made. People could not simply wait until order was restored.

In Shackle's (1949) own theory of decision–making under uncertainty the decision–maker's imagination, and the sources of the decision–maker's ideas are not explained; but much more is involved than working out the implications of established technologies and preferences. Instead of calculations based on what will happen, such as are required to launch Schumpeterian ventures, Shackle's decision–makers try to decide what can happen: in place of the imagined, deemed profitable, of Schumpeter's entrepreneurs, we have 'The Imagined, deemed Possible' (Shackle, 1979, p. 26).

Shackle has no time for the allocation of numerical probabilities to lists of contingencies which are known to be complete. Instead, he turns to Keynes' (1921) theory of probability, which is based on non–demonstrative logic. Keynes' question is: how can we assess the likelihood that a particular proposition is true, given the evidence currently available to the individual who is making the assessment? The concept of probability is thus applied to propositions, not to events (though of course some propositions may be about the occurrence of particular events). It is a concept which admits numerical measures, but only as a special, and relatively uncommon, category. Instead of applying Keynes' theory directly, Shackle inverts it, as Popper inverted the problem of verification, and focuses on the non–demonstrative logic of disbelief: how strong are the arguments for ruling out a possible future event, or a possible consequence of a contemplated action? What can prevent it, and are these obstacles in place, or likely to appear? Imagination is therefore constrained by logic and evidence, but free to explore whatever possible futures are reasonably credible.

An entrepreneurial venture is based on a conjecture. Success is not guaranteed by calculations conducted in a stable environment, or by anything else (except perhaps by selling the idea for cash), and failure after a full commitment is likely to be very costly for the innovator, and perhaps for many other people. Now although, in the end, plans must be tested in the market, it is possible to develop many kinds of surrogate tests which, in Keynes' (1921) terminology, may change the assessment of possible outcomes, and will certainly increase the weight of evidence behind that assessment, and therefore the confidence to accept, reject or modify a plan. The exploration and improvement of any new business idea should not rest on a probabilistic assessement of what will happen, but on a frank and imaginative appraisal of what can happen. The exploration of such possibilities is a major part of the activity of a research and development department; and it is in the organisation of an effective exploratory sequence that large firms are most likely to possess a comparative advantage within the process of innovation.

Popper's (1959) logic of scientific discovery is a logic of testing. Like Schumpeter, he has little to say about the origin of new ideas; indeed his fundamental argument for the open society is that no-one can say where new ideas will arise, and that therefore we should seek to avoid any barriers to entry into the business of idea generation. But once a conjecture has been put forward, then there is ample scope for logical analysis of its implications and prerequisites; and the investigation of these implications and prerequisites is an effective way of testing that conjecture. David Harvey (1995) has recently applied Popperian ideas to the entrepreneurial process. Shackle's formulation, in which the decision–maker examines a range of imagined futures in order to see which can be excluded, which are perfectly possible and which can be realised only if specific obstacles do not appear or can be circumvented, is directly applicable, as Suckling recognised, to the management of research, but with an important addition: a research department can investigate potential obstacles before the conjecture becomes a commitment. Indeed, the remit of a development project may be interpreted as the investigation, by experiment, modelling, market research, or any other available means, of every aspect of what is necessarily a complex conjecture, in an attempt to anticipate the results of market testing – and therefore to avoid exposing to the market those products which would fail that test. The neglect of this process is a major weakness in rational choice models of research and development.

The management of development projects is characterised by a great deal of procedural rationality, in the form both of scientific principles (which are themselves conjectures about patterns and causal connections) and of organised experience. This rationality, like the procedural rationality of Schumpeter's circular flow, often serves to prevent departures from established practice; much that has been imagined is deemed impossible and quietly discarded. Entrepreneurs and entrepreneurial firms who follow these procedures may therefore appear to possess the capacity of seeing things in a way which afterwards proves to be true.

It is important to recognise that the falsification of part of an entrepreneurial conjecture does not necessarily mean the abandonment of the project; it is often possible to imagine how the original conjecture might be amended to overcome the particular obstacle and try again. The variety of skills and specialist knowledge available in a large firm may allow innovative ideas to be shaped towards success in ways which are simply not available to the small firm or individual entrepreneur. Thus the common story of an original idea which is brought to successful fruition by someone other than the originator may be a story of complementary skills producing comparative advantage at different stages of the process. There appear to be relatively few examples of innovations in which the original conception was precisely realised, and even fewer in which the original conception turned out to be the most important aspect of the innovation; what proves to be true is not what was originally seen, and the capacity to imagine new combinations is not necessarily associated with the capacity to redesign an imagined combination into a successful form.

MANAGEABLE AND UNMANAGEABLE DECISIONS

'The boundedness of uncertainty is essential to the possibility of decision' (Shackle, 1969, p. 224). It is because Shackle does not impose the conventional limits on agents' expectations that some economists call his argument nihilistic. Their particular expertise lies in the constraints which are imposed by markets (or rather by their models of markets); but we might remember that earlier economists have ranged more widely. Adam Smith was particularly concerned with the constraints imposed by moral sentiments; and Marshall believed that social pressures might inhibit action, even among profit–seeking business men. Shackle discussed in various places and at various times many of the factors which make decisions manageable, such as the state of scientific knowledge, economic pressures, and social conventions; but none of these discussions, it seems fair to say, take us very far. One observation – that too many new entrants may spoil a market, and that this possibility may prevent any entry (Shackle, 1969, p. 174) – has been explored by G.B. Richardson (1960, 1990), and Shackle's (1963, pp. 1, 18) discussion of stereotypes – 'countless repetitions of a great number of diverse kinds of skill', which help to provide 'an orderliness in our surroundings that we rely on' – seems to point to, and in part beyond, the work of Nelson and Winter (1982); but, despite his interest in business, Shackle paid little attention to the constraints which may facilitate coordination within a group. He left much to be done.

The aspect to which he did give particular attention is the effect of time. Many constraints decay with time; therefore the longer the time–horizon the fewer the possibilities that can be confidently excluded. This is the core of the macroeconomic problem, as Shackle saw it – and as, he insisted, Keynes had seen it. Consumers find it impossible to make sensible decisions about many future purchases and therefore seek to preserve their freedom of action by accumulating financial assets; but by solving their own problems they accentuate the problems of businessmen who are seeking to decide what provision, by way of investment, they should make against future demands.

If these businessmen can find no good reason to exclude the possibility of severe losses from any investment that they can imagine, then they may reasonably decide not to make any investment. Moreover, since the range of uncertainty expands quite rapidly as one looks further into the future, it may seem sensible to disregard any consequences which are more than three or four years ahead; and Shackle demonstrated on several occasions that investment projects which are assessed over such a period are very unlikely to be sensitive even to quite large changes in the rate of interest. Recent history supports the view that where interest rate changes do appear to influence investment decisions, they work not by shifting well–defined projects across the margin of profitability but by changing businessmen's expectations about the possible outcomes of the projects themselves.

COORDINATION: SUCCESS AND FAILURE

The interaction between imagination and constraints is an appropriate focus for study by those who are interested in the problems of economic development and coordination. Shackle's position, that human beings flourish best in conditions where there is an intermediate degree of structure, and where imagination has a framework but a roomy framework – in which to operate, is remarkably similar to that of Herbert Simon; bounded imagination has many of the same implications as bounded rationality.

The coordination of economic activities does not primarily depend on the pre–reconciled choice of a general equilibrium or the pre–calculated Nash equilibria of fully specified games; it depends primarily on constraints, on the limits of what individuals deem possible. Many of these constraints are embodied in institutions; and Shackle and Simon both point the way to a study of institutions as a response to incomplete knowledge. (Simon has proceeded much further than Shackle, as indeed has Hayek). Because institutions are a response to incomplete knowledge, they cannot be rationally chosen (in the technical sense used by economists); they may have unexpected consequences, both beneficial and harmful, and are likely to change over time. Thus institutional economics must be evolutionary economics; and evolutionary economics must be institutional economics, for in a world of imperfect knowledge and of bounded rationality processes must be structured by institutions.

If institutions grip tightly, then life becomes a pattern of routine. Nothing novel that can be imagined is deemed possible. That is why Schumpeter's entrepreneur must be an outsider. In Schumpeter's model, entrepreneurs can act on their imagination only in a world of order; but the enactment of their imagined futures destroys the Walrasian equilibrium which is Schumpeter's stable economy and pushes those who are capable only of practising their routines beyond the limits of reason; new knowledge destroys old knowledge, as Shackle (1970, p. 21) observed, and creates a real business cycle.

Shackle did not seem to appreciate that unemployment in Keynes' and Schumpeter's theories had the same proximate cause: uncertainty had escaped the bounds within which people were capable of choosing. Perhaps this was because he emphasised the kaleidic quality of Keynes' analysis: there was no adequate basis for long run expectations, and so the commitment to long–lived capital projects depended on the vagaries of animal spirits. In Schumpeter's model, by contrast, it was the entrepreneur's imagination which inspired the sequence of events, and since this imagination was the prime source of economic development, unemployment was a price well worth paying. Schumpeter gives us a stark choice: we can preserve coherence only by excluding imagination and with it the possibility of improvement. A less extreme version of the same warning may be inferred from Smith's and Marshall's theory of progress through the evolution of knowledge. Schumpeter's vision is much closer to Shackle's than is generally recognised;

and Schumpeter has not been accused of nihilism. The interplay of imagination, uncertainty, knowledge, and institutions offers scope for an understanding of macroeconomic problems that lies outside the range of models which insist on rational choice equilibria, and may even permit some integration of economic theories.

SHACKLE'S LEGACY

Great economists always fail. As Shackle (1976, p. 516) observed, 'if all problems are to be soluble, we must be very careful what we admit to the category of problems'; and the problems created by the human condition are too complex to be soluble. The models, whether verbal, mathematical, or in the form of computer simulations, always omit or distort parts of the reality which turn out to be important; every attempt at improvement reveals a new difficulty. Yet in the process of failing, great economists have many successes, which give them pleasure and give us knowledge; and their failures provide the base from which their successors start. It is not difficult to see missed connections and unexploited opportunities in the work of George Shackle: since he raised fundamental issues, the possible connections were many and the opportunities diverse, sometimes obscure, and rarely easy to exploit. The ways in which economic systems attempt to improve knowledge and cope with uncertainty are of fundamental and pressing importance; they are the chief practical economic issues in present–day Britain and in many other countries. George Shackle's life as an economist was devoted to trying to understand them, and to explain them to others. No one has performed either task better.

George Shackle was a scrupulous and indefatigable scholar; he was also a gentleman, courteous, patient, generous, and enthusiastic about the work of others. He set himself the highest standards, yet had the lowest expectations for his own life; as a result he was continually delighted with his own good fortune. At the dinner in his honour in 1984 he put this down to luck (Shackle, 1990, p. 192); but if some people make their own luck, George Shackle commanded it by his refusal to seek it. He had the unconscious power to make other people behave better than they believed themselves capable of. He was a humble man of unshakable integrity, whose convictions were finely reasoned and rigorously tested; without this inner certainty, could he have probed so deeply into the implications of the deficiencies of human knowledge? Henry Boettinger called his life a pilgrim's progress; who is better fitted for the role of Pilgrim Father?

NOTES

1. This chapter is substantially derived from a memoir of George Shackle published in the *Proceedings of the British Academy* (Loasby, 1994). The British Academy 1994. Reproduced by permission from *Proceedings of the British Academy*, Volume 84, *1993 Lectures and Memoirs*. Some paragraphs have been adapted from 'The Imagined, Deemed Possible', published by the University of Michigan Press (Loasby, 1996), and is reproduced by permission of the University of Michigan Press.

   Prof. Loasby delivered a lecture based on this chapter at the special session in memory of George Shackle who was honorary president of EAEPE.

REFERENCES

Allen, D.H. (1968), 'Credibility Forecasts and their Application to the Economic Assessment of Research and Development Projects', *Operational Research Quarterly,* 19, 25–42.

Ansoff, H.I. (1965), *Corporate Strategy.* New York: McGraw–Hill.

Boettinger, H.M. (1967), 'Big Gap in Economic Theory', *Harvard Business Review*, July–August, 51–58.

Drucker, P.F. (1969), *The Age of Discontinuity,* London: Heinemann.

Frowen, S.F. (ed.) (1990), *Unknowledge and Choice in Economics,* Basingstoke and London: Macmillan.

Harvey, D. (1995), *Entrepreneurship and the Market Process,* London: Routledge.

Jefferson, M. (1983), 'Economic Uncertainty and Business Decision–Making', in J. Wiseman (ed.), *Beyond Positive Economics?* London: Macmillan.

Keynes, J.M. (1921), *Treatise on Probability,* London: Macmillan.

——— (1930), *Treatise on Money,* London: Macmillan.

——— (1936), *The General Theory of Employment Interest and Money,* London: Macmillan.

——— (1937), 'The General Theory of Employment', *Quarterly Journal of Economics*, 51, 209–223.

Loasby, B.J. (1994), 'George Lennox Sharman Shackle 1903–1992', *Proceedings of the British Academy*, 84, *Lectures and Memoirs 1993*, Oxford: Oxford University Press, 505–527.

——— (1996), 'The Imagined, Deemed Possible', in E. Helmstadter and M Perlman (eds.), *Behavioural Norms, Technological Progress, and Economic Dynamics*, Ann Arbor: University of Michigan Press, 17–31.

Marshall, A. (1919), *Industry and Trade,* London: Macmillan.

——— (1920), *Principles of Economics*, 8th edn. London: Macmillan.

Nelson, R.R. and S.G. Winter (1982), *An Evolutionary Theory of Economic Change,* Cambridge MA: Harvard University Press.

Perlman, M. (1990), 'The Fabric of Economics and the Golden Threads of G.L.S. Shackle', in S.F. Frowen, (1990) 9–19.

———— (1993), 'Rhetoric and Normativism: An Idiosyncratic Appraisal from the Standpoint of the History of Economic Thought', *Methodus,* 5, 1, 129–139.

Perrings, C. (1991), 'Reserved Rationality and the Precautionary Principle: Technological Change, Time and Uncertainty in Enviornmental Decision Making', in R. Costanza (ed.), *Ecological Economics,* New York and Oxford: Columbia University Press, 153–166.

Popper, K. (1959), *The Logic of Scientific Discovery,* London: Hutchinson.

Richardson, G.B. (1960, 1990), *Information and Investment,* Oxford: Clarendon Press.

Schumpeter, J.A. (1934), *The Theory of Economic Development,* Cambridge: Harvard University Press.

Shackle, G.L.S. (1949), *Expectations in Economics,* Cambridge: Cambridge University Press.

———— (1953), 'Economics and Sincerity', *Oxford Economic Papers,* 1, 1, 1–19.

———— (1963), 'General Thought–Schemes and the Economist', *Woolwich Economic Papers,* No. 2.

———— (1965), *A Scheme of Economic Theory,* Cambridge: Cambridge University Press.

———— (1966a), 'The Nature of Economic Thought', *Selected Papers 1955–1964.* Cambridge: Cambridge University Press.

———— (1966b), 'Policy, Poetry and Success', *Economic Journal,* 76, 755–767.

———— (1967), *The Years of High Theory: Invention and Tradition in Economic Thought, 1926–1939,* Cambridge: Cambridge University Press.

———— (1969), *Decision Order and Time in Human Affairs,* 2nd edition, Cambridge: Cambridge University Press.

———— (1970), *Expectation, Enterprise and Profit,* London: Allen and Unwin.

———— (1972), *Epistemics and Economics,* Cambridge: Cambridge University Press.

———— (1976), 'Keynes and Today's Establishment in Economic Theory: A View', *Journal of Economic Literature,* IX, 516–519.

———— (1979), *Imagination and the Nature of Choice,* Edinburgh: Edinburgh University Press.

———— (1990), 'Speech at Conference Dinner', 1984, in S.F. Frowen (1990), 192–196.

Smith, A. (1980), 'The Principles which Lead and Direct Philosophical Enquiries: Illustrated by the History of Atromony', in W.P.D. Wightman (ed.), *Essays on Philosophical Subjects* (1795), Oxford: Oxford University Press.

7. The Diffusion of Organisational Innovations Towards an Evolutionary Approach

Jorge Niosi

In the last fifteen years, simultaneously with the rise of Japanese foreign direct investment, the West has witnessed a major debate about the adaptability and diffusion of Japanese management techniques and organisational forms to Western enterprises. This debate started in Britain, where Japanese foreign direct investment first concentrated, but soon moved into the United States, Continental Europe and Canada. New words as 'Toyotism' (compared and opposed to 'Fordism') were coined, and many studies measured the extent of diffusion of these techniques – like Just-in-Time, technological cooperation among independent firms or total quality control – into different industrial settings. Evolutionary economics has remained marginal to this debate.

This chapter aims to develop an evolutionary analysis of the diffusion of organisational novelty, using as an empirical reference the debate on the emergence and spread of some Japanese organisational innovations. Evolutionary social sciences argue that organisations are structured through 'routines' (regularities in the behaviour of economic agents that these use to cope with uncertainty and risk) and that routines are somehow the 'genes' of organisations. Evolutionists, however, did not produce any coherent theory of how these organisational (including technological) routines are diffused from one firm to the other. We intend to go in this direction, by building theory on the routines that are closer to economics of technology, an area in which evolutionary analysts have by far made their most important contributions. The first part of this chapter recalls the essentials of evolutionary theories on routine creation. The second part develops some of the fundamentals of an evolutionary theory of routine diffusion. We conclude on the conclude on the usefulness of the evolutionary analysis in the study of organisational change through the adoption of management routines, most important of which are in the area of technology.

THE CREATION OF ROUTINES

The creation of routines is one in which bounded–rational agents (individuals within organisations, as well as organisations) develop new and improved new ways of doing things (Nelson and Winter, 1982; Hodgson, 1993; Baum and Singh, 1994). Organisational change takes place through the creation of new routines and the modification of existing ones. Variation can be gradual, if routines are slowly modified within a given organisation or adapted to organisations different from the innovative one; this type of routine modification is close to the Darwinian theory of genetic drift. Variation can also occur in sudden bursts of upheaval followed by long period of stasis or absence of change (Somit and Peterson, 1992). This process is far from logical, coherent and well–structured, but is best characterised by experimentation, tinkering and trial–and–error.

Technological innovation is also a process of search for alternative paths of action, but much more organised than the generation of routines. Technological innovation often takes place within established R&D facilities – corporate laboratories, design centers and the like – created with the goal of conducting technical change.

A converging approach of the firm, resource–based theory, posits that firms compete on strategic assets (consisting of knowledge, routines, capabilities, etc.) controlled by the firm and that enable the firm to conceive and implement strategies that improve their effectiveness and efficiency (Barney, 1991; Foss, 1993). These strategic assets are usually difficult to imitate by competitors, partially because of causal ambiguity, that is that rival firms are unable to link superior performance of competitors to the ownership and use of these resources.

The so–called Japanese organisational innovations show many different origins and patterns.[1] Some originated within the firms, like Just–in–Time (JIT) and concurrent engineering; others arose from corporations and external consultants, like total quality control (TQC); others, like technological cooperation developed, at least partly, within government laboratories and other government agencies. All are characterised by multiple restructuring and search, adaptation and the adoption of tentative forms.

Thus, methods for advancing quality had started in AT&T's Western Electric in the late 1800s and early 1900s and were applied first to the parts and components the company received from suppliers. Then they expanded to cover manufacturing and the design and installation of telephone equipment. In 1924, a physicist in the newly created AT&T's Bell Laboratories developed the first elements of statistical quality control that were to replace inspection to reduce defects and excessive variation of products. During World War II, the US Army and Navy procurement agencies put quality control in their contracts and encouraged the diffusion of the new routine. However, it was in Japan, through the Post–War occupation, that quality control was to spread more quickly in the early 1950s, first through the conferences of consultants J. M. Juran and W. E. Deming, two former employees of Western Electric. For nearly three decades, till the 1980s, Japanese firms had almost an exclusive use of this routine and had the opportunity to improve it in the field, while its use regressed in the United States (Juran, 1993; Main, 1994).

The basis of present–day JIT, appeared in Japan, as early as 1947, through the experimentation of Taichi Ohno, an engineer with Toyota (Florida and Kenney, 1993). It then spread towards Toyota suppliers (around 1955) and then to other Japanese automobile manufacturers in the late 1960s and early 1970s. It then migrated out of the auto industry in Japan, and into North American and European car industries in the 1980s (Cusumano, 1985; Womack et al., 1990).

Concurrent engineering was first developed in the 1950s in NTT by G. Taguchi under the name of Quality Function Deployment. It is based on the idea that each new product design project must be handled by a full–time multi–disciplinary task force (product design engineers, manufacturing engineers, marketing and finance personnel), in order to accelerate product design and bring forward the break–even point. R&D, thus, ceases to be confined to the R&D department but becomes a task for personnel of the whole company. In the early 1970s, the new routine spread to Mitsubishi Heavy Industries then to Mazda in 1978 in Japan and to many other firms and industries in the 1980s. In the United States, the largest auto, electronic and aircraft producing firms adopted it in the 1980s (Hartley, 1990).

Technological cooperation among firms is probably as old as the industrial revolution, but the chemical industry provided some of its more publicised cases. The German chemical firms conducted technological cooperation since the early twentieth Century; IG Farben and the Standard Oil of New Jersey (latter Exxon) exchanged technology since 1929 and up to the beginnings of World War II. Again, Japanese firms collaborated in technology matters before and after the second War (Gerlach, 1992; Levy and Samuels, 1991). What was new in the 1980s was the spread of cooperation to all other industries (Dodgson, 1993).

PATTERNS OF ROUTINE DIFFUSION

The diffusion of organisational routines is quite different from their creation, and much less understood. In the following part of this chapter we apply concepts and methods developed in the analysis of technological diffusion to the study of routine diffusion. This conceptual borrowing and comparison is based on the fact that both technology and organisation are intangible assets produced by the corporation and usually key to their competitive position. Thus, firms are interested in improving them and appropriating the benefits stemming from their investments in organisation and technology.

The Logistic Diffusion Curve and its Critics

According to Groliches and Mansfield, the pattern of technological diffusion is that of a logistic, S–shaped curve mapping the homogeneous diffusion of any new technology on a given population of firms.

Several authors have criticised the use of this epidemiological model to understand the spread of technological innovation (Davies, 1979). Davies argues that this model is based on two stringent assumptions: the 'infectiousness' of the disease must remain constant over time, and all individuals must have an equal chance of contracting it. In organisational terms, we can say that, for the neoclassical diffusion model to be true, the advantages of adopting a routine must remain constant over time, and all firms should have the same interest in adopting it and information about its financial characteristics (profitability and cost) should be homogeneously distributed. These two assumptions are probably too restrictive both for technology and organisation.

In fact, wide differences exist in the speed and rates of technology adoption according to firm, industry, and national context. There are firm and industrial (national and international) differences in technology diffusion patterns. According to Davies, large firms are more likely to be early adopters of technological innovations. This is due to several factors: the cost and risk of adoption is easier to be borne by large firms; because of their size, it is more probable that larger firms needed to replace old equipment at a given moment in time; and again, because of their size larger firms have a wider range of operating conditions than small and medium–sized enterprises (SMEs). Similarly, Colombo and Moscone showed that flexible automation (FA) appears first in large firms, only then in smaller ones (Colombo and Mosconi, 1995).

Industry is also a key explanatory variable in the diffusion of technological innovation: some industries are characterised by large firms and mechanical technologies (i.e., the car assembly industry) while others are mostly formed by SMEs and the predominance of chemical engineering (i.e. biotechnology). Flexible automation, thus, usually starts in mechanical industries then migrates towards other assembly activities and only afterwards is adopted by other industries.

Finally, national contexts are important in explaining the diffusion of technological innovation: the more the economic and technological information is widespread, and the industrial infrastructure is developed the greater the chances that countries become earlier adopters of technological innovations. Thus, in the Post War period, the new petrochemical industry migrated from the United States first to Western Europe and Japan (in the 1950s), where local markets and companies were able to assimilate the technology on the basis of the existing coal–based chemical activities, then to Eastern Europe (in the late 1960s) and finally to oil–rich developing countries in the 1970s (Spitz, 1988).

Firm–specific, industry–specific and national specific factors are also key in the spread of organisational innovations. Large firms usually have more opportunities and more resources to experiment with organisational innovations such as Just–in–Time, concurrent engineering or Total Quality Control. Nevertheless, SMEs are usually more prone to adopt some other routines, like technological cooperation, that saves crucial and often scarce resources available for R&D.

Industry is also an important variable to explain the diffusion of routines. For example, JIT appeared first in the auto industry (Cusumano, 1985; Womack et al., 1990; Florida and Kenney, 1993) then it spread to other assembly industries, like aircraft manufacturing. Conversely, technological cooperation appeared first in science–based industries, starting with the chemical industries in the early 1900s (Spitz, 1988), then spread into the electronic industries (in the 1950s), and only then appeared in the design of advanced materials and biotechnology (in the 1970s).

The national environment is also significant for the understanding of routine diffusion. The economic context may be more or less conducive to the adoption of innovative organisational forms. A study of Brazilian manufacturers of auto parts (Posthuma, 1992), identified nation–specific obstacles to the implementation of JIT. Among other difficulties, Posthuma found that Brazilian firms preferred to accumulate inventories as a security against inflation and the interruption of imported or locally–made supplies; they also preferred to buy materials in large quantities in order to obtain better prices than to buy them for shorter periods. In the unstable macroeconomic and macrosociological environment of Brazil, the fine–tuning provided by JIT proved less efficient than the traditional way of organising business. Similarly, research on technological collaboration in Canadian industry (Niosi, 1995) did not identify a single case (among more than a thousand alliances of over 130 firms) of North – South collaboration of Canadian and Latin American firms; in fact, the lack of R&D operations in Latin American firms was an obstacle for the establishment of North – South technological collaboration.

The diffusion of routines is a search process, involving much experimentation and tinkering, with periods of rapid spread of a successful pattern and others of creation of several competing variations of the similar routine. Firm–, industry–, and nation–specific factors contribute to the explanation of the specific patterns of diffusion of management routines.

How Quickly do Routines Leak ?

Research on technological diffusion is unanimous in underlining the fact that process development leaks out at a slower pace than product development, because the former is easier to protect through secrecy; it is thus more difficult and uncertain for rival firms to become acquainted with the new process and thus to evaluate its potential contributions to their own efficiency.

Organisational innovation is in several points similar to process innovation. First, major organisational innovations tend to spread slowly; our examples show that their diffusion has taken decades. Second, they are not voluntarily disclosed to rivals. Finally, at least in their first stages, they involve an important element of tacit knowledge and trial–and–error, which makes it more difficult for competitors to evaluate the merits of an emerging routine.

Product and process technological innovation are, at least partially, appropriated through patents, copyrights, trademarks and industrial design legislation (Schwarz, 1978). This type of legal protection involves a fair amount of disclosure and thus the possibility of imitation. Organisational innovation, conversely, is not protected by any legal device, and no public disclosure accompanies the intrafirm registration of the procedures and their performance.

The absence of legal protection for organisational novelty means, in principle, more difficult appropriability by the innovating firm and easier imitation by rivals. Also, many of the organisational innovations that are characteristic of the Japanese model must be diffused by the original innovator in order for him to capture the full benefits of the organisational novelty. For large assembling firms adopting JIT, for instance, some explanation of the new pattern to suppliers and clients is necessary. Thus, the large firm must 'teach' JIT to its suppliers (Cusumano, 1985; Womack et al., 1990). Similarly, government laboratories or science–based firms must devise jointly with their partners the contractual dimensions of their technological cooperation and thus contribute to spread the new routine.

This specific characteristic of organisational innovation makes it radically different from technological innovation, where firms strive to keep internalised as long as possible the results of their internal R&D in order to capture the full benefits of their innovation.

Population of Adopters

In the early phases of development of a new technology, it is difficult to determine precisely the future population of its adopters. Nobody could predict in the 1950s the future diffusion of the computer (IBM itself estimated in the 1950s that the machine could be sold to a few hundred customers); similarly, in the 1980s few could predict the future population of PC adopters.

In like manner, it is difficult to determine *ex–ante* the population of adopters of any organisational routine. In fact, the new routines evolve in the very process of their diffusion, as the new technologies change during their diffusion. They thus become adaptable to potential adopters not contemplated in their original version.

In some cases, only firms who have adopted a specific routine can adopt several other ones. Technological cooperation is a routine that has regular R&D as a precondition. Thus, the spread of technological alliances is confined to firms, industries and countries that conduct research and development. Similarly, concurrent engineering is confined to firms with design and R&D capabilities.

Creative Destruction and Obstacles

Joseph Schumpeter insisted on the fact that technological innovation is a process of creative destruction. Operating, even if technically obsolete, machinery and equipment is usually well fitted to the skills and physical capital of suppliers and customers. This equipment has to be destroyed if the diffusion of a technological innovation must take place. Diffusion is thus delayed by the persistence of old durable industrial facilities. Paul David, for example, has shown how the spread of electric power in industry since 1900 was slowed by the existence of existing plants using steam power (David, 1991).

This is also true in the realm of organisational innovation. Here, obstacles to the diffusion of organisational innovation come not only from imperfect information within rivals, but also from employees inside the potential adopting organisation. The inclusion of the new routine may eventually be beneficial for the organisation that adopts it, but detrimental to particular individuals and groups within it. Thus, while firms can benefit through the adoption of JIT, their supervisors and middle management can lose revenues (and even their employment) from the obsolescence of their skills, and they can raise against it (Florida and Kenney, 1993).

Diffusion and Adaptation

During its diffusion, technological innovation experiences permanent changes, as it is adapted to different markets and tastes, different countries with varying resource endowments and per capita revenues, and different existing technologies (Vernon, 1966; Utterback, 1979).

Similarly, the organisational innovation undergoes continuous adaptation and evolution in the very process of its diffusion, as conditions differ from one firm to another and complete observation and imitation is impossible. Routine patterns, like technological cooperation, JIT, or TQC will thus vary widely in their characteristics and degree of adoption from firm to firm and from one industry to the other.

Several models compete to understand how technological innovations evolve through time. In the product cycle model (Utterback, 1979) all major innovation is concentrated close to the original novelty, and then the pace of innovation falls down through time as the product or the process is standardised. For other authors (Abernathy et al., 1983) however, innovation undergoes periodical fluctuations through time, with bursts of renaissance of major novelty periodically shaking established industries. Thus, the development of electromechanical switching equipment transformed the telecommunications industry in the 1900–1915 period, as digital telecommunications reshaped it in the 1970s.

Similarly, quality control suffered a major change when in the 1920s it was transformed from an inspection–based to a prevention and statistically–based routine. Just–in–Time was also entirely transformed by the inclusion of software–based information flows in the 1970s and 1980s.

MODES OF DIFFUSION

Until 1850, migration was the most important mechanism of technological diffusion. Today, imitation and licensing are two of the predominant mechanisms through which technological spread takes place.

The mechanisms of routine emergence and diffusion among firms are different and have been scantily explored by evolutionary sociologists and economists. Some of these patterns are close to biological mechanisms. These include:

- the creation of new routines within new organisations and the differential selection of organisations possessing the adaptive traits compared to those that do not possess them (Hannan and Freeman, 1984, 1989). Examples of this type of creation are the new types of university–

industry collaboration related to the rise of the science–based industries (biotechnology, advanced materials, software).

- the creation of subsidiaries by firms: this is the equivalent of the genetic inheritance in biology. The parent firm transfers its routines to its subsidiaries, either at home or abroad. The specific advantages of this type of routine transmission, namely more precise transmission of information and internalised appropriation of knowledge, often explains that Japanese firms, in North America and Western Europe, prefer greenfield investments instead of the takeover of existing firms as they can transfer their patterns of organisation more easily (Abo, 1994).

Other diffusion mechanisms are distinctively social and have no equivalent in the biological world. They include:

- the voluntary disclosure of knowledge from the innovative firm to its suppliers in order to capture the full benefits of the innovation. This is the case with JIT and TQC.
- the flow of managers and technical personnel from one firm possessing the new routine to other, independent, firms using previous ones (Allen, 1977).
- the flow of organisational knowledge embodied in products, manuals, articles, (scientific, management and technical) and other writings. The Post–war teaching of W. E. Deming in Japan about organisation for quality control, for instance, was key in the migration of this routine from the US to that country.
- Informal networks of scientists, engineers and technicians working in different firms.

CONCLUSION

Organisational innovations are created in organisational environments much less structured than those surrounding technological innovation. The latter is often produced in the R&D laboratories of firms; the former come more often from tinkering and experimenting with different management schemes, using the whole firm (or at least part of it) as the laboratory.

New routines spread through a pattern that shows some similarities with the diffusion of technological novelty. Firm (size, presence or absence of

R&D activities, etc.), industry (i.e., types of technologies dominant) and national factors (like the national policies and institutions responsible for the spread of technological and managerial information) intervene in the diffusion of routines. In the process of diffusion, the innovation, whether organisational or technological, tends to change and adapt to different industries and national environments. Foreign direct investment by the innovative firms and differential survival rates for companies both contribute to the diffusion of routines and technology. Also, the diffusion of new routines – as the diffusion of technology – seems to be a process usually stretching through decades, witnessing long periods of slow spread and rapid periods of expansion into new nations and activities.

On other dimensions, the spread of new routines is different from technology diffusion. First, corporations tend to appropriate technological novelty through patents, secrecy and other means in order to reduce spillovers and imitation. They also prefer to internalise it, that is to transfer the new technology to foreign subsidiaries within the same enterprise. Conversely, organisational innovators need sometimes to be freely transferred to both domestic and foreign suppliers and customers in order for the leader to capture the full benefits of the novelty. Second, as organisational invention is not patentable, and cannot be protected by any other legal means, it tends to flood from firm to firm more freely than technology. However, as organisational novelty embodies a high share of tacit knowledge, its spread tends to involve more variation and adaptation than technological innovation. Third, and linked to the previous points, organisational novelty often flows through specific mechanisms, like the migration of personnel from one firm to the other and through the activities of consultants; networks of industrial scientists and engineers also contribute to the diffusion of knowledge about new routines. Finally, one of the most important conclusions of this analysis is that innovation creation and innovation diffusion are thoroughly related processes, particularly when it comes to the area of technological routines.

The bounded–rationality assumption of evolutionary theory points also to another dimension of the diffusion process that was not studied here, namely the learning processes, both individual and organisational, that take place within the firm during the spread of these routines. But this should be the theme of a very different kind of analysis.[2]

NOTES

1. In this chapter we shall confine ourselves to a few corporate routines that are at the core of what is called 'The Japanese corporate model' (Aoki, 1990; Elger and Smith, 1992; Abo, 1994).
2. There is a first analysis of these learning processes (Cole, 1994).

REFERENCES

Abernathy, W., K. Clark and A. Kantrow (1983), *Industrial Renaissance*, New York: Basic Books.

Abo, T. (1994), *Hybrid Factory*, New York: Oxford University Press.

Allen, T. (1977), *Managing the Flow of Technology*, Cambridge, MA: MIT Press.

Barney, J. (1991), 'Firm Resources and Sustained Competitive Advantage', *Journal of Management*, 17, 1.

Baum, J. and J.V. Singh (eds.) (1994), *Evolutionary Dynamics of Organisations,* Oxford: Oxford University Press.

Colombo, M. and R. Mosconi (1995), 'Complementary and Cumulative Learning Effects in the Early Diffusion of Multiple Technologies', *Journal of Industrial Economics* XLIII.

Cusumano, M. (1985), *The Japanese Autmobile Industry. Technology and Management at Nissan and Toyota*, Cambridge MA: The Council of East Asian Studies of Harvard University.

David, P.A. (1991), *Computer and Dynamo. The Modern Productivity Paradox in a Not–too–Distant Mirror*, Stanford, CA: CEPR Discussion Paper #172.

Davies, S. (1979), *The Diffusion of Process Innovations*, Cambridge: Cambridge University Press.

Dodgson, M. (1993), *Technological Collaboration in Industry*, London: Routledge.

Elger, T. and C. Smith (eds.) (1992), *Global Japanisation?*, London: Routledge.

Florida, R. and M. Kenney (1993), *Beyond Mass Production, The Japanese System and Its Transfer to the US*, New York: Oxford University Press.

Foss, N. (1993): 'Theories of the Firm: Contractual and Competence Perspectives', *Journal of Evolutionary Economics*, 2, 2.

Gerlach, M.L. (1992), *Alliance Capitalism. The Social Organisation of Japanese Business*, Berkeley: University of California Press.

Hannan, M.T. and J.H. Freeman (1984), 'Structural Inertia and Organisational Change', *American Sociological Review*, 49, April.

——— (1989), *Organisational Ecology*, Cambridge, MA: Harvard University Press.

Hartley, J.R. (1990), *Concurrent Engineering*, Cambridge, MA: Productivity Press.

Hodgson, G.M. (1993), *Economics and Evolution*, Cheltenham: Edward Elgar.

Juran, J.M. (1993), 'Made in USA. A Renaissance in Quality', *Harvard Business Review*, 83, 4, July–August.

Levy, J. and R. Samuels. (1991), 'Institutions and Innovation: Research Collaboration as Technology Strategy in Japan', in L. Mytelka (ed.), *Strategic Partnerships in the World Economy*, Rutherford, Fairleigh Dickinson Press.

Main, J. (1994), *Quality Wars. The Triumph and Defeats of American Business*, New York: Free Press.

Nelson, R.R. and S.Winter (1982), *An Evolutionary Theory of Economic Change*, Cambridge: Belknap Press of Harvard University.

Niosi, J. (1995), *Flexible Innovation. Technological Alliances in Canadian Industry*, Montreal and Kingston: McGill–Queen's University Press.

Posthuma, A. (1992), 'Japanese Production Techniques in Brazilian Automobile Firms', in T. Elgers, T. and C. Smith (eds.), *Global Japanisation?*, London: Routledge.

Schwartz, M.A. (1978), *Imitation and Diffusion of Industrial Innovations*. (Ph.D. Dissertation Economics, University of Pennsylvania) Ann Arbor: University Microfilms.

Somit, A. and S.A. Peterson (1992), *The Dynamics of Evolution. The Punctuated Equilibrium Debate in the Natural and the Social Sciences*, Ithaca and London: Cornell University Press.

Spitz, P.H. (1988), *Petrochemicals. The Rise of An Industry,* New York: Wiley.

Utterback, J. (1979), 'The Dynamics of Product and Process Innovation in Industry', C. Hill and J. Utterback (eds.), *Technological Innovation in a Dynamic Economy*, New York: Pergamon.

Vernon, R. (1966), 'International Investment and International Trade in the Product Cycle', *Quarterly Journal of Economics,* 80, 2.

Womack, J.P., D.T. Jones and D. Roos (1990), *The Machine that Changed the World*, New York: Macmillan.

8. The Variety and Dynamics of Capitalism

Robert Boyer

One of the major events of the last decade has been the unexpected and dramatic collapse of Soviet regime type societies. Most observers have analysed this structural crisis as the direct consequence of two of the systemic features of this regime : the concentration of political power by the communist party and related nomenclatura, and the centralisation of economic decisions by Gosplan. Thus, conventional economists have been active in advising the new governments and have put forward a very simple equation :

$$Capitalism = Private\ property\ rights + Markets$$

which was supposed to replace the wrong mix of political and economic institutions:

$$Socialism = Collective\ property + Gosplan$$

Thus capitalism has won..., but practitioners and social scientists discovered soon that there is not a single capitalism but a large variety, and that differences between them do matter (Albert, 1991; Aoki, 1995; Dore, Boyer, Mars (eds.), 1994; Berger, Dore (eds.), 1996). In this chapter different systems of capitalism will be discussed and the question will be raised whether the dynamics of the systems will result in the dominance of one type of capitalism namely the Anglo–American model, i.e. a market led configuration.

WHY DO ECONOMIES DIFFER ?

Arguments why different capitalist systems exist stem from a large variety of disciplines ranging from economics to political sciences.

- The first argument flows directly from the recent advances of micro economic theory of imperfect information: as soon as no complete contract can be drafted, nor all contingent markets organised, many second best solutions can be given to the same economic issue. Therefore from a strict neoclassical standpoint, commodities markets display a lot of configurations (Stiglitz, 1987). The argument is still stronger for the allocation mechanisms for labour, credit and finance and even durable consumer goods, which show far more complex relationships than typical commodities. Thus a multiplicity of institutional settings can be observed in order to solve the same informational problem and no one is *a priori* superior.
- Political scientists add a quite different argument: the variety of economic institutions explicitly derives from the intricacy of the political process (Hibbs, 1987) which leads to institutionalised compromises. The diversity of political institutions seems somehow correlated with the diversity of capitalisms (Boismenu, 1995; Zysman and Cohen, 1987). The methods for solving conflicts among alternative principles and diverging interests differ drastically from one country to another. This is why a constitutional order is so important (Figure 8.1): it informs and channels the evolution of institutions and organisations and therefore it induces a strong path dependency (North, 1991, 1996). For instance, the same issue is solved by private law and jurisprudence in the United States and by public jurisdiction in France, and these differences are piling up decade after decade and finally define quite different capitalisms (Cohen–Tanugi, 1984). More generally, the same issue is solved by negotiation, state intervention or market contracts, depending on the constitutional order reflected in different institutional forms and organisations.
- Specialists of technical change and evolutionary economists have developed fairly sophisticated models built upon the role of increasing returns to scale (Dosi, 1988, 1991). This is a quite general phenomenon which arises through a large variety of mechanisms: typical technical returns to scale, role of the number of adopters in the selection of a communication technique or social norm, impact of radical innovations

on subsequent developments, constitution of technological and productive paradigms, tacit knowledge and its diffusion within an industrial district. Then, initial choices, which seemed marginal and reversible, turn out to propel the economic system along a trajectory, featuring a strong path dependency (Arthur, 1994). This applies to economic geography (Krugman, 1992), the evolution of conventions and social norms (Boyer and Orléan, 1992), the constitution of networks, the emergence of technical norms. When all these mechanisms are added, no surprise if strong localised or sectoral specificity tends to perpetuate.

- Finally, the same evolutionary framework can be extended to the issue of co–evolution and the complementarity of institutions, organisations and economic specialisation (Aoki, 1995; Dosi, Fabiani, Freeman and Aversi, 1993). The institutions of capitalism can no more be analysed in isolation, since they have to be mutually compatible. This complementarity is the more important, the more distant the economy is away from the idealised Walrasian world, in which individuals are only coordinated and socialised by the price mechanisms. As soon as constitution, institutions and organisations are created to overcome the limits of individual information gathering and use (Favereau, 1989), the central issue is the compatibility of a complete institutional architecture. Institutional economics is one of the rare and serious alternatives to Walrasian economics and their contemporary legacy, since it deals with the central question of political economy: how to organise a decentralised economy?

Figure 8.1 summarises some of the previous arguments and builds upon the primacy of a constitutional order over institutional forms and organisations. Thus from a theoretical standpoint, both variety of institutional architectures and their path dependence are possible or even likely.

There are many theoretical reasons for the diversity of capitalisms, but do empirical evidences confirm such a variety? Are there as many capitalisms as cultural values, political traditions and economic specialisation? A recent research has collected a large number of statistical indexes in order to capture the determinants of innovations for twelve OECD countries (Amable, Barré and Boyer, 1997) Data analyses and statistical clustering techniques deliver a suggestive taxonomy: four major brands of capitalism were coexisting at the end of the 1980s. This totally inductive method produces results easily to be interpreted within the present framework.

Figure 8.1 The building blocks of an institutional analysis of capitalism

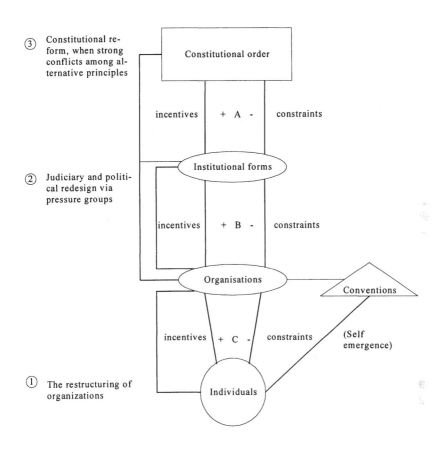

Top-down   : From the constitution to individuals: a clear hierarchy

A ___ B ___ C

Bottom-up   : Emerging disequilibria and conflicts call for a revision of
upper level rules of the game:

1 ___ 2 ___ 3

Degree of persistence : Constitutional order > Institutional forms >
Organisations > Individual behaviours

MARKET LED CAPITALISM

The processes of evolution differ from one type of capitalism to the other. In Market Led Capitalism (see Figure 8.2) the self–interested individual and the selection through competition are central. Figure 8.2 shows how market mechanisms shape the whole socio–economic order from labour to education and innovation.

Individuals and families invest in education in accordance with the expected private rates of return of each track and generally there is few professional training, since it cannot be appropriated by the recipients. External flexibility (exit) is the important method for adjusting labour markets, which are segmented according to the degree of skills of individuals, the specificities of sectors and regions. Since the Fordist collective bargaining on wages has been seriously eroded, income evolution may vary drastically according to skills, localisation and the firm considered.

The concept of fairness is limited to the objective that each talent or competence should be paid its price. In the system of Market Led Capitalism innovation is governed by the question of appropriability, and the patent system is designed in order to try to work out a trade off between incentives to innovate and speed of diffusion of the technological advances associated to these innovations. Venture capital and a whole spectrum of financial instruments allows a permanent renewal of entrepreneurs in sunrise sectors. The institutions of the labour market and the process of innovation lead in market systems like the United States and United Kingdom to a specialisation in activities where knowledge is easily coded and formalised: pharmaceuticals, publishing, software, leisure industry, and high tech sectors like aircraft building. Central in the market led model is the 'market for corporate control', which disciplines management to behave according to the interest of the shareholders. This together with the characteristics of the external labour market result in short term dynamism, radical innovations, and quick adaptation to disturbances and variations in the environment. But simultaneously, the system shows its weaknesses for sectors which require a lot of coordination among interdependent firms.

Coordination of activities of firms can take place through competition or organisation, like strategic alliances and industrial groups. Generally speaking competition in the Market Led Capitalism contributes to the efficiency of short term dynamics, but fails when organised coordination is needed that aims at long term dynamics and efficiency (see below).

Figure 8.2 Market Led Capitalism

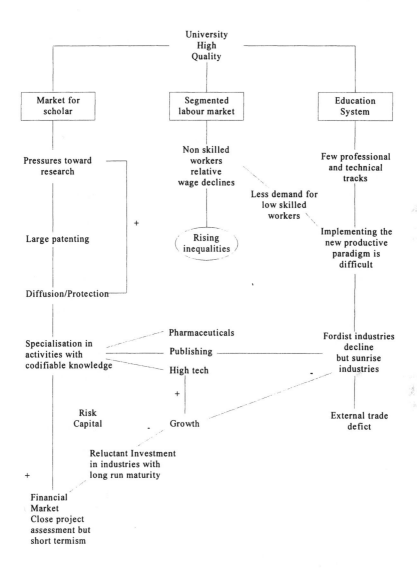

Although the general level of unemployment is relatively low in countries of the market led type, the systems allow for (or even call for) the deepening of inequalities. More generally, market led capitalisms tend to under–invest in the public goods which would benefit the poorest part of the population (public transportation infrastructures, general education, preventive health care).

MESO CORPORATIST CAPITALISM

In the system of Meso Corporatist Capitalism, of which Japan is an illustration, not the external labour and capital markets feature, but the internal ones. At meso level large industrial groups have internalised labour and capital markets with a crucial role for the main bank and the network of related or affiliated companies. This so–called internal organisation of markets is supplemented with an external regulation of public institutions. The institutions in the corporatist type of capitalism coordinate behaviour of members of the different groups; the coercion of markets is replaced by coordination of organisations. Coordination is not limited to the interior of the firm (by opposition to micro–corporatist) nor does it require strong nation wide economic policy (in contrast with typical state led capitalism). For instance, wage increases are coordinated and synchronised by the *Shunto*, and equivalent mechanisms, generally less explicit, are operating for innovation, trade, foreign investment and so on.

This configuration is frequently misunderstood and confused with another brand of capitalism. For the tenants of Market Led Capitalism, the Japanese economy is only an evidence for archaism and obsolete institutions which should be replaced by American–inspired regulations and organisations. Clearly, this is a misinterpretation of a typical capitalist trajectory, even if permeated by some specific Japanese features (Landes, 1998). Conversely, some observers tend to present Japan as a State Led Capitalism, more or less in accordance with the French trajectory. Again, the role of State might have been important after World War II, but since the 1970s large *keiretsus* have taken the initiative and coordinated most of their activities, with a residual, if not at all minimal, role of the State. Similarly, the Japanese capitalism is not a minor variant of a social–democratic configuration since enterprise unions operate at a decentralised level, contrary to the strong and highly centralised unions in Sweden or Austria (see below). Furthermore, the general welfare is kept minimal in Japan, whereas it is the cornerstone of the social democratic capitalism.

The distinctive feature of this capitalism is the meso level at which coordination takes place. It expresses itself at the level of the educational system, the labour market and the strategy of the large firm (Figure 8.3).

The central role of the large corporation explains the structuring of the labour market between regular and non–regular workers; the large firm has its own internal labour market. Similarly, the secondary education system delivers a rather high and homogeneous degree of general knowledge, but the specific competencies required by the firm are learned by internal job mobility and on the job training. Therefore, this system is specially strong in coordinating complex production processes (automobile, consumer electronics and robotics), but conversely, rather weak in sectors where innovations are basic science driven such as the biomedical industry, chemistry, aerospace, and the like. The interdependencies inside industrial–financial groups (keiretsu) at meso–level create also inefficient reciprocities which makes the Meso Corporatist Capitalism weak in sectors of banking, insurance and distribution.

SOCIAL DEMOCRATIC CAPITALISM

There is a third way to solve the recurring social and economic problems and unbalances associated to capital accumulation and development. If social partners are well organised in a very small number of unions and associations, which takes into account the whole range of interests of their members, then it is possible to negotiate mutually advantageous compromises. In the social democratic socialism, of which Scandinavian countries, Austria and the Netherlands are examples, tri–partite institutions offer the possibility to cope efficiently with pressing issues, like preserving competitiveness, promoting innovation in order to keep productivity and standards of living rising, emerging social problems, such as the crisis of work organisation, or the environmental problems. Countries belonging to this third category have in common to be small open economies, which need to be competitive to survive in the long run.

The pursuit of general interest and the concern for social justice permeate nearly all economic and political institutions (Figure 8.4). The educational system is organised in order to give a good basic education, whereas special institutions are devoted to retrain workers when their competence become

Figure 8.3 The 'meso–corporatist' capitalism

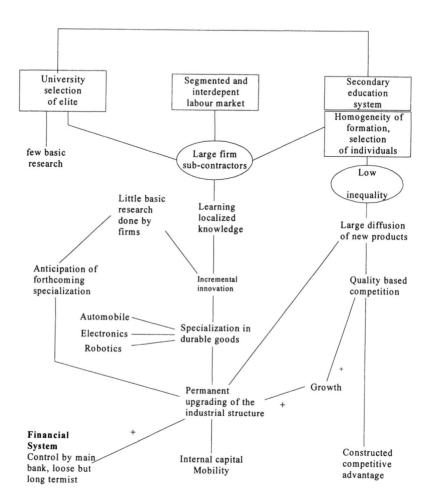

Figure 8.4 Social Democrat Capitalism

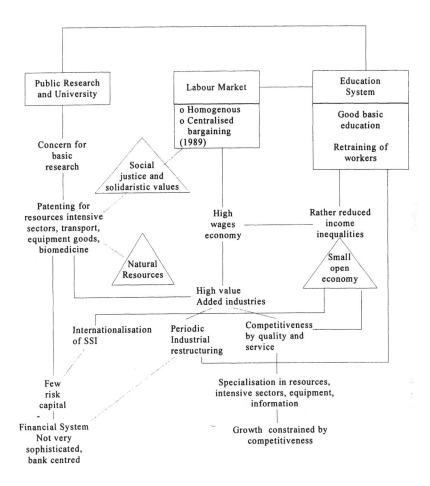

obsolete. The labour market is actively organised by public authorities, which minimise external flexibility and promote a permanent up–grading of skills in response to external competition and technological advances. The research is undertaken within public institutions and is guided towards highly specific directions to improve the value added content of the products derived from natural resources. Furthermore, the system is focused on innovations in order to solve ecological problems, to organise social welfare and security, to design goods with a special premium concerning quality and servicing, just to sustain a high wage economy with minimal income inequalities.

All these institutions are complementary and the social–democratic architecture is quite different from the market led or meso–coporatist configuration. The social democratic capitalism has been developing an original industrial trajectory with a high degree of specialisation, which is not just duplicating that of foreign competitors. The economies of the social democratic countries are strong, because of their long term orientation and specific investments in physical and human resources. Also the processes of adaptation seem to be efficient: gradual restructuring with commitments of different interest groups taking together care of an 'organised adaptation' instead of an hard 'shake out'. As a consequence these type of economies are strong in sectors driven by natural resources (gas, oil, agriculture) that are linked to industrial research and production activities with highly value adding characteristics (for example, the food and agri–business complexes). The weaknesses of the social democratic system are located in the interlocking interdependencies resulting in rigidities. It takes often high external pressure and quite some time to set the adaptation process described above into motion. Changing the institutional forms and organisations depicted in Figure 8.1 are not realised in the short term.

STATE LED CAPITALISM

The last brand of capitalism, of which France, Italy and Spain are often presented as illustrations, is built on still another coordinating principle. Contrary to the social democratic configuration, worker unions are weak and divided and even business associations do not play a major role in the coordination and defence of firm's interests and strategies. Bargaining rarely takes place between the two social partners; public authorities have to induce such a process by various incentives. At odds with the meso–

corporatist capitalism, private firms and large corporations are not strong and innovative enough to develop a coherent strategy. The market ideology of *laissez–faire* is far from accepted contrary to the market led configuration. Therefore the only arrangement left derives from public interventions in all domains, including production. Public enterprises and public spending are therefore very important in the production of goods which would be provided by private firms elsewhere. Relationships between the educational system, the labour market, the capital market and the role of the public sector are depicted in Figure 8.5.

The State, either central or regional, has an overwhelming role in economic life. The education system is essentially public, aims at the transmission of general knowledge and selects an elite who works as public servants or managers of nationalised and state–related firms. By contrast, professional training is weak, since social partners cannot agree on curricula and wage systems which would induce apprenticeship. The labour markets are highly regulated by the social welfare state. Research, basic and applied, is organised within public specialised institutes which do not have necessarily good connections with private production firms, which are supposed to use productively their results. Therefore, the most successful innovations take place within or in close relation with public firms and concern mainly infrastructure and welfare or state–related expenditures. The State Led Capitalism is especially strong in transport equipment, aircraft, weapons, and pharmaceutical industry. By contrast, this capitalism is not well equipped to be competitive in the financial sector, in the sector of consumer goods and industrial equipment, or in sectors where differentiation by quality is important.

Thus, different economic institutions induce different industrial specialisation. American and Japanese specialisation seem to be in many cases more complementary than rivalry. If confirmed, this would be good news about their international relations. More generally, internationalisation could well deepen the national specificity of each institutional architecture. In a sense, no system is absolutely superior to another and therefore there is room for the coexistence of a significant variety. Within a well organised international regime all the four types of capitalisms may coexist and develop their relative competitive advantages, which is driven by the nature and the coherence of their institutional architecture.

Figure 8.5 The State Led Capitalism

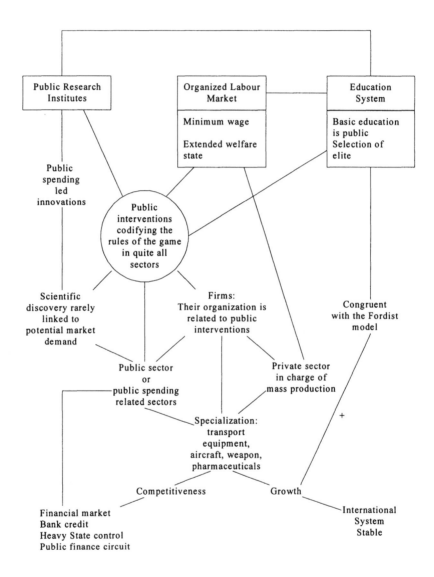

THE SURPRISING 1990s : WILL A FORM OF GRESHAM LAW FOR CAPITALISM PREVAIL ?

A frequent argument in favour of trade and finance liberalisation stresses that the emerging international regime will push the efficiency of all forms of capitalism into one direction: regime competition is assumed to select the most efficient constitutional order, institutions and organisations. The conventional belief in the efficiency of markets is extended to entire economic systems. However, efficient selection is questionable also in the case of the survival of the fittest economic system. In reality national governments, as well as large multinational enterprises, aim at controlling the forces of globalisation and competition in their own interest. The international pressures might very well destabilise national architectures, especially those which foster long term perspectives. It might very well be the case that 'bad capitalism drives out good capitalism'.

Nowadays, international forces exert their influence upon many aspects of national economic activity, but it is a novelty which should be put into historical perspective (Boyer, 1993).

- During the XIXth century, each national capitalism was severely constrained by the international monetary regime and foreign competition. In a sense, the wage labour nexus had to be flexible and highly reactive with few social and economic rights granted to workers. Wage and employment flexibility were absolutely necessary to keep domestic production price in line with the global price stability, which was implied by the Gold Standard. Similarly, the very concept of national economic policy was absent, because the interventions of the Central Bank had not any counter–cyclical objective and they were only following the trends set by the market. In the language of the French 'Regulation School' the two leading institutional forms were the international regime and the form of competition. Thus the competitive wage–labour nexus was hierarchically dependent from these two key institutions.
- The post World War II Fordist era displays a quite different configuration of institutional forms. After the turmoil of the inter–war period and the structural changes implemented after 1945, the building block of the new social and political order is then the capital–labour compromise, which is recognising unprecedented rights to workers. They are institutionalised and concern direct wage formation, access to welfare and a permanent

improvement in standards of living of workers. But the other institutional forms had to change in order to cope with these far reaching reforms. The dynamism of consumption and demand mitigates competition which became oligopolistic. Since the nominal wage is now set through a bargaining process or the implementation of an indexation formula, monetary policy has to adapt and for instance accept that inflation becomes permanent. Last but not least, when a country cannot cope with the foreign competition because inflation was higher than in the rest of the world, it is easy to adjust the exchange rate, given the stability of the Bretton–Woods system. By contrast with the previous century, forms of competition and monetary regimes are now structurally determined by the Fordist wage–labour nexus.

• The last two decades have experienced a significant change. Because of the success of each national regime to organise mass production efficiently, exportation is pushed. Because of the extension of world trade, economies have become more and more interdependent and the relative autonomy of the Fordist wage–labour compromise can no longer be maintained. The insertion into the international trade and financial flows become determinant for monetary policy, which is under the permanent scrutiny of the financial international community. Similarly, the competition regime, which used to be enforced at the national level according to quite contrasted conceptions of anti–trust policies, becomes more and more an international issue. For instance, the Single Market is associated with a rise of an ambitious European competition policy, whereas the World Trade Organisation as well as OECD tend to play an increasing role in setting new rules of the game. Clearly the source of competitive advantage and the related market shares between firms, regions and nations are drastically refined. The whole architecture of post–World War II institutional forms is altered by these transformations. Even the budgetary policy is now constrained by the assessment of financial markets and can no more sustain all the entitlements which were supporting the previous wage–labour nexus. Structurally, the hierarchy of institutional forms tends to look like the configuration observed for competitive capitalism. Again, the wage–labour nexus transformations are conditioned by the forces of competition and the return to the objective of price stability.

This structural change is not without consequences with respect to the viability of each brand of capitalism, since it introduces criteria of selection and viability which are quite different from the post World War II era.

SHORT TERM FLEXIBILITY AGAINST EFFICIENCY?

A priori, the viability of any capitalist system depends on its capability to satisfy a mix of three different criteria. First, systems ought to be dynamically efficient; competitiveness in terms of prices and innovations improves the standard of living. This was a key criteria during the Golden Age of the 1960s, given the competition between the capitalist western economies and the soviet type regimes. Actually, the firms benefited from rather high profits and workers from real wage increases and near full employment. Second, democratic constitutions have given a say to citizens, mainly wage earners, about the content of economic policy, taxation, public goods and income distribution. So next to dynamic efficiency, economic systems should fulfill the criterion of fairness and social justice. It can been argued that reduction of inequalities and dynamic efficiency have been closely associated since World War II until the early 1990s (Boyer, 1991). Thirdly, the most conventional argument stresses the ability of capitalism to react to innovation, to experiment with new products and organisations, to respond flexibly to uncertainty and business fluctuations, to correct quickly past investment errors by highly reversible price systems. The Austrian school, which has become so influential again in the 1980s, seems to have imposed its vision of capitalism: it should react easily to disturbances and this property is captured by the criterion of short run flexibility. This criterion becomes specially important if growth rates drastically slow down, when short run dynamics becomes erratic, or at least quite difficult to predict, and of course if financial markets frequently change their assessment about the relative competitiveness of various economies.

In the 1990s the criteria of dynamic efficiency and social justice seem to be replaced by the one of short run flexibility (Figure 8.6). Some of the representative social democrat capitalisms experienced the most severe crisis since the inter–war period. Diagnosis: the inadaptability is due to cosy relationships that shelter economic actors from market pressures. Simultaneously, State Led Capitalism is blamed for being sclerotic and irrationally attached to too generous welfare schemes and too much income redistribution. Even the meso-corporatist capitalism, which was so admired and tentatively copied during the 1980s, is considered to be archaic and inefficient. Especially, the 'Asia crisis' at the end of the 1990s gave rise to a wide range of criticism by political scientists as well as economists. The Japanese economy is now viewed as archaïc in terms of financial management, badly run by the Ministry of Finance, whereas the

Figure 8.6 A general evolution towards short run efficiency at the cost of long run performance and social justice?

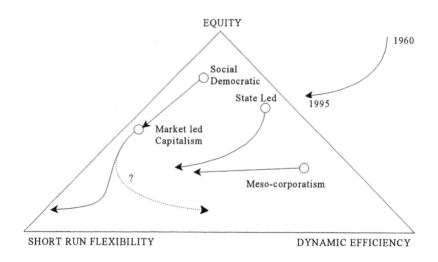

employment stability and seniority wages are blamed for blocking the recovery, inhibiting the restructuring of firms and the diffusion of new technologies. Some American economists do even declare that for the first time, Japan has to become capitalist. The only way out of the current political and financial crisis would be to adopt the American style capitalism, which should take place as soon as market forces would defeat the bureaucrats! The intrinsic rigidity of all capitalisms except the market led one is deemed to be the source of the problems experienced by Japan and Europe as well.

The US economy is playing a major role again in setting what should be the rules of international relations and sound economic policies. Other capitalisms experience severe difficulties in redesigning their basic institutions and their business and political elite tend to consider market led capitalism more and more as the norm. It seems that the system, that is relatively unfair and less efficient in the long run, but highly reactive in the short term, is driving out the more solidaristic and efficient ones, precisely because the latter are quite clumsy in reacting to a rather erratic international system. Will the Gresham law apply to capitalism? It would be tempting to conclude so, but the very reference to this monetary theory introduces some caveats, since it has been true only during quite exceptional periods of high uncertainty and major unbalances.

CAPITALISM AGAINST CAPITALISM UNDER THE PRESSURE OF INTERNATIONALISATION

It is dangerous to prolong the present trends over a long period. First, according to a Polanyian argument, it would be not surprising if some political and social protests were soon blocking the general process of 'commodification' of the society. Second, the long run history of advanced capitalist countries shows the permanence of strong social and economic differentiation, deeply embedded into each societal system of values and political institutions. Third, it would be dubious to simply extrapolate the present trends and especially the power of financial markets indefinitely. Therefore the ruling of the short run flexibility criteria could quite soon be replaced by a more balanced mix, which would give a chance to all the three other forms of capitalism.

REFERENCES

Albert M. (1991), *Capitalisme contre capitalisme*, Paris: Seuil.
Amable B., R. Barré, and R. Boyer (1997), *Les Systèmes d'Innovation à l'Ère de la Globalisation*, Economica, Paris.
Aoki, M. (1995), 'Towards a Comparative Institutional Analysis: Motivations and Some Tentative General Insights', *Working Paper Stanford University*, October 4.
Arthur, B. (1994), *Increasing Returns and Path Dependence in the Economy*, Ann Arbor: The University of Michigan Press.
Berger, S. and R. Dore (1996), *Globalisation and National Diversity*, Ithaca: Cornel University Press.
Boismenu, G. (1995), 'Modèles Politico–institutionnels et Politique Macroéconomique', *Etudes Internationales*, Montréal: Institut Québecois des Hautes Etudes Internationales, Juin.
Boyer, R. (1993), 'D'une série de "National Labour Standards" à un 'European Monetary Stardard?', *Recherches Economiques de Louvain*, Vol. 59, No. 1–2, 119–153.
Boyer, R. and D. Drache (eds.) (1996), *States Against Markets. The Limits Of Globalisation*, London: Routledge.
Boyer, R. and A. Orléan (1992), 'How do Conventions Evolve?' *Journal of Evolutionary Economics*, No. 2, 165–177.
Boyer, R. and Y. Saillard (eds.) (1995), *Théorie de la Régulation. L'État des Savoirs*,

Paris: La Découverte.

Cohen–Tanugi, L. (1984), *Le Droit Sans l'État. Sur la Démocratie en France et en Amérique*, Paris: Presses Universitaires de France.

Dore, R., R. Boyer and M. Zoe (eds.) (1994), *The Return to Incomes Policy*, London: Pinter Publishers.

Dosi, G. (1988), 'Sources, Procedures and Microeconomic Effects of Innovation', *Journal of Economic Literature*, September, 1120–1171.

––––––– (1991), 'Perspectives on Evolutionary Theory', *Science and Public Policy*, Vol. 18, No. 6, December, 353–361.

Dosi, G., S. Fabiani, C. Freeman and R. Aversi (1993), 'On the Process On Economic Development', WP C.C.C. No. 93–2, Berkeley: University of California, January.

Favereau, O. (1989), 'Marchés Internes, Marchés Externes', *Revue Economique*, No. 2, Mars, 273–328.

Hibbs, D.A. Jr. (1987), *The Political Economy of Industrial Democracies*, Cambridge MA and London: Harvard University Press.

Hollingsworth, R. and R. Boyer (eds.) (1997), *Contemporary Capitalism: the Embeddedness of Institutions*, Oxford University Press, to appear.

Krugman, P. (1992), *Economic Geography*, Boston: MIT Press.

Landes, D. (1998), *The Wealth and Poverty of Nations. Why Some Are So Rich and Some So Poor*. New York: W.W. Norton.

North, D.C. (1991), *Institutions, Institutional Change and Economic Performance*, Cambridge and New York: Cambridge University Press.

––––––– (1996), 'Economic Performance Through Time', in: L.J. Alston, T. Eggertsson, D.C. North (eds.) *Empirical Studies in Institutional Change*, Cambridge University Press, 342–355.

Sabel, C.F. (1997), 'Constitutional Ordering in Historical Context', in F.W. Scharpf, (ed.) *Games in Hierarchies and Networks*.

Shonfield A. (1967), *Le Capitalisme d'Aujourd'hui. L'État et l'Entreprise*, Paris: Gallimard.

Soskice, D. (1991), 'Reinterpreting Corporatism and Explaining Unemployment: Coordinated and No–coordinated Market Economies', in R. Brunetta and C. Dell Áringa (eds.), *Labour Relations and Economic Performance*, Basingstoke: Macmillan, 170–211.

Stiglitz J.E. (1987), 'The Causes and Consequences of the Dependence of Quality on Price', *Journal of Economic Literature*, Vol. XXV, Mars, 1–48.

Zysman, J. and S.S. Cohen (1987), *Manufacturing in Matters*, Basic Book.

9. Understanding Varieties in the Structure and Performance of National Innovation Systems: The Concept of Economic Style

Alexander Ebner

INTRODUCTION

Current debates in economic theory and policy are shaped by topics such as national competitiveness. The corresponding challenge of analysing the impact of technological innovation on economic growth has fuelled a renaissance of Schumpeterian ideas. Related to these is the systems of innovation approach which puts the analytical focus on the manifold relations between institutions, organisations and technology, especially regarding their interaction in the innovation process. This chapter follows a Schumpeterian approach in suggesting that the integration of theory and history within a dynamic conceptual framework is crucial for the analysis of innovation. It shall be emphasised that historically rooted structural and institutional varieties specify the performance of national innovation systems. A major distinguishing feature of these national systems is, for instance, the matter of investment patterns which has been differentiated according to notions such as short–termism and which has been related to certain types of economic behaviour, industrial structures or specific organisational modes of coping with technological and institutional change. Hence a historical and comparative approach to systems of innovation should consider the individual 'gestalt' of an innovation system and take into account the interdependence of the various elements by which it is constituted.

It is therefore suggested that the concept of economic style which has risen to prominence within the research tradition of the German Historical School might serve as a useful conceptual device for comparative systems of innovation. The economic style notion encompasses economic attitudes, socio–economic structures, technological specificities and endogenous growth dynamics in order to denote the recurring institutional, organisational and technological patterns of an economic formation. Furthermore the economic style concept reflects the high degree of compatibility among Schumpeter's theory of economic development and those approaches to institutional and technological change which have been elaborated by major scholars of the German Historical School. This undererpins once more the indispensable but rather implicit influence of the German Historical School on the formulation of a Schumpeterian economics in general, as well as on the system of innovation approach in particular.

This chapter proceeds in four sections. First, an outline of the systems of innovation approach is provided with special reference to comparative–historical research perspectives. As these considerations are based upon genuinely Schumpeterian concepts, second, a discussion of the institutional aspects of Schumpeter's theorising is presented which combines the matter of entrepreneurial activities with the aspect of an embedding institutional variety. Third, the concept of economic style which has been designed for the historical and institutional comparison of economic formations is discussed. This is put in the context of Schumpeter's original approach, especially his idea of analysing the institutional dynamics of economic change by the means of an economic sociology. Finally, the advantages of relating the economic style perspective to comparative innovation systems is examined and applied to the most recent discussions on the persisting national varieties of capitalism.

APPROACHING SYSTEMS OF INNOVATION: INSTITUTIONS, TECHNOLOGY AND HISTORY

The emergence of a Schumpeterian paradigm in economics results from the structural crises which have affected the OECD–countries since the 1970s and fuelled theoretical as well as policy concerns with structural unemployment, industrial competitiveness and technological innovation. Schumpeterian ideas emphasise the evolutionary character of capitalist economic life. They provide the background for the systems of innovation approach which examines the role of institutions and organisations for the generation, modification and diffusion of technologies within a territorial setting. Innovation processes are described as cumulative, marked by the interaction of various agents which are acting within a specific institutional set–up. With reference to the notion of Schumpeterian competitiveness, defined as efficiency in allocating resources to promote technical, product and organisational innovations (Dosi et al., 1989), it may be declared that the systems of innovation approach is concerned with the institutional and organisational foundations of that kind of competitiveness. Consequently, Freeman's pioneering definition denotes systems of innovation in a broad sense as 'the network of institutions in the private and public sector whose activities and interactions initiate, import, modify and diffuse new technologies' (Freeman, 1987, p. 1). Lundvall adds the following more specific assumptions:

> First it is assumed that the most fundamental resource in the modern economy is knowledge and, accordingly, that the most important process is learning... Second it is assumed that learning is predominantly an interactive and, therefore, a socially embedded process which cannot be understood without taking into consideration its institutional and cultural context (Lundvall, 1992, p. 1).

The examination of interdependencies among institutions, organisations and technology in a nation–state framework was typical until recently, when the complementary role of supranational, regional or sectoral configurations has been recognised (Edquist, 1997). This multi–level perspective of the systems of innovation approach is accompanied by a comprehensive analytical framework which resembles various theoretical traditions. In order to provide an orientation, I shall emphasise the essential characteristics of the various arguments and distinguish between structuralist, evolutionary and neo–Schumpeterian biased research concepts. The structuralist strand is concerned with the role of industrial structures and inter–firm relations. It focuses on the notion of user–producer relationships in the sense of innovation supporting interactions and knowledge transfers between producers and users of certain technologies and products. User–producer relationships facilitate the communication of user needs and technological opportunities. They are thus identified as the basis of interactive learning which is perceived as the major aspect of continual knowledge creation and diffusion (Lundvall, 1985, 1992). Industrial structures and the institutional set–up establish the general framework for systemic processes of interactive learning and hence define the shape and performance of an innovation system. Related to the matter of learning by interacting, the prominent role of industrial structures within the structuralist SI perspective is due to the fact that the relation between production and learning resembles the post–Schumpeterian ideas of Perrouxian economic structuralism which has stressed the strategic importance of inter–firm and sectoral linkages for analysing economic growth patterns (Andersen and Lundvall, 1988). This conceptual proximity to the structuralist notion of national systems of production, perceived as systemic inter–firm linkages which proceed the flow of goods, knowledge, and information is reflected in the standpoint that systems of innovation are well described as subsets of national production systems (Niosi and Bellon, 1996).

Due to the project of elaborating a non–linear and non–deterministic approach to innovations, an evolutionary perspective on the dynamic of technological change is a commonly shared motive within the systems of innovation approach (Edquist, 1997). Some rather abstract and more specific evolutionary conceptualisations of innovation systems still have been formulated recently. This perspective draws from related theories of technological change which point at elements of the innovation process such as a firm's search routines and the selective role of the market environment as well as the likewise selective social context (McKelvey, 1996). Technological change is characterised as a cumulative local phenomenon which is to be perceived as an evolutionary process based upon the systemic introduction of novelty and the creation of diversity. While the level of the firm provides a focal point of evolutionary analysis, the role of institutions is acknowledged with respect to the matter of variety. Saviotti (1996), for instance, maintains that variety is an indispensable feature of open dynamic systems. Distinguishing between output variety, process variety and institutional–organisational variety he proposes that an exploration of qualitative changes in the economic system, such as technological change in the course of economic development, needs to take into account diverse actors, activities and types of output which together constitute a particular system of innovation.

The neo–Schumpeterian research agenda is mainly concerned with the economic role of formal institutions and organisations involved in innovation activities. In addition to firms, which constitute the primary terrain where technological learning is taking place, further elements such as R&D facilities, education and training programmes or patent systems are integrated into the analysis of interactions. Systems of innovation are then described as networks of innovation–related institutions, whose emergence is portrayed as a result of the historical evolution of capitalist economies, that is, as a result of the institutionalisation of science and technology in the socio–economic sphere. This points at the Schumpeterian argument that technological as well as social innovations are the source of economic growth and development in capitalist market economies (Freeman, 1987, p. 1). Another major Schumpeterian issue is taken to the fore by relating the institutional–organisational dimension of innovations to the dynamic of technological and institutional change as it is denoted by the concept of the 'techno–economic paradigm'. Such a paradigm is defined as an ideal type of productive organisation, basically constituted by specific patterns of business organisation, radical and incremental innovations, innovator-entrepreneur types, as well as modes of investment, consumption and distribution (Freeman and Perez, 1988). A techno–economic paradigm emerges gradually, taking advantage of specific input factors of production. Its diffusion enforces a restructuring of the productive system which results in a mismatch with the institutional set–up. A temporarily stable reconfiguration may be established by the conflict–ridden adaption of the institutional set–up to the requirements of the dominant paradigm. National systems of innovation provide those institutional and organisational means which are essential for coping with paradigm changes and thus for defining a country's position in the hierarchy of the global economy. The corresponding long wave dynamic is characterised by the technological leadership of those countries which are best equipped for meeting the techno–economic paradigm requirements, as every new paradigm configuration corresponds with an ideal typical 'best practice' type of national innovation system and thus allows for catch–up growth. Outstanding examples of that particular role of national innovation systems are, of course, latecomer economies such as Germany in the 19th and Japan in the 20th century (Freeman, 1987).

Summing up, the systems of innovation approach explores the institutions–organisations–technology nexus which coins innovation-related interaction modes and technological learning processes within various settings, primarily national economies but also micro– and macro–regions. A major common theme is the institutionalistion of science, technology and learning as attributes of the endogenous dynamic of capitalist market economies. This aspect is of utmost importance, for the dominant role of technological and organisational innovations distinguishes capitalism from any other preceeding historical formation. As Freeman and Soete note:

> Technical innovation contributes to the everlasting uncertainty and evolutionary turmoil,
> which are so characteristic of capitalism. The growth of capitalist firms, industries and
> nations is not just a matter of the quantitative increase of inputs and outputs, ..., but of the
> qualitative transformation of the structure of the economy through successive waves of
> technical change (Freeman and Soete, 1997, p. 31).

Thus it may be proposed that systems of innovation are a characteristic feature of the institutional specificity of capitalism.

While institutions constitute the conceptual core of the NIS approach, a commonly shared definition of the term 'institution' has not yet been achieved. Some authors favour a formal definition of institutions (Nelson and Rosenberg, 1993; Freeman, 1987), while others refer to the Veblenian notion of social behaviour regularities (Johnson, 1992). Consequently further attempts of integrating formal and informal institutions and relating them directly to the innovation process have been formulated. According to Edquist and Johnson (1997) institutions may enable innovations as they carry information, reduce uncertainty, provide incentives, and frame various modes of governance and cooperation. Institutions therefore shape the particular modes of interactive learning and thus the outcome of the innovation process. Moreover they coin the organisational behaviour of firms and other subjects of innovation. Hence 'it is difficult to imagine innovations that are not to some extent formed by the institutional set–up' (Edquist and Johnson, 1997, p. 51). Regarding the policy conclusions it follows therefore that a purposeful innovation system design is not feasible, for any design strategy will be limited by unintended consequences and externalities of the actions of the economic agents. There is thus no necessary convergence towards a first best scheme but a real typical variety of possible institutional configurations for coping with a new paradigm within an innovation system. This implies the possibility of a persisting divergence of national economies (Freeman, 1995).

The acknowledgement of institutional varieties points at the matter of comparative research which is in fact a constitutive element of the systems of innovation approach, for the major questions point at reccurring growth patterns: 'Why do some countries catch up rapidly at some periods and others move slowly or not at all?' (Freeman, 1995b, p. 23). An examination of this matter is in accordance with the approach of 19th century German political economist Friedrich List, who is in addition to Schumpeter appreciated as the conceptual founding father of the national systems of innovation perspective (Freeman, 1987; Lundvall, 1992). List's 'National System of Political Economy' (1841) reconsidered the situation of latecomer economies and emphasised the role of science, education and technological knowledge for the industrialisation efforts of national economies.[1] This cross–national perspective is well reflected in the actual comparison of different national systems of innovation (Nelson and Rosenberg, 1993), while comparative analyses of regional or continental ensembles, such as East Asia versus Latin America, have been elaborated additionally (Freeman, 1996). Especially the growth performance of the Japanese economy has provided a thoroughly examined research object which points at the limits of a purely quantitative empirical comparison due to the qualitative character of institutional configurations. From this point of view it is not enough to measure and compare systems of innovation by taking into account quantitative data sets, for an understanding of innovation processes requires additionally the analysis of ideologies and cognitive frameworks (Maddison, 1994). It is necessary to combine the comparative analysis of organisations and formal institutions with the impact of institutional–cultural elements on the structure and performance of innovation systems. Hence the role of social belief systems and ideologies as incentives or disincentives for the acquisition of scientific knowledge and the corresponding modes of technological learning have been underlined as a promising facets of the systems of innovation approach (Edquist and Johnson, 1997).

As a complement to the comparative perspective it has been proposed that an integrated historical perspective is of substantial importance. As a first approximation to this matter of integrating theory and history it has been emphasised that knowledge and learning share cumulative traits, a standpoint which is underlined by acknowledging the complex and continual character of innovation processes (Lazonick, 1994). Edquist (1997) refers to the matter historical time which marks the path–dependent sequence of invention, innovation and diffusion. A historical perspective does not simply refer to 'the past' but to a conceptualisation of economic processes as indetermined and irreversible. Regarding the Schumpeterian credo of economic change as a dynamic process in historical time, it may be proposed that actually existing systems of innovation are to be understood as essentially historical ensembles. This corresponds with recent attempts to develop a theoretical framework for a 'reasoned history' of economic growth, encompassing the historically rooted interrelatedness of economic processes with the spheres of science, technology, politics and culture (Freeman, 1995b). Ideas like these point at the opportunities offered by a reconsideration of Schumpeter's theorising, especially with regard to its institutional–historical facets, for the elaboration of a reasoned history resembles Schumpeter's very own approach to economic sociology. Consequently, a comparative–historical perspective on innovation systems might benefit from an examination of Schumpeter's approach to the institutions–technology nexus.

SCHUMPETER REVISITED: INSTITUTIONAL VARIETY AND EMBEDDED INNOVATIONS

Schumpeter's works were influenced by diverse theoretical schools, hence a general classification of his ideas proves difficult and is still subject to fierce controversies. Following Perroux (1965, p. 72) I would propose that Schumpeter's thought represents a synthesis of the Austrian and Lausanne schools of economics, accompanied by the German Historical School's institutional approaches as formulated by Max Weber and Werner Sombart. In what follows I will concentrate on a largely undervalued aspect of Schumpeter's theorising: his historical and institutionalist orientation which was due to his relations with the German Historical School, in particular with their representatives Max Weber, Sombart and Spiethoff. First of all it will be useful to discuss the institutional aspects of Schumpeter's theory of innovation and his genuine concept of capitalism, which leads to the matter of institutional variety.

Schumpeter defines capitalism as follows: 'capitalism is that form of private property economy in which innovations are carried out by means of borrowed money, which in general, though not by logical necessity, implies credit creation' (Schumpeter, 1939, p. 223). This capitalist credit economy is additionally characterised by specific social and institutional patterns. On the one hand, these are constituted by the capitalist civilisation, which represents all those institutional features which are essential characteristics of capitalism as an individual historical formation. Examples are the specific rationality related to the use of money as unit of account or the intellectual attitude of modern science. A common drive for quantification and rationalisation gives capitalism its historically unprecedented character. (Schumpeter, 1942, p. 123n). On the other hand, the typical features of capitalism are necessarily paralleled by pre–capitalist institutional elements and social strata. Actually existing capitalism is an amalgamation of pre–capitalist and capitalist elements. While innovations repeatedly dissolve and renew economic structures in the successive 'gales of creative destruction', a decomposition of the pre–capitalist and finally even capitalist institutional and social spheres is taking place. Thus Schumpeter formulates rather provocatively:

> In breaking down the pre–capitalist framework of society, capitalism thus broke not barriers that impeded its progress but also flying buttresses that prevented its collapse. That process, ... was not merely a matter of removing institutional deadwood, but of removing partners of the institutional stratum, symbiosis with whom was an essential element of the capitalist schema. Having discovered this fact ... we might well wonder whether it is quite correct to look upon capitalism as a social form sui generis or, in fact, as anything else but the latest stage of the decomposition of what we have called feudalism (Schumpeter, 1942, p. 139)

The role of institutions in Schumpeter's approach is not simply one of constraining the capitalist process, but instead also one of enabling and supporting. Thus Schumpeter is conceptually interested in grasping the particular 'motive power' of the various agents within the economic process (Rothschild, 1986). This statement applies well to his concept of the entrepreneur, whose function of introducing innovations keeps the capitalist growth engine in motion. Innovative entrepreneurial functions are characterised by the capability for creative response. In contrast to an adaptive attitude which denotes reactive adaptions to a change in market data, creative response is neither predictable nor determined. Schumpeter therefore maintains that creative response is the decisive counter–force against the general drive for rationalisation and depersonalising automatisation of the capitalist process which may in the long run, due to an institutional transformation, result in the bureaucratic leviathan of state–socialism (Schumpeter, 1947). With creative response present, the future course of capitalist formations remains indetermined.

Entrepreneurial motivation is not guided by the kind of profit motive which characterises the economic attitude of capitalists, who provide the entrepreneur with the necessary capital funds and hence represent the typically capitalist motive sphere. The entrepreneur views profits not as ends in themselves but as means to achieve further ends. He may, for instance, strive for the material well–being of his family. Not surprisingly the latter is said to be subject to devaluation and decomposition (Schumpeter, 1942, pp. 156–163). The entrepreneur is thus driven by motivations which are basically alien to the capitalist rationale and represent an element of aristocratic leadership which resembles a Nietzschean 'will to power' (Schumpeter, 1908, p. 618). In the course of fulfilling their functions, entrepreneurs are strangers in the value setting of capitalist rationality. Their function is not based upon social or institutional sameness and nearness but rather upon distance and difference. It follows that the reproduction of capitalism depends on the persisting variety of institutional and structural forms which are the result of asymmetrical change. Innovations are thus embedded in an institutional set–up which is marked by a necessary degree of historically rooted variety.

The constitutive role of variety is also prevalent in the way Schumpeter conceptualises differences in the institutional set–up of nation–states. On the topic of national institutional specificities and their further impact he suggests in rather general terms:

> at any given time, every nation has a certain class structure and a certain civilisation. The concept of civilisation comprises a system of beliefs, a schema of values, an attitude to life, a state of the arts, and so on. This ... will in general determine a nation's behaviour in its foreign and domestic affairs... (Schumpeter, 1948, p. 429).

While Schumpeter held sympathy for the idea of historically rooted national regularities in habits and thoughts, subsumed under the term Volksgeist which has been prominent among the idealist–historicist tradition of German political philosophy, he still rejected any metaphysical implication. Instead he argued that national characteristics in the institutional sphere represent social values which have been set up by dominant ruling groups and classes in a certain historical context and exhibit a high degree of inertia (Schumpeter, 1929). He concludes:

> Social structures, types and attitudes are coins that do not readily melt. Once they are formed they persist, possibly for centuries, and since different structures and types display different degrees of this ability to survive, we almost always find that actual group and national behaviour more or less departs from what we should expect it to be if we tried to infer it from the dominant forms of the productive process (Schumpeter, 1942, p. 12).

Hence national economies differ in terms of the structured variety of production modes as well as social, institutional and organisational configurations. It is concluded 'that the spirit of a people or a time is never an architectural unity' (Schumpeter, 1929, p. 214, my translation). A comparative analysis of the growth performance of various economic formations needs to take into account these various factors. Schumpeter therefore opted for a comparative institutional analysis of economic growth. This manifestation of the interdependence between institutions, technology and economic growth exposes further implications concerning the necessity of a holistic view, as he puts forward:

economic growth is not autonomous, being dependent upon factors outside of itself, and since these factors are many, no one–factor theory can ever be satisfactory. That is to say, such theories as that economic growth is a function, chiefly, of the objective opportunities of the environment, of increase in population, of the 'spirit' of a nation's civilisation, of technological progress (increasing 'control over nature') can never be adequate....But if we tried to use mathematics, we would immediately run up against the difficulty that some of the most important of these interdependent factors cannot be quantified... (Schumpeter, 1947, p. 4n).

Schumpeter hence formulates the outline of an institutional and historical approach to economic dynamics which should capture the specific 'gestalt', that is, the interdependent structured whole of the object under examination. This perspective of Schumpeter's has been influenced by the ideas of 'gestalt psychology' which are portrayed as highly useful for establishing a non–metaphysical concept of society for they contain that 'individual elements of any set of elements are not perceived or appraised individually but as part of the definite set in which they occur' (Schumpeter, 1954, p. 798). Relating the matter of variety to the method of contextualisation the Schumpeterian credo then maintains that economic action is embedded in social relations which are open to multiple possibilities of change while the corresponding economic phenomena are to be viewed in the context of an unitary 'gestalt' configuration (De Vecchi, 1995, p. 8n).

All these historical–institutional aspects as well as their methodological implications may be subsumed under the category of 'economic sociology' which is described in the 'History of Economic Analysis' as one of the four major research techniques among economic theory, statistics, and economic history. With reference to Max Weber's notion of a social economics, Sozialökonomie, Schumpeterian economic sociology denotes a typified, stylised or reasoned economic history, for it transcends the usual theoretical question of how people behave and what effects their behaviour produces, and asks instead why they behave the way they do (Schumpeter, 1954, p. 20). It follows: 'Economic sociology covers, first, the facts of economic behaviour from which economists forge certain assumptions and, second, the institutions that characterise the economic organisation of the societies to be studied' (Schumpeter, 1954, p. 544).

Uncovering the variety of motives and economic attitudes is a major contribution of economic sociology to the whole body of economics and characterises the latter as a genuine social science: 'Economics lacks the benefits that physics derives from laboratory experiments...but enjoys instead...man's extensive knowledge of the meanings of economic actions' (Schumpeter, 1954, p. 16). According to Swedberg (1989) economic sociology is hence designed to address the institutional framework of the economic process, while the matter of business cycles or economic systems, for instance, is to be analysed by both economic sociology and formal economic theory.

The idea of economic sociology as an institutional approach to economic dynamics can be traced througout Schumpeter's works. It is closely related to the research programme of the German Historical School as formulated by Gustav von Schmoller and continued by the 'youngest' Historical School's representatives Max Weber, Werner Sombart and Arthur Spiethoff. It should be emphasised that the term 'historical' as it was used within the German Historical School and repeatedly also by Schumpeter does not simply denote an account of the past in a narrative–descriptive sense, but a dynamic concept of economic development which has become established in the works of Schmoller.[2] Therefore it has been suggested that the model of economic sociology, in Schumpeter's view, was that of the German Historical School (Shionoya, 1997, p. 278).[3] Consequently, as derived from methodological considerations and conceptual intentions, an explicit 'Schmoller–Weber–Schumpeter nexus' has been identified (Shionoya, 1991).[4]

Schumpeter argued against the idea of a unitary meaning of history and the related assumption of an uniform linear development nations or civilisations. His own approach of indetermined social evolution implies that social conditions become historical individuals in historical time. Consequently Schumpeter was well aware that speaking of innovations demands speaking of capitalism as an epochal economic formation. This amounts to saying that capitalism exhibits a specific 'economic style', which is, according to Schumpeter, primarily derived from the unique roles of the monetary sphere and the mode of credit–creation (Schumpeter, 1926a, p. 107).[5] This notion of economic style denotes a comprehensive conceptual framework which is set in the tradition of the German Historical School. In fact Sombart and Spiethoff elaborated on that notion as a comparative approach which should provide insights for a historical perspective on economic formations by pointing at the matter of economic action, institutional variety and technological change. An outline of that economic style approach, and the corresponding 'economic gestalt theory' is presented in the following section.

TOWARDS A COMPARATIVE–HISTORICAL FRAMEWORK: THE CONCEPT OF ECONOMIC STYLE

The economic style notion emerged from the German Historical School as a reflection of a definition of economics as a cultural science in the tradition of humanities and the arts (Schefold, 1994). Economic phenomena have been viewed as time–conditioned, that is, as research objects which are to be understood by viewing them in their particular historical–cultural context. The point of view that historical phenomena have to be treated individually as coherent developing entities of various interdependent elements was basically kept throughout all strands of the German Historical School (Betz, 1988). The concept of economic style was soon mobilised against the deterministic stages theories of economic development. List's proto–historicist elaborations, for instance, were marked by a developmental optimism which characterised socio–economic evolution as progress in material wealth and ethical standards. The post–Schmollerian 'youngest' Historical School subjected that kind of developmental optimism to a revision by pointing at the individual 'gestalt' of economic formations while the idea of capitalist degeneration replaced the belief in a feasible combination of economic and ethical progress (Schefold, 1996a, p. 187n).

A point of departure for the critique on capitalist perfection was the debate on the historical evolution of modern capitalism. Sombart presented the notion of 'economic system' which should grasp the economic, social and institutional features of epochal economic formations (Sombart, 1916, p. 14n). These economic systems encompass three dimensions: first a specific economic spirit, representing the dominant economic attitudes, principles, and norms; second an individual historical form of economic order which denotes typical regulations as well as other economic and social relations; third a specific mode of using technology and accumulating technological knowledge. Sombart's major work 'Modern Capitalism' combines the historical analysis of the evolution of modern capitalism with the concept of economic systems and characterises capitalism as a coherent configuration of economic institutions, organisations, and technology. Sombart's position on the role of technology is well described by the formulation that science and technology become endogenous elements of the capitalist process in the course of economic development (Krabbe, 1996). While technology is an important topic in Sombart's works, he still identifies economic spirit as the major characteristic and driving force of capitalist evolution. Consequently, he used the Gestaltidee of economic systems as the key concept of his increasingly hermeneutical concept of economics (Sombart, 1930).

Schumpeter's idea of combining abstract theory with institutional perspectives was also pursued by Arthur Spiethoff, who used Schumpeter's and Sombart's names when he differentiated between 'pure theories' which may abstractly grasp those elements common to all known historical formations, and an 'economic gestalt' theory, which should serve an analysis of time–conditioned economic life (Spiethoff, 1932). While Schumpeter had felt uncomfortable with possible hermeneutical exaggerations of the style perspective (Schumpeter, 1926b, p.50), it was Spiethoff who maintained that economic styles should be subject to empirical falsification and thus redirected the style notion back to the Schmollerian position, Schumpeter himself referred to. Hence in contrast to Sombart and in accordance with Schumpeter, Spiethoff's economic style perspective should be compatible with formal and abstract theories. Spiethoff's work on economic styles is nonetheless built upon Sombart's economic systems concept and explictly strives for its empirical perfection (Spiethoff, 1932). With references to List, Schmoller and Sombart, Spiethoff defines an outline of his approach as follows:

> Most economic phenomena are time–conditioned and are rooted in specific geographical areas. They are subject to change over time and cannot be treated, therefore, with the help of concepts and theorems purporting to be of universal applicability. Economic theory can deal with those phenomena only by differentiating patterns of economic life, patterns which have come into being in the course of the historical process. As a matter of fact, as many patterns must be delimited as there are essential and typical differences in the basic economic institutions. Patterns of this kind are here called economic styles (Spiethoff, 1952, p. 132)

Economic styles reflect a coherent system of interdependent elements, which are rooted in specific institutional configurations: 'the concept of economic style ... reflects the properties which make out of an institutional setup a unique case of economic life... The concept of economic style is the tool with the help of which uniformities in time are made available for theoretical research' (Spiethoff, 1952, p. 137). According to Spiethoff, economic styles are outlined by the following basic characteristics, elaborated as a preliminary compilation of criteria (Spiethoff, 1932, p. 76n, my translation):

I. Economic spirit: 1. Moral attitude. Striving for the Kingdom of God, striving for economic success as an indicator of divine vocation; community interests act as guideline; striving for the most sublime earthly happiness of the individual. 2. Spiritual motives of economic action. Fear of punishment, religious–moral motives (altruism, sense of duty, urge for moral action), partly moral motive (sense of honour, urge for action, enjoyment of work), egoistic motive (striving for personal economic advantage), personal impulse, striving for power. Depending on the strength of the motives the aim followed is material wealth or self–sufficiency. 3. Intellectual attitude. Habitual or innovating attitude, resulting in varieties of technology.

II. Natural and technological foundation: 4. Population density. 5. Natural population dynamics. Static, slowly, moderately, rapidly increasing. 6. Production of goods with or without division of labour. 7. Intellectual work and manual work united or separated. 8. Organic or inorganic–mechanistic realisation of technology.

III. Constitution of society: 9. Size of the economic sphere of society. 10. Social cohesion. Kinship, force, contract. 11. Social division of labour and composition of society.

IV. Economic constitution: 12. Proprietary constitution. Either free or state– or socially–owned property of capital goods, combined with free property of consumption goods. Socially–owned property of consumption goods (and capital goods). 13. Constitution of the production of goods. Self–sufficient economy: production of requirements under unified guidance. Regulated market production: production of goods in economic units under regulation of production und price–formation by social organs consisting of entrepreneurs, workers, consumers (planned economy), or by political organs. Free market production: production in economic units free according to market constellation. 14. Constitution of distribution. Generalised compensation, regulated special compensation, free special compensation, altruism. 15. Constitution of labour. Cooperative, forced or hierarchised by contract. According to a combination of the possibilities no. 12 to 15 the whole economic constitution presents itself as: planned guidance, or regulated free constitution, or free constitution.

V. Economic dynamism: 16. Economic process. Continual economy, progressing economy, economic process in continuous alternation between upswing and stagnation.

This catalogue reflects the comprehensive conceptual and theoretical range of the German Historical School. The first topic of economic spirit reflects Schmoller's and Sombart's works, but it mirrors additionally the influence of Max Weber's sociology of religion and his elaborations on the institutional–cultural preconditions for capitalist develoment. In fact Weber has been classified as a major scholar of the economic style perspective (Müller–Armack, 1943). Furthermore the explicit way of grasping the institutional foundation of technology and technical change deserves some attention. Spiethoff refers to the dominant attitudes towards technological change within a range of habitual or innovating attitudes, a perspective similar to Schumpeter's innovation theory.[6] Next to the criterion of economic spirit, the natural and technological foundation as well as the social and economic constitution are mentioned as style elements. Most of these aspects are also part of Sombart's approach. Especially the matter of technology is based upon Sombart's proposal that capitalism dissolves the organic procedures of craftsmanship and establishes a technological system with inorganic–mechanic features. The criteria of social and economic constitution include the modes of allocation and the social distribution of property rights. Finally the catalogue pinpoints the issue of economic dynamics which is seen as an endogenous element of economic styles, for all style dimensions are interdependent. Business cycles are classified as phenomena with a specific capitalist character, a perspective which bears evidence of Spiethoff's own contributions to research on long wave dynamics.

Spiethoff's approach to economic styles encompasses material–structural as well as institutional–cultural elements without establishing a hierarchy of priorities, thus representing the variety of material and institutional characteristics of an economic formation on conceptually equal terms.[7] Spiethoff's approach complements the Schmoller–Weber–Schumpeter nexus of economic sociology and hence echoes decisive conceptual relations among Schumpeter and the 'youngest' Historical School.[8] Even more than that, both the economic style approach and the corresponding Schumpeterian ideas on economic dynamics are highly relevant for the discussions within modern institutional economics. The variety aspects of Schumpeter's theory of economic development, for instance, have been interpreted in terms of systems theory (Hodgson, 1988). The impurity principle defines that each functional system contains impurities which are not typical of the whole, but which are nevertheless necessary for the reproduction of that particular system. The principle of dominance suggests that every system exhibits a dominant functional structure. Consequently socio–economic systems represent diversified pluralities which exhibit a dominant economic structure by which they may be classified (Hodgson,

1988, p. 167n). Moreover the impurity principle implies a holistic research perspective:

> the impurity principle suggests a break from the Cartesian mechanistic mode of thinking where phenomena are broken down into determinate elements or parts, and through their aggregation we build up a picture of the whole. What is suggested is that parts themselves are multi–facetted and inter–penetrating (Hodgson, 1988, p. 168).

This corresponds with Schumpeter's theorising on the 'gestalt' of economic growth phenomena and also with the methodological background of Spiethoff's economic gestalt theory, which encompasses the phenomenological concepts of the economic style approach. The unifying common aspect of that rather diverse philosophical context is provided by the rejection of Cartesian mechanistic notions (Schefold, 1996b, p. 313).[9]

In spite of its conceptual advantages the economic style perspective was replaced by approaches to a plan–market dichotomy since the German economic systems debate in the late 1940s and kept its dominance during the period of East–West systems conflict. Historical–institutional perspectives gave way to the assumption of an universal economic calculus while topics such as cultural values or technological change were abandoned almost completely (Schefold, 1994). Since the breakdown of state socialism and the emergence of the East Asian New Industrialising Countries (NICs), it is even more vital to reconsider the institutional and technological features of the varieties of market capitalism on a continental, national or regional scale. This change of research perspectives towards a complementary institutional perspective is reflected by the formation of a 'new comparative economics'. Rosser, Rosser and Marina (1996) for instance differentiate in Polanyian terms between traditional–customary, market and command mechanisms of allocation, while Angresano (1996) proposes an evolutionary–institutional approach to comparative economics and refers, of course, to the tradition of economic sociology.[10]

It is a central suggestion of this chapter to reconstruct a genuinely Schumpeterian framework for the comparison of economic formations, especially regarding those elements of an economic formation which support innovations as the major driving force of economic evolution. The concept of economic style offers the advantage that it grasps the totality of various real typical economic formations, for it treats, among others, the historically specific interdependence of institutions and technologies as endogenous sources of economic change. In the following section I shall follow the practice of combining concepts of the 'old' institutionalism with the modern economics of innovation and thus relate the notion of economic styles to the comparative analysis of innovation systems.[11]

A COMPARATIVE–HISTORICAL VIEW ON INNOVATION: STYLES, SYSTEMS AND TRAJECTORIES

Comparative studies within the systems of innovation approach have been primarily concerned with national systems, although framed by the debates on globalisation and regionalisation. Some authors have envisaged a decreasing competence of the nation–state in governing the challenge of globalistion by means of a neo–mercantilist 'techno–nationalism' as the national character of innovation systems seems to be endangered by regional or supranational interactions (Nelson and Rosenberg, 1993). Nevertheless Lundvall (1992) stresses the continuous relevance of the nation–state as an institutional form endowed with unparalleled policy competences and important as a provider of cultural symbolism which shapes the capability for interactive learning. Thus it has been suggested that 'nation–states, national economies and national systems of innovation are still essential domains of economic and political analysis' framed by evolving local, regional or supranational systems of innovation (Freeman and Soete, 1997, p. 315). A prominent method for delineating national systems is provided by identifying the several links among the system units which facilitate the exchange of goods, information, knowledge and other resources (Niosi et al., 1993). Possibilities for measuring the 'nationalness' of innovation systems are therefore offered by quantitative analyses of patent systems, the location of R&D facilities or material input–output structures (Patel and Pavitt, 1994; Lundvall, 1996). These quantitative procedures are limited by the qualitative character of national innovation systems, for national specificities are to a large extent derived from institutional configurations. Nelson and Rosenberg note that 'the policies and programs of national governments, the laws of a nation, and the existence of a common language and a shared culture define an inside and outside that can broadly affect how technical advance proceeds...national differences and boundaries tend to define national innovation systems, partly intentionally, partly not' (Nelson and Rosenberg, 1993, p. 16). Similarly, Lundvall accentuates that 'basic differences in historical experience, language, and culture will be reflected in national idiosyncrasies in the internal organistion of firms, the types of inter–firm relationship, the role of the public sector, the structure of financial institutions, and the nature, organisation and volume of research and development' (Lundvall, 1992, p. 13). Therefore it has been concluded: 'As long as we can identify national cultures, we should expect national differences in production and innovation' (Johnson, 1992, p. 39).[12]

These assertions hint at the institutional embeddedness of innovation processes and thus at patterns of economic growth and development as a result of institutional and structural specificities. Patterns such as these are stylised by the notion of national trajectories which complements the concept of techno–economic paradigms by stressing the institutional impact on shaping the actual form of a paradigm as it crystallises within the national system. National technological trajectories hence result from specificities in industrial structures, economic linkages, the social organisation, and government–economy relations (Dosi et al., 1989). Indeed they represent the performance of a national system of innovation. The conclusion is: 'Technology, like market processes, is not disembodied. It develops in communities; it has local roots. The processes of learning that drive its development are shaped by the community and institutional structure, and consequently the technological trajectories can only be defined in reference to particular societies' (Zysman, 1994, p. 130).

Although the systems of innovation approach as well as the notion of national trajectories consider the co–evolution of institutions and technology, it is evident that both of these concepts mirror the simplifying assumption that national economies exhibit high degrees of institutional–structural homogeneity which facilitate cooperative relations among the economic agents.[13] The systems of innovation approach reformulates the Schumpeterian scheme by taking into consideration the evolution of a systemic entrepreneurship which integrates the Schumpeterian functionaries of innovation within an interactive system. Hence an important element of innovation systems are the various modes of interaction among individual and collective agents (Edquist, 1997). It is therefore a significant question which institutional configurations enable an innovation system to fulfill the entrepreneurial function of creative response. While it is of course true that the notions of homogeneity and cooperation mirror important aspects of economic life, they still exhibit an implicit determinism which neglects the matter of institutional and structural varieties as well as the conflicts which might arise from these. Innovations in Schumpeter's terms result from conflicts between entrepreneurial agents and their habitual environment. This has been articulated by scholars of technological evolution such as Paul David, who proclaims economics as a historical science and maintains that 'real economic actors function within many varieties of networks – social, and kinship–related, as well as commercially transactional and technological. Each of these potential webs of interaction and positive reinforcement into which individual agents may be drawn provides a theatre for the unfolding of historical dramas' (David, 1993, p. 211). Innovation processes are therefore embedded in the same sense as any economic action is embedded in a specific system of social relations which have been characteristic elements of pre–capitalist economic formations and whose importance may have decreased but still persists in the age of modern market capitalism (Granovetter, 1992).

Consequently national systems may be stylised as segmented layers of institutions and production modes which integrate several regional and local ensembles such as technopoles and industrial districts with all their particular forms of industrial, technological and institutional logic (Garrouste and Kirat, 1995, p. 235n). The corresponding amalgamation of capitalist and pre–capitalist institutions and structures marks the existing varieties of national innovation systems and their persisting divergence. As Hodgson puts it: 'given the potential variety of systemic combinations, and the reality of path dependency and cumulative causation, an immense variety of institutions and forms are possible' (Hodgson, 1996, p. 419). The economic style notion captures that variety of forms underneath the surface of the national productive fabric, for the difference between an epochal economic style in Spiethoff's terms and the corresponding notion of national economic styles is basically a matter of the degree of abstraction. Consequently it may be suggested that the varieties of national systems of innovation, their structural features as well as their particular performance, reflect the features of the corresponding national economic styles.

Although the economic style approach stems from a tradition of economic thought which has rejected the use of metaphors from the natural sciences, a basic congruence with evolutionary theorising may be postulated, especially concerning the analytical focus on economic dynamics and the conceptual integration of notions such as cumulative causation. Specific implications of the economic style perspective for the structuralist innovation systems dimension can be related to the standpoint that sectoral and firm structures coin the interactive relations in the innovation process and hence the specificities of knowledge transfers and learning procedures. Economic styles then represent the historical core of these various modes of interactive learning as well as the related modes of cooperation and governance. Similar conclusions may be applied to the neo–Schumpeterian macro–perspective, where countries cope with techno–economic paradigms on the basis of the possession of natural resources plus social, cultural and political factors. As the long wave dynamic does not result in a revolving tabula rasa, it follows that the continuity of certain social, institutional and structural economic elements exceeds the successive industrial, technological and institutional disruptions. In addition to the spheres of change and restructuring which may constitute the periphery of an economic style, it is necessary to reconsider those recurring patterns which constitute the core of a national economic style and which will support the rather invariant modes of coping with as well as shaping a techno–economic paradigm. This element of continuity represents the historical core of the economic style of a national system.[14]

The economic style approach attempts to uncover the gestalt of an economic formation by reconstructing its historically individual shape as well as its inherent variety of forms and interdependencies. Functionalist as well as culturalist approaches to the comparative advantage of capitalist 'models' may be useful for providing ideal typical comparative perspectives, but they are inadequate for grasping the real typical character of economic formations.[15] With regard to the debate on competing capitalist variants, Patel and Pavitt (1994) have stylised two types of innovation systems. Myopic systems are typical for the USA and the UK where demand–led investment in technology dominates. In the dynamic German and Japanese systems long–term investment in technology is prevalent. Different performance profiles are then derived from specificities in financial systems, methods of management and attitudes towards financial and technical competence. In a similar fashion Tylecote (1996) has compared Anglo–Saxon and German–Japanese types of market capitalism. He relates investment patterns and modes of technological learning to the hegemonial social attitudes towards labour, technology and innovation. These procedures of subsuming economic phenomena under a dichotomic taxonomy which orders national systems according to ideal typical features hints at the advantages of an economic style perspective on the various capitalist 'models', for it should aim at a holistic view by grasping the real typical individuality of national systems.[16]

Some guiding principles for reconstructing the core elements of national economic styles as well as for relating them to particular systems of innovation are of course necessary. The following chart distinguishes four constitutive dimensions: (1) the economic dimension comprises elements such as economic growth patterns, trajectories of technological change, sectoral configurations, firm structures and the structure of the financial system which may be analysed concerning modes of finance and investment. Moreover the topics of industrial relations and income distribution complete the economic core dimension of an economic style. (2) The institutional dimension is concerned with the shape and impact of formal and informal institutions. The aspect of economic attitudes may be related to the matter of incentives for knowledge acquisition as well as to the social acceptance of economic and technological change. Additionally national ideologies may be examined, for instance, with regard to social mobilisation capacities. (3) The social dimension comprises the stratification and coherence of the social sphere which represents the material substance of a particular mode of economic growth and development. (4) The political dimension accentuates the role of the nation–state. Here the degree of political interference with the economic sphere as well as the institutionalisation and regulation of social interests may be explored.

This catalogue denotes the focal points for an analysis of national economic styles with regard to the varieties of national systems of innovation. It aims at an illustration of the concerns of the economic style approach, not at a rigorous operationalisation. Therefore it is designed to support a view on the innovation performance of national economies which combines the matter of institutional variety and coherence with the matter of economic dynamics. By doing so the major questions of Schumpeter's approach to economic theory and economic sociology shall be pursued within a comparative–historical framework.

CONCLUSION

The systems of innovation approach examines those networks of institutions which support technological and organisational innovations. The basic argument of this chapter has been that a comparative–historical perspective on national systems of innovation benefits from insights and concepts which are provided by the Schumpeterian approach to economic sociology and the related traditions of the German Historical School. One of these is the concept of economic style which denotes the essential properties of

Table 9.1 Economic styles and national systems of innovation

Dimensions	Characteristics and Elements
Economic Dimension	Pattern of economic growth and technological change Financial system and pattern of investment Sectoral and firm structures Industrial relations and income distribution
Institutional Dimension	Regularities in social behaviour and economic attitudes National ideology and symbolism Codified law and property rights
Social Dimension	Social structuration Social cohesion Intensity of social conflicts and modes of cooperation
Political Dimension	Pattern and range of government and state activities Structure of the political system Modes of political regulation and governance

economic formations. Economic styles encompass institutional and organisational configurations, the endogenous dynamics of economic growth and technological change, as well as the socio–economic structuration of an economic formation.

These economic styles have been designed for a historical comparison of epochal formations but they are also useful as real typical frameworks for the comparison of national economies and the variety of forms by which these are characterised. It is that particular historically rooted variety of institutional forms and modes of interaction which has a decisive impact on the structure and performance of national innovation systems, for it supports the endogenous capabilities of creative response.

Research areas for an application of the economic style perspective on comparative systems of innovation are manifold. A first example is provided by the growth and innovation performance of East Asian economies. Moreover the prospects of European integration and thus of an European system of innovation may be examined in the light of the economic style perspective. This might contribute to further progress in comparative research on innovation systems as well as to a more reflective and sensitive way of technology and innovation policy–making.

NOTES

1. Note that Lists's 'National System' denotes not an empirical object but a systematic theoretical approach which should counter Quesnay's 'Natural System of Political Economy' as well as Adam Smith's allegedly 'cosmopolitan' ideas.
2. Veblen himself, who has been regarded as the pioneer of an evolutionary approach to institutional economics, pointed at the importance of Gustav von Schmoller's works on the dynamics of socio–economic evolution. Veblen states that: '... the distinguishing characteristic of Professor Schmoller's work, .., is that it aims at a Darwinistic account of the origin, growth, persistence, and variation of institutions, in so far as these institutions have to do with the economic aspect of life either as cause or effect... In this line of theoretical inquiry Professor Schmoller is not alone, ...; but the seniority belongs to him, and he is also in the lead as regards the comprehensiveness of his work' (Veblen, 1901, p. 264n). While Veblen goes on to deny that Schmoller was a genuine evolutionary theorist, which is quite in accordance with Schmoller's reservations regarding metaphors from the natural sciences, the appreciative character of this statement is well designed to counter inadequate judgements still prevalent in many accounts of the German Historical School.
3. This has been emphasised repeatedly by Schumpeter himself. In his first major volume Schumpeter differentiates between phenomena such as commodity exchange which are relevant for static economic theory, and dynamic problems such as technological change which should be analysed by a combination of theoretical and historical research. He notes that the most valuable contributions to this matter have been delivered by the German Historical School (Schumpeter, 1908, p. 617). In the 'Theory of Economic Development' this aspect is continuously underlined (Schumpter, 1926a, p. 90n). Therefore Schumpeter not only kept a mediating position during the '*Methodenstreit*', but even recommended Schmoller's approach as a conceptual source for the integration of theory and history (Schumpeter, 1926b). In the 'Business Cycles' it is maintained that economic change evolves in historical time and thus enforces an institutional approach to economic dynamics (Schumpeter, 1939, p. 220). Finally, in the 'History of Economic Analysis' economic sociology is said to be borrowed from 'German practice', that is, from the Schmollerian research programme. (Schumpeter, 1954, p. 21).
4. For a comprehensive discussion of methodological topics and conceptual differences between Schmoller, Weber and Schumpeter see Shionoya (1991). For example, Schumpeter is sceptical concerning the possible hermeneutic exaggeration of the method of *Verstehen* which, according to Max Weber, sets human motives in relation to meaningful phenomena.
5. The term Wirtschaftsstil has been translated as 'type' in the 1934 English edition of the 'Theory'. This is inadequate because the correct term 'economic style' is of course rooted in humanities and the arts and thus reflects the metaphorical orientation of the German Historical School towards the latter.
6. A comparable argument has been put forward more recently by Basalla (1988), who remarks that the generation of innovation responds to a specific cultural context which defines whether certain artifacts are needful. He differentiates between static and dynamic, respectively innovative cultures, based upon the appreciation and acceptance of novelty and change.
7. Spiethoff's approach offers the analytically most comprehensive perspective of the economic style literature. Müller–Armack for instance, who developed the concept of Germany's social

market economy, stressed the impact of economic attitudes as derived from religious world views. Religious hegemony thus was his criterion for delineating economic styles (Müller–Armack, 1943).

8. Stolper comments on Spiethoff that he were 'static in proposing to construct...any number of possible economic sytems by combining 20 variables in all possible ways.' He goes on to remark that 'Schumpeter could not have been more different' (Stolper, 1988, p. 16). This contrasts with Schumpeter's own statements on Spiethoff which are consistently appreciative. For example, Spiethoff's theory of business cycles is portrayed as the most indispensable influence on Schumpeter's own theorising on economic turbulence (Schumpeter, 1926a, p. 320 and p. 332). In the 'History of Economic Analysis' this positive verdict is still valid, for Spiethoff is said to have exhibited 'an outstanding performance in the field of business cycle research' (Schumpeter, 1954, p. 816). Moreover Spiethoff is characterised as a major scholar of economic sociology (Schumpeter, 1926a, p. 377). Thus Schumpeter goes on to describe Spiethoff's notion of economic style as 'highly interesting' (Schumpeter, 1954, p. 816). In contrast to that, Schumpeter's comments on Sombart are more ambiguous and range from critical acclamation in the mid–1920s to an almost complete rejection later on.

9. It is noteworthy that the term 'economic gestalt theory' has been introduced by the translator of Spiethoff's 1952 article on the historical validity of economic theories with explicit reference to phenomenology and gestalt psychology (Spiethoff, 1952, p. 135, translator's note).

10. In fact the approach of economic sociology has recently experienced a renewal as a sociological analysis of economic phenomena in a broad sense (Smelser and Swedberg, 1994). This chapter does not subscribe to that definition of economic sociology and follows Shionoya, who insists on the original Schumpeterian programme which is closer to the concerns of the 'youngest' Historical School as well as to modern institutional economics (Shionoya ,1997, p. 324).

11. This practice is also followed by de la Mothe and Paquet (1996, p. 23n) who take the basic elements of Åkerman's institutionalist theory of economic development as a point of reference for the identification of certain sub-games or 'sub–processes' which are then reformulated in a modern evolutionary framework.

12. Porter, who has labeled himself a Schumpeterian, links institutional configurations to the matter of competitiveness as he formulates on the persisting role of nations: 'Competitive advantage is created and sustained through a highly localised process. Differences in national economic structures, values, cultures, institutions and histories contribute profoundly to competitive success' (Porter, 1990, p. 19).

13. This assumption bears resemblance to the Japanese ideology of consensual decision–making and cultural–ethnical homogeneity. Not surprisingly the concept of national trajectories has been designed for the analysis of Japanese competitiveness (Dosi et al., 1989). Similarly, the systems of innovation approach has been very much concerned with the Japanese case and uses the homogeneity assumption as an explicit simplification (Lundvall, 1992, p. 3).

14. Jamison maintains that 'even though there is an international technological development process, to which all countries must accomodate themselves, or a kind of technological imperative, there are significant differences as to how the accomodation takes place. There is also, ..., a cultural imperative in the process of technological development' (Jamison, 1991, p. 308). He concludes that patterns of industrial innovations cannot be separated from cultural patterns and traditions. Related to such a point of view is the topic of 'social capability' as a precondition for catch–up growth which includes institutional factors such as attitudes towards economic efforts (Hurwicz, 1995, p. 124).

15. Recent applications of the economic style notion to the debate on capitalist 'models' have focused almost exclusively on the impact of cultural values on economic behaviour (Klump, 1996). This seems to reduce economic styles to economic cultures. Such a perspective may be

compatible with single–factor approaches to economic styles, such as Müller–Armack's (1943), but not with Spiethoff's (1932) economic 'gestalt' approach.

16. This emphasis on real types in comparative–institutional analysis distinguishes Schumpeter's and Spiethoff's ideas from Max Weber's method of ideal types which are abstracted from the complex representations of economic life.

REFERENCES

Andersen, E.S. and B.–Å. Lundvall (1988), 'Small National Systems of Innovation Facing Technological Revolutions: An Analytical Framework' in C. Freeman, and B.–Å Lundvall (eds.), *Small Countries Facing the Technological Revolution*, London: Pinter, 9–36.

Basalla, G. (1988), *The Evolution of Technology*, Cambridge: Cambridge University Press.

Betz, H.K. (1988), 'How does the German Historical School Fit?', *History of Political Economy*, 20 (3), 409–430.

David, P.A. (1993), 'Path–Dependence and Predictability in Dynamic Systems with Local Network Externalities: a Paradigm for Historical Economics' in D. Foray, and C. Freeman (eds.), *Technology and the Wealth of Nations*, The Dynamics of Constructed Advantage, London: Pinter, 208-231.

De la Mothe, J. and G. Paquet (1996), 'Evolution and Inter–Creation: the Government–Business–Society Nexus' in J. De la Mothe and G. Paquet (eds.), *Evolutionary Economics and the New International Political Economy*, London: Pinter, 1–34.

De Vecchi, N. (1995), *Entrepreneurs, Institutions and Economic Change: The Economic Thought of J.A. Schumpeter (1905–1925)*, Aldershot: Edward Elgar.

Dosi, G., L. Tyson and J. Zysman (1989), 'Trade, Technologies, and Development: A Framework for Discussing Japan' in C. Johnson et al. (eds.), *Politics and Productivity: The Real Story of Why Japan Works*, New York: Ballinger, 3–38.

Edquist, C. (1997), 'Systems of Innovation Approaches: Their Emergence and Characteristics' in C. Edquist (ed.), *Systems of Innovation: Technologies, Organisations and Institutions*, London: Pinter, 1–35.

Edquist, C. and B. Johnson (1997), 'Institutions and Organisations in Systems of Innovation' in C. Edquist (ed.), *Systems of Innovation: Technologies, Organisations and Institutions*, London: Pinter, 41–63.

Freeman, C. (1987), *Technology and Economic Performance: Lessons from Japan*, London: Pinter.

——— (1995b), 'History, Co–Evolution and Economic Growth', IIASA *Working Paper*, WP–95–76, September.

——— (1996), 'Catching–Up and Falling–Behind. The Case of Asia and Latin America' in J. de la Mothe and G. Paquet (eds.), *Evolutionary Economics and the New International Political Economy*, London: Pinter, 160–179.

Freeman, C. and C. Perez (1988), 'Structural Crises of Adjustment, Business Cycles and Investment Behaviour' in G. Dosi et al. (eds.), *Technical Change and Economic Theory*, London: Pinter, 38–66.

Freeman, C. and I. Soete (1997), *The Economics of Industrial Innovation*, Third Edition, London: Pinter.

Granovetter, M. (1992), 'Economic Action and Social Structure. The Problem of Embededdness' in M. Granovetter and R. Swedberg (eds.), *The Sociology of Economic Life*, Boulder: Westview Press, 53–81.

Hodgson, G. M. (1988), *Economics and Institutions: A Manifesto for a Modern Institutional Economics*, Oxford: Polity Press.

—— (1996), 'Varieties of Capitalism and Varieties of Economic Theory', *Review of International Political Economy*, 3 (3), 381–434.

Hurwicz, L. (1995), 'Social Absorption Capability and Economic Development' in B.H. Koo and D.H. Perkins (eds.), *Social Capability and Long–Term Economic Growth*, London: Macmillan, 123–141.

Jamison, A. (1991), 'National Styles in Technology Policy. Comparing the Swedish and Danish State Programmes in Microelectronics and Information Technology' in U. Hilpert (ed.) *State Policies and Techno–Industrial Innovation*, London: Routledge, 305–327.

Johnson, B. (1992), 'Institutional Learning' in B.–Å. Lundvall (ed.), *National Systems of Innovation: Towards a Theory of Innovation and Interactive Learning*, London: Pinter, 23–44.

Klump, R. (1996), 'Einleitung' in R. Klump (ed.), *Wirtschaftskultur, Wirtschaftsstil und Wirtschaftsordnung: Methoden und Ergebnisse der Wirtschaftskulturforschung*, Marburg Metropolis, 9–20.

Krabbe, J.J. (1996), 'Nature and Technology as Economic Categories: Sombart in the Mainstream' in J.G. Backhaus (ed.), *Werner Sombart (1863–1941) — Social Scientist*, 3 Vols., Vol. 2: His Theoretical Approach Reconsidered, Marburg: Metropolis, 57–64.

Lazonick, W. (1994), 'The Integration of Theory and History. Methodology and Ideology in Schumpeter's Economics' in L. Magnusson (ed.), *Evolutionary and Neo–Schumpeterian Approaches to Economics*, Boston: Kluwer, 245–263.

List, F. (1841), *Das Nationale System der Politischen Oekonomie*, Stuttgart and Tübingen: Cotta'scher Verlag.

Lundvall, B.–Å. (1985), *Product Innovation and User–Producer Interaction*, Aalborg: Aalborg University Press.

—— (1992), 'Introduction' in B.–Å. Lundvall (ed.), *National Systems of Innovation: Towards a Theory of Innovation and Interactive Learning*, London: Pinter, 1–22.

—— (1996), 'National Systems of Innovation and Input-Output Analysis' in DeBresson, C. et al. (eds.), Economic Interdependence and Innovative Activity: An Input–Output Analysis, Cheltenham: Edward Elgar, 356–363.

Maddison, A. (1994), 'Explaining the Economic Performance of Nations, 1820–1989' in W.J. Baumol et al. (eds), *Convergence of Productivity. Cross–National Studies and Historical Evidence*, New York: Oxford University Press, 22–61.

McKelvey, M. (1996), *Evolutionary Innovations: The Business of Biotechnology*, Oxford: Oxford University Press.

Müller–Armack, A. (1943), *Genealogie der Wirtschaftsstile. Die Geistesgeschichtlichen Ursprünge der Staats– und Wirtschaftsformen bis zum Ausgang des 18 Jahrhunderts*, Stuttgart: Kohlhammer.

Nelson, R.R. and N. Rosenberg (1993), 'Technical Innovation and National Systems' in R.R. Nelson (ed.), *National Innovation Systems: A Comparative Analysis*, Oxford: Oxford University Press, 1–18.

Niosi, J., P. Saviotti, B. Bertrand and M. Crow (1993), 'National Systems of Innovation' in Search of a Workable Concept', Technology in Society, 15, 207–227.

Niosi, J. and B. Bellon (1996), 'The Globalisation of National Innovation Systems' in J. de la Mothe, P. John and G. Paquet (eds.), *Evolutionary Economics and the New International Political Economy*, London: Pinter, 138–159.

Patel, P. and K. Pavitt (1994), 'National Innovation Systems: Why they are important and how they might be compared', *Economics of Innovation and New Technology*, 3 (1), 77–95.

Perroux, F. (1965), 'La Pensée Économique de Joseph Schumpeter: Les Dynamiques du Capitalisme' in F. Perroux (1993), *Euvres Complètes, Vol.VI, Théorie et Histoire de la Pensée Économique: Marx, Schumpeter, Keynes*, Grenoble: Presses Universitaire de Grenoble, 2nd. ed., 57–334.

Porter, M. (1990), *The Competitive Advantage of Nations*, London: Macmillan.

Rosser, J. Barkley and Rosser and V. Marina (1996), *Comparative Economics in a Transforming World Economy*, Chicago: Irwin.

Saviotti, P. P. (1996), *Technological Evolution, Variety and the Economy*, Cheltenham: Edward Elgar.

Schefold, B. (1994), 'Nationalökonomie und Kulturwissenschaften: Das Konzept des Wirtschaftsstils' in K.W. Nörr, et al. (eds.): *Deutsche Geisteswissenschaften zwischen Kaiserreich und Republik. Zur Entwicklung von Nationalökonomie, Rechtswissenschaft und Sozialwissenschaft im 20. Jahrhundert*, Stuttgart: Steiner, 215–242.

——— (1996a), 'The German Historical School and the Belief in Ethical Progress', in N.F. Brady (ed.), *Ethical Universals in International Business*, Berlin: Springer, 173–196.

——— (1996b), 'Are Economic Theories Historically Specific?' in M.C. Marcuzzo, et al. (eds.): *The Economics of Joan Robinson*, London: Routledge, 300–316.

Schumpeter, J.A. (1908), *Das Wesen und der Hauptinhalt der theoretischen Nationalökonomie*, Berlin: Duncker und Humblot.

——— (1926a), *Theorie der wirtschaftlichen Entwicklung. Eine Untersuchung über Unternehmergewinn, Kapital, Kredit, Zins und den Konjunkturzyklus*, 2nd ed., Berlin: Duncker und Humblot.

——— (1926b), 'Gustav v. Schmoller und die Probleme von heute', *Schmollers Jahrbuch für Gesetzgebung, Verwaltung und Volkswirtschaft im Deutschen Reiche*, 50 (1.1), 1–52.

——— (1929), 'Das soziale Antlitz des Deutschen Reiches' in J.A. Schumpeter (1953), *Aufsätze zur Soziologie*, Tübingen: Mohr, 214–225.

────── (1939), Business Cycles, *A Theoretical, Historical and Statistical Analysis of the Capitalist Process*, New York: McGraw Hill.

────── (1942), *Capitalism, Socialism and Democracy*, London: Allen and Unwin.

────── (1947), 'Theoretical Problems of Economic Growth', *The Journal of Economic History*, Supplement VII, 1–9.

────── (1948), 'Wage and Tax Policy in Transitional States of Society' in J.A. Schumpeter (1991), *The Economics and Sociology of Capitalism* ed. by R. Swedberg, Princeton: Princeton University Press, 429–437.

────── (1954), *A History of Economic Analysis*, New York: Oxford University Press.

Shionoya, Y. (1991), 'Schumpeter on Schmoller and Weber: A Methodology of Economic Sociology', *History of Political Economy*, 23 (2), Summer, 193–219.

────── (1997), *Schumpeter and the Idea of Social Science: a Metatheoretical Study*, Cambridge: Cambridge University Press.

Smelser, N. J. and R. Swedberg (1994), 'The Sociological Perspective on the Economy' in N.J. Smelser and R. Swedberg (eds.), *The Handbook of Economic Sociology*, Princeton: Princeton University Press, 3–26.

Sombart, W. (1916), *Der moderne Kapitalismus. Historisch–systematische Darstellung des gesamteuropäischen Wirtschaftslebens von seinen Anfängen bis zur Gegenwart*, 6 Vols., Vol.1.1, Die vorkapitalistische Wirtschaft, repr. 1987, München: dtv.

────── (1930), *Die drei Nationalökonomien. Geschichte und System der Lehre von der Wirtschaft*, 2nd edition 1967, Berlin: Duncker & Humblot.

Spiethoff, A. (1932), 'Die Allgemeine Volkswirtschaftslehre als geschichtliche Theorie. Die Wirtschaftsstile', *Schmollers Jahrbuch für Gesetzgebung, Verwaltung und Volkswirtschaft im Deutschen Reich*, 56 (2.2), 51–84.

────── (1952), 'The 'Historical' Character of Economic Theories', *The Journal of Economic History*, XII (2), Spring, 131–139.

Stolper, W. F. (1988), 'Development: Theory and Empirical Evidence' in H. Horst (ed.), *Evolutionary Economics. Applications of Schumpeter's Ideas*, Cambridge: Cambridge University Press, 9–22.

Tylecote, A. (1996), 'Managerial Objectives and Technological Collaboration: The Role of National Variations in Cultures and Structures' in R. Coombs et al. (eds.), *Technological Collaboration: The Dynamics of Cooperation in Industrial Innovation*, Cheltenham: Edward Elgar, 34–53.

Veblen, T. (1901), 'Gustav Schmoller's Economics' in T. Veblen (1994), *The Collected Works of Thorstein Veblen, Vol.VIII: The Place of Science in Modern Civilisation and other Essays*, London: Routledge, 252–278.

Zysman, J. (1994), 'Dynamic Diversity: Institutions and Economic Development in Advanced Countries' in R. Delorme and K. Dopfer (eds.), *The Political Economy of Diversity: Evolutionary Perspectives on Economic Order and Disorder*, Aldershot: Edward Elgar, 126–146.

10. Capabilities, Tacit Knowledge and Systemic Change: Hungary Compared with other Emerging Market Economies

Wim Swaan

INTRODUCTION

This chapter is concerned with the development of capabilities in post–socialist economies, in particular in Hungarian industry. As will be set out below, the emergence of well functioning markets is not merely a matter of creating appropriate incentives and institutions at the macro level, but strongly interacts with the development of capabilities. This argument relies on the growing literature acknowledging the role of capabilities or competence in the competitiveness of firms and nations and the high costs involved with transferring capabilities across organisations (Nelson and Winter, 1982; Prahalad and Hamel, 1990; Porter, 1990; Chandler, 1990; Teece, 1993; for applications to post–socialist economies see Swaan, 1996 and Swaan and Lissowska, 1996). With internalisation and mobility in capital and technology advancing, the performance of an economy increasingly depends upon the quality of labour and the degree to which the institutional infrastructure is supportive of innovation (Nelson, 1993).

While the importance of capabilities at a theoretical level is increasingly acknowledged and few economists would deny the importance of managerial and organisational skills in the process of post–socialist transformation, measurability of this aspect encounters substantial difficulties. This chapter presents a way of measuring developments in the Hungarian economy by contrasting them to developments in other countries. Comparative data are presented on the assessment of level of organisational and managerial skills in a couple of countries at a comparable level of development, based on the World Competitiveness

Report. This will give some indication of the level of capabilities attained, both of the strengths and weakneses of the Hungarian economy.

CAPABILITIES AND ECONOMIC PERFORMANCE

Below a brief overview is presented of the growing literature on the role of capabilities in the competitiveness of firms and nations. Radosevic (1994) puts this literature in a useful framework, by pointing to the simultaneity of incentives, institutions and capabilities in shaping economic performance. In the Eastern European context, much of the literature and the policy debate has focussed on the role of incentives: price and trade liberalisation, privatisation and tax reform. Increasing attention has been paid to the role of institutions (see for instance, Schmieding, 1993). Yet, for incentives and institutions to have an impact on performance, actors need to be able to respond in an appropriate way: if the capabilities to this are inadequate, response is delayed or will even be totally absent (Swaan and Lissowska, 1992, pp. 92–95; Radosevic, 1994, pp. 89–91). As was argued by Teece (1993, following Chandler, 1990) markets are not an exogenous constraint determining the behaviour of business organisations: rather, markets are created by business organisations and their specific competencies. This view is related to Schumpeter's argument (1934, 1939) on the role of entrepreneurs in economic development.

An implication of the foregoing is not that the role of incentives would be less important. On the contrary, without strong and stable incentives, actors are not willing to commit themselves to long term investments which are required for building capabilities. Similarly, in the absence of an appropriate institutional framework actors may be withheld from investing in developing their capabilities (Pelikan, 1992). The argument is that the development of effective incentive structures is not merely an exogenous policy issue, but may initially be hindered by inadequate capabilities, or by inappropriate institutions.

The interaction between incentives, institutional change and economic performance has been dealt with in detail by North (1990). In the presence of transaction costs in the market, in political decision making and in the cultural transmission of values, institutional change may be retarded or completely blocked, even if it would be in the long term interest of actors to bring about change. Choices made in the past, including the adaptation of particular mental models or policy regimes, may accordingly lead to path dependence. Similar arguments have been made by Coleman (1990) on the development of social norms and by Jones (1995) on the interaction between the role of culture and the incentives structures in the economy.

TACIT KNOWLEDGE AND POST SOCIALIST ECONOMIES

As was argued by Michael Polanyi (1958), a considerable part of human knowledge is tacit or personal: it is difficult to articulate and can only be acquired through practice and imitation of skilled masters. Such relatively simple activity as swimming, for instance, requires a coordination of movements of which even experienced swimmers are not completely aware, let alone that they would be able to transfer their skills easily to other people.

Similar to individual knowledge, organisational knowledge is partly tacit: it is difficult to articulate and neither the management, nor other participants in the organisation may be completely aware of its content. The knowledge of a firm cannot be reduced to a book of blueprints, or to the knowledge of its engineers and scientists. Instead, the firm's knowledge can be considered to be embodied in the routines that develop as a response to the tacit character of knowledge (Nelson and Winter, 1982, pp. 99–124, following Polanyi, 1958).

Acknowledging the importance of tacit organisational knowledge, firm specific knowledge (or the 'core competence of the firm') is increasingly recognized as one of the key factors of a firm's competitiveness (Wernerfelt, 1984; Prahalad and Hamel, 1990; Hamel and Prahalad, 1994). Given the high costs of creating competencies (even by imitating), actors may be better off by teaming up with international market leaders, than by acting on their own. Teaming up might take place through various forms: strategic alliances between existing entities, transfer of ownership of an existing firm, or individuals joining a newly set up firm. This is not something special for post–socialist economies: it is equally valid for actors in developed market economies and emerging market economies, as is witnessed by the increased importance of strategic alliances and foreign direct investment all over the world (Badaracco, 1991; Hamel, 1991).

While cooperation between international market leaders and domestic actors is not at all typical for post–socialist economies, the existing stock of individual and organisational capabilities in these economies is likely to pose special problems. Since tacit knowledge develops through experience, it is closely related to the institutional structure in which it developed (Murrell, 1992a, 1992b). The basis for acquiring marketing and organisational capabilities can be given through standard education, but thorough command of these skills can only be acquired through practice, for instance, by following examples of others. In post–socialist economies such examples are largely absent, as in the past in the centrally planned economy quite different capabilities were required to be successful.

The Measurement of Capabilities: a Comparison with Countries of a Comparable Level of Development

Very useful data on the level of capabilities can be found in the *World Competitiveness Report* (1994). Apart from a host of published statistical data, the World Competitiveness Report presents the results of a survey among businessmen and experts in the countries concerned, who are asked to evaluate 129 aspects of their countries' competitiveness as compared to other countries.[1] From these, 28 survey questions are related to the level of capabilities and will be considered in the current analysis: 12 in Management, 7 in Science and Technology, and 9 on Miscellaneous aspects of the quality of human capital. Table 10.1 lists the factors concerned and the valuation by Hungarian respondents.

Admittedly, asking people to evaluate aspects of their own country's competitiveness introduces a great deal of subjectivity. In some countries people may be likely to systematically overestimate their countries' performance, whereas in other countries people may appear to be notorious pessimists. While this calls for caution in interpreting the survey data as an indication of absolute strength of an economy, it at least gives an indication of the relative strengths and the relative weaknesses of an economy. Even pessimists are likely to assess different aspects of their economy in different degrees of pessimism, thereby giving an indication of their relative valuation of these aspects. A comparison with the relative valuation of respondents in other countries might then give valuable information on the strengths and weaknesses of different economies.[2]

While the World Competitiveness Report originally focussed on developed market economies, an increasing number of newly industrialising countries and post–socialist countries are included. Among the post–

Table 10. 1   Aspects of competitiveness related to economic capabilities: assessment by Hungarian respondents and ranking among 41 countries

(1)	**Management**	(2) Valuation	(3) Ranking
6.16	Entrepreneurship and innovation	5.52	37
6.17	Risk taking and initiative	4.13	41
6.20	Use of information technology	4.17	36
6.21	Organisation of the workspace	2.83	41
6.22	Implementation of strategies	3.11	41
6.23	Willingness to delegate authority	4.37	31
6.25	Intercultural understanding	5.32	29
6.26	International business experience of senior management	4.59	38
6.31	Total quality management	3.09	41
6.33	Customer orientation	3.91	35
6.34	Time required for product development	2.67	41
6.35	Time required for maketisation of a product	2.76	41
	Science & Technology		
7.20	Availability of qualified engineers	7.03	11
7.24	Effectiveness of basic research in relation to long term development	3.37	33
7.25	Education of science in compulsory schools	5.47	15
7.36	Effectiveness of technological strategies	3.11	41
7.37	Sourcing of technology by domestic companies	1.98	41
7.39	R&D in key industries compared to competitors	1.82	41
7.41	Level of production technologies	2.31	40
	Human Capital, Miscellaneous Aspects		
8.21	Availability of skilled labour	6.13	15
8.22	Availability of competent senior managers	4.02	36
8.28	Educational system	4.15	25
8.34	Level of compulsory education	5.43	23
8.36	Computer literacy	3.41	39
8.37	Economic literacy among the population	3.23	36
8.38	Companies' efforts at retraining employees	4.13	40
8.50	Willingness of employees to be retrained	4.64	38
8.56	Values of society and economic competitiveness	3.93	38
	Average valuation of 28 factors selected	3.95	

Source: *World Competitiveness Report 1994*

(1) For ease of reference the original table numbers from the World Competitiveness Report are reported here.
(2) The average valuation of the Hungarian economy relative to other economies as perceived by Hungarian respondents on a continuous 0–10 scale. In the questionnaires, respondents are asked to evaluate each aspect on a discrete 1–6 scale. Average values per country are then transported to the scale reported here (World Competitiveness Report 1994, p. 627).
(3) Ranking of Hungary among 41 countries.

socialist countries, Hungary was added to the group in 1992, followed by Poland and the Czech Republic in 1994. In the 1994 issue, upon which the analysis will be based here, a total of 41 countries were covered, including 18 countries outside the OECD (as against only 10 in the 1991 report).

From the perspective of the competitiveness of the Hungarian economy it is especially instructive to make a comparison with countries of a comparable level of development. The usual comparison with developed market economies might be useful as setting a goal to reach for, it does not throw much light on the relative strength and weaknesses of the Hungarian economy. Thus, a comparison will be made with 6 countries ranked immediately above Hungary in terms of GDP per capita at purchasing power parity, and 6 countries ranked immediately below it. This group includes all post–socialist countries covered in the 1994 report (Hungary, Poland and the Czech Republic), one other European country (Greece), three countries from South–East Asia (Korea, Malaysia and Thailand), and six Latin American countries (Venezuela, Mexico, Chile, Brazil, Argentina and Colombia).

The 28 factors that were selected are divided into four groups according to the following criteria (for details see the explanation in the table):

- ranking of factors by Hungarian respondents (column 3) relative to ranking by respondents in the reference group of countries (column 5);
- absolute ranking of factors by Hungarian respondents (column 3);
  in Table 10.2 a comparison is presented between Hungary and the reference group of countries of a comparable level of development.
- difference between valuation for Hungary (column 2) and the average valuation for the reference group (column 4);
- ranking of Hungary among all 41 countries covered by the World Competitiveness Report (column 1).

Consider briefly the robustness of the classification of aspects as strong (I), potentially weak (II), weak (III) and extremely weak (IV). Regarding category IV (extremely weak), there can be little doubt as to the weakness of the Hungarian economy. The factors in these category are ranked very low by Hungarian respondents and have in each case a lower ranking than the one implied by the average valuation of the reference group (or an equal

Table 10.2   Aspects of competitiveness related to economic capabilities: Hungary compared with countries of a comparable level of development

	Ranking of Hungary among all 41 countries	Valuation by Hungarian respondents (in brackets ranking among the factors selected)	Average valuation for Reference group of 13 Countries (in brackets ranking among the factors selected)	Difference between Hungary and the reference group, relative to the standard deviation of the 13 values	Ranking of Hungary, Poland and the Czech Republic among 41 countries **
	[1]	[2] [3]	[4] [5]	[6]	[7]
I. Strong					
1. Availability of qualified engineers (7.20)*	11	7.03 (1)	5.52 (4)	+1.11	[7]
2. Availability of skilled labour (8.21)	15	6.13 (2)	4.96 (8)	+1.36	
3. Education of science in compulsory schools (7.25)*	15	5.47 (4)	4.10 (22)	+1.13	
4. Level of compulsory education (8.34)	23	5.43 (5)	4.29 (20)	+0.62	
5. Educational system (8.28)	25	4.15 (11)	3.62 (25)	+0.48	
II. Comparable level or potentially weak					
6. Intercultural understanding (6.25)	29	5.32 (6)	5.36 (6)	-0.04	
7. Willingness to delegate authority (6.23)	31	4.37 (9)	4.64 (12)	-0.41	
8. Use of information technology (6.20)	36	4.17 (10)	4.71 (11)	-0.59	HPC 6
9. Availability of competent senior managers (8.22)	36	4.02 (14)	4.37 (18)	-0.38	
10. Customer orientation (6.33)	35	3.91 (16)	4.40 (17)	-0.51	
11. Effectiveness of basic research in relation to long term development (7.24)	33	3.37 (18)	3.62 (26)	-0.32	
III. Weak					
	[1]	[2] [3]	[4] [5]	[6]	[7]
12. Entrepreneurship and innovation (6.16)*	37	5.52 (3)	6.35 (1)	-1.16	
14. Willingness of employees to be retrained (8.50)	38	4.64 (7)	5.64 (3)	-1.0	IIPC 6
International business experience of senior management (6.26)	38	4.59 (8)	5.38 (5)	-0.77	HPC 6
15. Companies' efforts at retraining employees (8.38)	40	4.13 (13)	4.91 (9)	-0.97	HPC 3
16. Values of society and economic competitiveness (8.56)	38	3.93 (15)	5.31 (7)	-1.14	HPC 6
17. Computer literacy (8.36)	39	3.41 (17)	4.36 (19)	-1.14	
18. Economic literacy among the population (8.37)	36	3.23 (19)	4.08 (23)	-0.81	

continued on next page

Table 10.2 Aspects of competitiveness related to economic capabilities: Hungary compared with countries of a comparable level of development (continued)

	Ranking of Hungary among all 41 countries	Valuation by Hungarian respondents (in brackets ranking among the factors selected)	Average valuation for Reference group of 13 Countries (in brackets ranking among the factors selected)	Difference between Hungary and the reference group, relative to the standard deviation of the 13 values	Ranking of Hungary, Poland and the Czech Republic among 41 countries **
IV. Extremely weak					
19. Risk taking and initiative (6.17)	41	4.13 (12)	5.85 (2)	-1.85	HPC 3
20. Implementation of strategies (6.22)	41	3.11 (20)	4.74 (10)	-1.50	HFC 6
21. Effectiveness of technological strategies (7.36)	41	3.11 (21)	4.42 (16)	-1.55	HFC 6
22. Total quality management (6.31)	41	3.09 (22)	4.48 (14)	-1.72	HFC 6
23. Organisation of the workspace (6.21)	41	2.83 (23)	4.13 (21)	-1.45	HFC 3
24. Time required for marketization of a product (6.35)	41	2.76 (24)	4.62 (13)	-2.00	HPC 3
25. Time required for product development (6.34)	41	2.67 (25)	4.46 (15)	-2.21	HPC 6
26. Level of production technologies (7.41)	40	2.31 (26)	3.79 (24)	-1.46	HPC 6
27. Sourcing of technology by domestic companies (7.37)	41	1.98 (27)	3.37 (27)	-1.45	HPC 6
28. R&D in key industries compared to competitors (7.39)	41	1.82 (28)	3.11 (28)	-1.51	HPC 6
Average valuation of 28 factors selected		3.95	4.59		

* The numbers in brackets refer to the original table numbers of the World Competitiveness Report.
** HPC 3: the three countries are the bottom three among all 41 countries; HPC 6: the three countries are among the bottom six of 41 countries

The factors have been classified into four groups by the following criteria:
- ranking of factors by Hungarian respondents (column 3) relative to ranking by respondents in a group of 13 countries of a comparable level of development, as listed in table 2 (column 5);
- absolute ranking of factors by Hungarian respondents (column 3);
- difference between valuation for Hungary and the average valuation for the reference group of 13 countries, relative to the standard deviation of the 13 values (column 6);
- ranking among all 41 countries covered by the World Competitiveness Report (column 1).

I. Strong
- ranked higher by Hungarian respondents from the reference group of 13 countries
- positive difference in valuation

II. Comparable level or potentially weak
- ranked equal or higher by Hungarian respondents than by respondents from the reference group of 13 countries
- small negative difference between valuation for Hungary and the average valuation for the reference group of 13 countries (less than around 0.5 times the standard deviation of the 13 values; value of column 6 between 0 and around –0.5)

III. Weak
- the remaining factors (not classified under I., II. or IV.)

IV. Extremely Weak
- ranked lower by Hungarian respondents than by respondents from the reference group of 13 countries
- large negative difference between valuation for Hungary and the average valuation for the reference group of 13 countries (more than around 1.5 times the standard deviation of the 13 values: value of column 6 below around –1.5)
- valuation for Hungary lowest or one but lowest among all 41 countries covered by the World Competitiveness Report (40 or 41 in column 1).

ranking as regards the bottom two factors). Moreover, the difference in valuation for these factors between Hungary and the reference group is so large that this cannot be attributed only to pessimism of Hungarian respondents or optimism from respondents of other countries. Similarly, there can be little doubt on the strength of the Hungarian economy for factors in group I. For factors in categories II and III some caution is in order.

Table 10.2 gives a revealing picture of the strengths and weaknesses of the Hungarian economy regarding the capabilities of domestic actors. The group of capabilities in which the Hungarian economy can be considered (very) strong (category I) either involve a high level of definable, transferable knowledge (high level of education, row 3–5) or types of tacit knowledge which are not related to commercial application and marketisation (availability of qualified engineers and skilled labour, row 1–2).

On the other hand, as regards the aspects in which the Hungarian economy is extremely weak (category IV), it is noteworthy that they are almost all related to complex organisational capabilities involving a high degree of market related tacit knowledge and complex (inter) organisational cooperation: the effectiveness of strategies, the time required for product development and marketisation, the implementation of total quality management and the level of technology and research and development (row 20–28). Indeed, among the more complex organisational capabilities listed in the table, only the use of information technology (row 8) and the degree of customer orientation (row 10) can be considered of comparable to the reference group of countries.

With regards to the level of research and development and technologies (row 21, 22, 25, 26, 27, 28) it should be obvious that these are not only a matter of individual and organisational capabilities, but may also be due to a lack of resources. The availability of financial resources for technological development is indeed valued very low by Hungarian respondents (2.29, compared to an average for the reference group of 4.49, difference relative to standard deviation −1.81; World Competitiveness Report 1994, Table 7.42). However, financial resources alone cannot compensate for technological disadvantages and insufficient capabilities, all the more since technological development requires complex cooperation within and among organisations.

From the factors classified in the two middle categories, some are worth examining in more detail. Although both the willingness of employees to be retrained (row 13) and companies' efforts at retraining employees are ranked in the upper half by Hungarian respondents (7th and 13th respectively), it is striking that they are on average ranked even higher in the reference group (3rd and 9th respectively). The relative undervaluation of this aspect is worrying, as retraining at firm level is a key aspect of enterprise restructuring in post–socialist economies. It is also noteworthy that the relative valuation of formal education (row 3, 4 and 5) versus company training (row 13 and 15) is precisely reverse in Hungary as it is in the reference group: in Hungary formal education is strong and company training relatively weak, whereas in the reference group formal education is on average very weak and company training strong.

Another factor worth mentioning is the effectiveness of basic research (row 11): although not ranked very high by Hungarian respondents (18th), it is not ranked as low as in the reference group (26th). This seems to confirm the picture revealed above of strong transferable skills and non market related tacit skills, compared to extreme weakness in complex organisational capabilities needed for commercial application and marketisation.

Most of the other factors in categories II and III are related to individual skills (such as computer literacy, row 17) or to individual and social attitudes (such as intercultural understanding, row 6, and values of society and economic competitiveness, row 16).

A brief comparison of Hungary with Poland and the Czech Republic, which are both included in the group of 13 countries considered above, shows that the three Central Eastern European countries frequently find themselves at the bottom of the overall listing of 41 countries. In 4 from the 28 factors listed in Table 10.2, the three countries form the bottom three of 41, in another 10 they are among the bottom 6 (table 10.2, column 7, indicated by HPC3 and HPC6 respectively). From the factors judged extremely weak for the Hungarian economy (category IV), in all but one the Czech and the Polish economy might be considered comparably weak. The same holds, *mutatis mutandis*, for the strong aspects of the Hungarian economy (category I). In addition, the absolute difference in valuation between Hungarian, Czech and Polish respondents is surprisingly small for the aspects considered here. Differences in valuation are usually smaller than 1, except for 8 factors for the Czech Republic (4 positive, 4 negative) and 5 for Poland (2 positive, 3 negative).

The similarity between the three countries is confirmed by principal components analysis of all factors considered in the World Competitiveness

Report (1994, pp. 30–45). Not only are the three countries very close to each other in all of the major 8 headings considered (Domestic Economic Strength, Internationalisation, Government, Finance, Infrastructure, Management, Science & Technology, People), in some of these headings they form together a clear outlier as compared to the other 38 countries (in Government, Finance, Management and People).

CONCLUSION

The main findings are summarised in Table 10.3. This provides confirmation of the conjectures advanced in section 1. In comparison with newly industrialising countries of a comparable level of GDP per capita, the capabilities represented in the Hungarian economy are weaker, the more they involve tacit aspects, the more they are related to marketisation and the more they require complex cooperation. While basic, technical skills are very strong, and individual and social attitudes vary from acceptable to weak, the application of knowledge in complex cooperation is extremely weak. This also implies that huge efforts are required. Changes in complex organisational capabilities require concerted action.

Although the government and its agencies can and should provide appropriate incentives and may play a role in building supportive institutions for such concerted action, the process of building complex organisational and technological capabilities can ultimately only be undertaken by active innovative firms with a clear strategy.

The findings confirm the conjecture put forward in the beginning of this chapter that knowledge structures are closely related to the institutions and the economic system in which they were developed. The combination of a high level of technical, transferable skills and a low level of relevant tacit skills is indeed rare in economic history, as the social stock of tacit and technical skills mostly have developed in mutual interaction. Systemic disintegration has led to a destruction of the value of accumulated tacit knowledge.

Very similar findings were reached by Child and Markóczy (1993) in a comparative analysis of Hungarian and Chinese managerial behaviour. These appeared to show many similarities, such as:

- reluctance of managers to make decisions and accept responsibility;
- unwillingness to share information;

Table 10.3   A typology of economic capabilities: strengths and weaknesses of the Hungarian economy

	High degree of tacit Aspects (as opposed to Definable, easily Transferable Knowledge	High degree of market related aspects	Capabilities requiring complex cooperation to be effective
STRONG Formal education (row 3, 4, 5) technical skills (row 1, 2, 11, 17)	(x)		
NEUTRAL OR WEAK Company training (row 13, 15)	x	x	
individual and social attitudes (row, 6, 7, 12, 16, 18, 19)	x	x	(x)
EXTREMELY WEAK Organisational Capabilities Requiring complex Cooperation (row 9, 10, 14, 20, 23, 24)	x	x	x
technological capabilities requiring complex cooperation (row 8, 21, 22, 25, 26, 27, 28)	x	x	x

x: strongly present
(x):   weakly present
Row numbers refer to Table 10.2.

- absence of effective systems for selecting and firing employees. Although Child and Markóczy (1993) did not explicitly consider the role of tacit skills in managerial behaviour, they too see managerial behaviour in Hungary and China first of all as a result of similar systems of industrial governance. In particular, they argue that managerial skills are not in the first place related to the extent of industrialisation, but to the character it took. In socialist countries the bureaucratic nature of industrialisation did not encourage the development of market oriented capabilities. This differs considerably, for instance, from industrialisation in South East Asia, which although more recent, took place in institutional structures much better geared to the development of market capabilities. In this sense, post socialist countries have to make up for their relative disadvantages.

An interesting question in this respect is the relation between current performance and the reform process, which in Hungary has a much longer history than in other post-socialist countries. The main advantage of these reforms was that they formed a preparation for the process of radical institutional change. Issues such as private ownership and the functioning of markets were not anymore totally alien to actors in the economy. Paradoxically, however, the slightly favourable heritage of socialist reforms may have even put a constraint on the speed of the transformation process. The changes that occurred until 1989 all took place within the framework of a socialist economic system. Quasi market–oriented attitudes arose in an environment of bureaucratic bargaining, often in exchange for centrally allocated resources. Enterprises got accustomed to bargaining for subsidies and exemptions and in the importance of finding ways to evade official regulations. The drive for autonomy that has characterised Hungarian enterprises during the 1980s has facilitated entry into the private sector and the disintegration of the system: by 1988, enterprises did apply their political clout to oppose market–oriented reforms as they had done on earlier occasions. Yet this drive for managerial autonomy has also hampered the transfer to more effective governance structures (for more details see Bod and Hall, 1992; Crane, 1991; Mihályi, 1993; Swaan and Lissowska, 1996). The impact of the heritage of socialist reform was aggravated by ineffective economic policy, at least until early 1995, in particular by the lack of a clear policy strategy. Although this is partly endogenous to the structure of interest group 5 inherited from the socialist reform era, a more effective policy would have certainly been possible.

The high level of education and technical skills implies large potential advantages for the Hungarian economy. This can, however, only be reaped if substantial progress is made in developing the required capabilities in commercial application. Mere awareness of this dichotomy is also important. Foreign managers and consultants have sometimes been unaware of the high level of education and technical skills and ended up teaching things that are by long familiar. Domestic actors, on the other hand, have not always been aware of the importance of tacit aspects of skills: some have considered restructuring mainly as a process of acquiring financial capital and equipment.

Above a measurement of the level of capabilities in the Hungarian economy is provided at one particular point of time. This allows us to compare Hungary with other emerging market economies, against the background of the history of the socialist economic system in force prior to 1989. The data and the method that were used, however, do not allow to make inferences about the precise speed of behavioural change since 1989. Evidence from a wide variety of studies, both in the scientific literature and in the business press, gives a mixed picture (see for instance, Török, 1993; Laki, 1994; Carlin, van Reenen and Wolfe, 1995; Estrin, Brada, Gelb and Singh, 1995). From the point of view of what would be desirable in absolute terms, the process of behavioural change has not always been satisfactory. However, from the point of view of the initial conditions, the magnitude of the tasks to be accomplished and the uncertainty actors had to face, impressive changes have been going on. At any rate, it would be premature and incorrect to interpret the results in terms of a culturally and historically determined pattern. The data presented in this chapter in fact do not suggest anything more than that behavioural change has not been instantaneous and has not been completed by 1994. Findings different from this would indeed have been surprising in view of the theoretical behavioural literature.

NOTES

1. For the 1994 report (World Competitiveness Report, 1994, p. 22) the questionnaire was completed by 2851 respondents in 41 countries, implying an average of 70 per country. The response rate was 17%.
2. A more detailed discussion of the validity and robustness of the data is given in Swaan (1995).

REFERENCES

Badaracco, J.L. Jr. (1991), *The Knowledge Link: How Firms Compete through Strategic Alliances*, Boston: Harvard Business School Press.

Bod, P.A. and J.B. Hall (1992), 'Toward an Autonomy Preference Theory of the East European Firm', *Eastern European Economics* 30 (4), 57–67.

Carlin, W., J. van Reenen and T. Wolfe (1995), 'Enterprise Restructuring' in Early Transition: the Case Study Evidence from Central and Eastern Europe', *Economics of Transition* 3 (4), 427–495.

Chandler, A.D. Jr. (1990), *Scale and Scope: The Dynamics of Industrial Capitalism*, Cambridge: The Belknap Press of Harvard University.

Child, J. and L. Markóczy (1993), Host–country Managerial Behaviour and Learning in Chinese and Hungarian Joint Ventures, *Journal of Management Studies* 30 (4), 611–631.

Coleman, J.S. (1990), *The Foundations of Social Theory*, Cambridge: The Belknap Press of Harvard University Press.

Crane, K. (1991), Institutional Legacies and the Economic, Social and Political Environment for Transition in Hungary and Poland, *American Economic Review* 81 (2), Papers & Proceedings, 318–322.

Estrin, S., J.C. Brada, A. Gelb and I. Singh (1995), *Restructuring and Privatisation in Central Eastern Europe: Case Studies of Firms in Transition*, Armonk, New York: M.E. Sharpe.

Hamel, G. (1991), Competition for Competence and Inter-partner Learning within International Strategic Alliances', *Strategic Management Journal* 12, Special Issue, Summer, 83–103.

Hamel, G. and C.K. Prahalad (1994), *Competing for the Future*, Boston: Harvard Business School Press.

Jones, E.L. (1995), Culture and its Relationship to Economic Change, *Journal of Institutional and Theoretical Economics* 151 (2), 269–285.

Laki, Mihály (1994), Firm Behaviour During a Long Transitional Recession, *Acta Oeconomica* 46 (3–4), 347–370.

Mihályi, P. (1993), Hungary: a Unique Approach to Privatisation - Past, Present and Future, in I. P. Székely and D.M.G. Newbery (eds.), *Hungary: an economy in transition*, Cambridge: Cambridge University Press, 84–117.

Murrell, P. (1992a), Evolutionary and Radical Approaches to Economic Reform, *Economics of Planning* 25 (1), 79–95.

—— (1992b), Conservative Political Philosophy and the Strategy of Economic Transition, *East European Politics and Societies* 6 (1), 3–16.

Nelson, R.R. (ed.) (1993), *National Innovation Systems: a Comparative Analysis*, New York: Oxford University Press.

Nelson, R.R. and S.G. Winter (1982), *An Evolutionary Theory of Economic Change*, Cambridge: The Belknap Press of Harvard University.

North, D.C. (1990), *Institutions, Institutional Change and Economic Performance*, Cambridge: Cambridge University Press.

Pelikan, P. (1992), The Dynamics of Economic Systems, or How to Transform a Failed Socialist Economy, *Journal of Evolutionary Economics* 2 (1), 39–63.

Polanyi, M. (1958), *Personal Knowledge: Towards a Post-Critical Philosophy*, London: Routledge & Kegan Paul.

Porter, M.E. (1990), *The Competitive Advantage of Nations*, New York: The Free Press.

Prahalad, C.K. and G. Hamel (1990), The Core Competence of the Corporation, *Harvard Business Review* 68 (3), 79–91.

Radosevic, S. (1994), Strategic Technology Policy for Eastern Europe, *Economic Systems* 18 (2), 87–116.

Schmieding, H. (1993), From Plan to Market: on the Nature of the Transformation Crisis, *Weltwirtschaftliches Archiv* 129 (2), 216–253.

Schumpeter, J.A. (1934), *The Theory of Economic Development*, Oxford: Oxford University Press.

——— (1939), *Business Cycles*, New York: McGraw Hill.

Swaan, W. (1995), Capabilities and Competitiveness of the Hungarian Economy: a Comparative Analysis, Budapest: Institute of Economics, Hungarian Academy of Sciences, *Discussion paper* MT-DP 36.

——— (1996), Behavioural Constraints and the Creation of Markets in Post-socialist Economies, in B. Dallago and L. Mittone (eds.), *Economic Institutions, Markets and Competition: Centralisation and Decentralisation in the Transformation of Economic Systems*, Cheltenham: Edward Elgar, 221–240.

Swaan, W. and M. Lissowska (1992), Enterprise Behaviour in Hungary and Poland in the Transition to a Market Economy: Individual and Organisational Routines as a Barrier to Change, in W. Blaas and J. Foster (eds.), *Mixed Economies in Europe: An Evolutionary Perspective on their Emergence, Transition and Regulation*, Aldershot: Edward Elgar, 69–102.

——— (1996), Capabilities, Routines and East European Economic Reform: Hungary and Poland Before and After the 1989 Revolutions, *Journal of Economic Issues,* 30 (4), 1031–1056.

Teece, D.J. (1993), The Dynamics of Industrial Capitalism: Perspectives on Alfred Chandler's Scale and Scope' , *Journal of Economic Literature* 31 (1), 199–225.

Török, A. (1993), Trends and Motives of Organisational Change in Hungarian Industry' *Journal of Comparative Economics,* 17 (2), 366–384.

Wernerfelt, B. (1984), A Resource-based View of the Firm, *Strategic Management Journal* 5 (2), 171–180.

World Competitiveness Report 1994 , Geneva/Lausanne: IMD/World Economic Forum.

11. An Evolutionary Analysis of Technology Policy[*]

Vanessa Oltra

INTRODUCTION

The purpose of this chapter is to explore the economics of technology policy from an evolutionary perspective. More precisely the objective is to analyse the mechanisms underlying the evolution of technology and policy and to emphasise the interactions between technological change, industrial structure and technology policy.

Firstly we focus on the objectives of technology policy. We propose a differentiated analysis of technology policy, according to the objectives and the mechanisms it seeks to influence. We differentiate between three types of technology policy: research incentive policy, innovation policy and policy at the level of selection mechanisms.

Finally we study the mechanisms driving the evolution of technology policy. We underline the learning capacities and the specificities of the policy maker. In the same way as that of technology, the evolution of technology policy is based on learning and selection processes. We analyse the relationships between innovation and industrial dynamics, and argue that there is a co–evolution of technology, industrial structure and technology policy.

---

[*] I am grateful to P. Cohendet, P. Llerena and M. Yildizoglu for their helpful comments on a previous version of this chapter.

186

THE OBJECTIVES AND INTERVENTION MECHANISMS OF TECHNOLOGY POLICY

The general purpose of technology policy is to stimulate the process of technical change and to support the processes of creation, utilisation and diffusion of technological and scientific knowledge. In this section, we propose to divide this general objective into three parts, in order to present a taxonomy of technology policy. We differentiate between three types of technology policy according to whether the objective is to increase research incentives, to support the innovation process or to act upon the selection mechanisms.

RESEARCH INCENTIVE POLICY

The purpose of this type of policy is to overcome the lack of private incentive, which is due to the uncertainty inherent to the innovation process, to deal with the appropriation problems and to reduce the cost of research activities. To increase private incentive can consist either in reducing the cost of research activities, or in raising the private returns of innovations. This kind of policy does not act upon the competences and the abilities to innovate of firms, but concerns the economic and financial sides of the innovation process. The aim is to increase the level of research investment, and not to improve its efficiency.

The neoclassical analysis focuses on this type of technology policy. The lack of private research incentive corresponds to a market failure which is linked to the uncertainty and to the public character of technologies and innovations. The problem is to determine a research incentive mechanism in a context of uncertainty and asymmetries of information. This issue is developed in Principal–Agent theory which is devoted to the analysis of incentive mechanisms in a context of hidden action and hidden information. This theory deals with the determination and the implementation of the optimal incentive mechanism. There are two main differences between this approach and the evolutionary one. First of all, given the radical uncertainty and the bounded rationality assumptions, the evolutionary theory assumes that agents are not able to implement the optimal action which is not known anyway. As a consequence, the analysis deals with the way individual actions combine to solve specific problems, to learn and to find better solutions. The second difference is linked to information asymmetries. Principal–Agent models assume that agents have private information, not known by the Principal, and that they send signals to disclose partly this information. Thus the informational advantage is on the side of agents and entails moral hazard phenomena. In our technological context, it is impossible to assume any informational advantage. Indeed the policy maker is not endowed with the same information as firms and, above all, does not interpret information in the same way. In certain cases, the policy maker is less informed than firms on the technological state and the private research level. In others, thanks to its specific function, it has better knowledge of past experiences and of the results of scientific research. This means that the policy maker is neither better nor more informed than firms, but differently. As a consequence, the question is not to deal optimally with information asymmetries, but to study how the firms and the policy maker learn, adapt and interact. The emphasis is no longer on the information asymmetries, but on the uncertainty and on the learning capacities of agents. In this context Principal–Agent theory is not adapted to the analysis of research incentive policy, mainly because of its microeconomic foundations and its optimisation objective.

Generally speaking, the aim of research incentive policy is to increase the level of private research incentives, while maintaining a certain equilibrium between private incentive and diffusion. Three types of policies are advocated. The first one is the mechanisms which aim at increasing the appropriation degree of innovations, such as patent systems, intellectual property rights and licences. The other type is technology policy whose objective is to decrease the cost of research activities, thanks to R&D funding, subsidies or tax credit. The last one consists in acting upon the demand side by increasing the commercial opportunities and the potential applications of innovations thanks to procurement policies. This set of policies is also considered in the neoclassical analysis. Indeed, for this type of technology policy, the specificities of the evolutionary approach are more at the level of the microeconomic foundations and efficiency criteria, than at the level of the intervention mechanisms advocated.

Innovation Policy

We call innovation policy every policy which aims at acting upon the abilities to innovate and the technological knowledge and competences of firms. We differentiate these policies according to the stages oftechnological evolution, that is to say according as the system is in a transition stage or in an evolution stage along a given technological trajectory.

Transition stages correspond to the emergence of a new technological paradigm which is defined as a set of technological artefact and heuristics that provides a new potential of developments and improvements (Dosi, 1988). These stages are characterised by radical innovations which bring new technological or scientific artefacts. These radical innovations constitute a source of qualitative variations and potential economic growth. At this level, the aim of technology policy is to act upon the technological environment and the abilities to innovate of firms, in order to favour the emergence of a new technological paradigm. The purpose is to sustain and to stimulate exploration activities and variety creation. In general, the policies are industry or technologyoriented, in order to support or to speed up the evolution of this industry or this technology, for strategic or commercial reasons. It is a question of improving the efficiency and the competitiveness of a specific industry or technology, or of solving new technicoeconomic problems (for instance, environmental issues). At this stage of technological evolution, cooperative research programmes, involving different organisations like firms, research centres or universities, constitute the main innovation policy. Indeed, to sustain cooperation among firms and to develop the relationships between public and private research allows the exploitation of positive externalities and increasing returns in research activities, as well as the reduction of duplication in R&D. In this cooperation process, the policy maker acts as a 'catalyst'. The development of the relationships between private and public research is also a way of turning scientific research to more industrial issues and of exploiting with more efficiency the economic value of basic research. Other technology policies are important at this stage of technical evolution such as procurement policies, which give an impulse to research for the development of new technologies, basic research funding, and the creation of research centres or technological infrastructures.

The exploitation of a technological paradigm corresponds to a technological trajectory (Dosi, 1988). At this stage the aim of technology policy is to sustain the processes of learning and adaptation to the new paradigm, as well as to favour the emergence of incremental innovations which allow improvement of the initial technological artefact. Thus the purpose is to support the exploitation and the diffusion of new technologies. During this stage, innovation and diffusion policies are interdependent. Indeed, to sustain the diffusion and the assimilation of a new technological artefact also favours the emergence of incremental innovations. At the same time the improvements of the new technology stimulate its diffusion. Thus the phenomena of mutual reinforcement of innovation and diffusion are crucial to the development of a new technology. This is the reason why it is important not to consider independently innovation and diffusion policies. At this level technology transfer policies have a key role, since they contribute to the processes of diffusion and incremental innovations. Indeed information policies, the aim of which is the diffusion of new technological and scientific knowledge, as well as technology transfer mechanisms, based on cooperation or collaboration between public research centres and firms, entail an improvement of knowledge, technological competences and absorptive capacities of firms. Cohen and Levinthal (1990) define the absorptive capacity of firms as their ability to assimilate and to integrate in their knowledge base new external information and knowledge. These abilities are built progressively by firms and have a fundamental role in their processes of leaning and innovation. Cohen and Levinthal (1990) consider that the R&D investment of a firm is an indicator of its absorptive capacity. R&D activities allow, at the same time, an improvement of the firm knowledge base and an increase in its absorptive capacity. Thus R&D public funding policies allow not only an increase in private incentives, but also an improvement of firms technological competences and absorptive capacities. This means that this type of technology policy can also contribute to the diffusion of new technologies and to the evolution along a technological trajectory.

TECHNOLOGY POLICY AND SELECTION MECHANISMS

Technology policies also have an important part to play at the level of selection mechanisms which, contrary to the innovation process, tend to decrease the variety within the system. We can differentiate the policies the aim of which is to influence the selection of technologies from those which try to act upon the selection at the level of firms. At the level of the selection of technologies, the policy maker has to deal with technology competition and lockin phenomena which are due to the cumulativeness of the process of technical change and to the existence of network externalities in the adoption process. In presence of increasing returns to adoption the competition among several technologies generally leads to the selection of one and only technology. There are increasing returns to adoption when the returns from the adoption of one technology by the next user is an increasing function of the number of early adopters. In this context the objective of technology policy is to influence the pace and the direction of the selection of technologies, while maintaining a diversity of technical options and avoiding lockin into an inferior technology. A technology is called 'inferior' if it does not correspond to the technology which would produce the most benefice if it was adopted by all users. The technology producing the most benefice as a standard is called 'superior' (Cowan, 1991). Given the lack of information about technologies at the beginning of the adoption process, the problem for the policy maker is to evaluate the immediate returns on technologies, the potential improvements along the learning curve and the increase in information linked to the utilisation of technologies. There is a tradeoff between immediate return and gain in information (Cowan, 1991). David (1987) emphasises three generic technology policy problems in such a context of technology competition:

The 'narrow policy windows': in presence of network externalities, 'there may be only comparatively brief and uncertain 'windows in time' during which effective public policy interventions can be made at moderate resource costs' (David, 1987). Thus the time period for a potential intervention tends to be relatively brief.

The 'blind giants paradox': the policy maker has greater power to influence the trajectories of technologies and the outcome of the selection at the beginning of the adoption process, that is to say when information on the competing technologies is most lacking. The power of the policy maker declines through time, while the quantity and quality of the information on the technologies is increasing.

The 'angry orphans problem': the selection will leave some groups of users 'orphaned' who will have sunk investments because they did not adopt the technology selected by the market or the policy maker.

In this context the objective of technology policy is limited to an increase in the expected future returns on adoptions and in the probability of lockin into a superior technology. But the risk of lockin into an inferior technology can not be completely avoided. A range of technology policies are relevant to deal with lockin problems, depending on the period of the potential intervention and on the type of information available (Soete and Arundel, 1993):

> At the beginning of the adoption process, if there is no information available on the competing technologies or if this information is not sufficient, an active public intervention is not necessary and the role of the policy maker is limited to the collection of knowledge and information on the competing technologies. It is a question of observing the experimentation stages and maintaining the different technical options.

If some information is available about the advantages or the superiority of a technology before a lockin occurs, the role of technology policy is to influence the adoption process in order to favour the diffusion of this technology. In this case regulations, standardiation, subsidies to adoption and procurement policies constitute the main policies to influence the diffusion.

If a lockin into an inferior technology already occurred, the aim of technology policy is to redirect investments and diffusion, either by supporting search for new technical options, or by subsidising an alternative technology.

At the level of firms the market selection tends to evict the least effective firms. The competition among firms is largely based on their technological competences and abilities to innovate at the level of the production process, the product design or the organisation. The evolution of industrial structures is strongly linked to the evolution of the technological knowledge and competences of firms. But at the same time industrial structures influence the technological opportunities and the pace of the technical change process. The objective of technology policy is to maintain a certain heterogeneity of firms and a sufficient degree of competition. The basic goal is to reach an equilibrium between static and dynamic efficiency, that is to deal with the 'Schumpeterian tradeoff'. On the one hand, a competitive industry allows the extraction of a higher social surplus in the short run, in comparison with a more concentrated industry where firms can exploit their monopoly power. On the other hand, the higher level of profits in the monopolistic case leads to more research activities and increases both the probability to innovate and the surplus in the long run. Moreover market structure influences the speed with which transient rents of innovators are eroded away by imitators, so that perfect competition is incompatible with innovation. But at the same time too weak competition may reduce the incentives to innovate. That is the reason why it is important to maintain at the same time a certain level of competitive pressure and enough private research incentives. This is the role of industrial policies, such as regulation policies or antitrust laws which aim at acting upon the evolution of industrial structures.

This analysis of technology policy foundations and objectives emphasises their specific and dynamic character. Technology policies must adapt to the pace and to the different stages of the process of technical change, but also follow the evolution of industrial structures. Thus there are strong interdependent relationships between the evolution of technologies, industrial structures and technology policy.

THE CO–EVOLUTION OF TECHNOLOGY, INDUSTRIAL STRUCTURE AND TECHNOLOGY POLICY

In this part, we study the interactions between the evolution of technology, industrial structure and technology policy. Before explaining the co–evolution of these three elements, we focus on the mechanisms guiding the evolution of technology policy.

Bounded Rationality and Specificities of the Policy Maker

Technology policies are determined within public institutions which are characterised by a specific organisational structure. There are different sequential and complementary levels of intervention, from the determination of the main policy goals to the implementation of intervention mechanisms. The bounded rationality assumption is also applicable to the policy maker. Indeed it is not justified to assume that the policy maker has better cognitive capacities than other agents, a superior knowledge and understanding of market behaviour and technological opportunities, and less informational constraints. The policy maker is in the same situation as the firms it seeks to influence, that is to say it also has to operate under the constraints of localised, imperfect and uncertain information (Metcalfe, 1993). Obviously this calls into question the neoclassical approach which considers the policy maker as a social planner, that is able to determine the Pareto equilibrium and to maximise social welfare. Given the uncertainty inherent to the innovation process, these arguments are stronger in the precise case of technology policy. The policy maker has to deal with a lack of information and strong uncertainty, not only at the level of the firms that constitute the target group of the policy, but also at the level of the technological state and the outcomes of innovative activities. These constraints are stronger during transition stages, that is to say when a new technological paradigm is emerging.

This leads us to call into question the idea of an omniscient and omnipotent policy maker. It is not its superior rationality which characterises the policy maker and which differentiates it from firms, but its particular position on the market, as well as its ability to give incentives and to provoke coordination. The policy maker does not have to cope with the same competitive pressures and selection as firms. Contrary to firms, it has, by definition, a certain 'monopoly power', since it does not operate in a market in competition with other policy makers, and it is not threatened by potential entrants (except in the case of elections). The capacity of the policy maker to give incentives is linked to its allocation and redistribution power, and permits it to influence the decision process and behaviour of firms by providing private incentives in addition to those provided by the market (for example, thanks to public funding policies). As to its ability to coordinate, it gives it the capacity to influence the outcomes of selection mechanisms and to incite firms to coordinate. For instance, this is the case with network policies and cooperative research programmes which incite firms to coordinate and to cooperate, or standardisation policies which determine the outcome of the selection mechanism by requiring firms to coordinate and to use the same technological standard. These specific abilities to give incentive and to coordinate enable the policy maker to substitute itself for the market and to impose on firms new constraints which entail changes in their decisions and behaviour.

These arguments lead us to reject the assumption of an optimising policy maker and to consider it more as an adaptive agent. For various reasons such as informational constraints and radical uncertainty, but also political myopia, pressure group activity, or the separation of tax payers from the beneficiary of policy, technology policy can fail (Metcalfe, 1993). Thus it is important to take into account policy failures as well as market failures, and to analyse how policy makers learn and adapt in the light of experience.

Learning Process and Evaluation of Technology Policy

Learning processes have an important part to play in the evolution of technology policy. May (1982) emphasises three types of learning in the framework of public policy:

1. 'Instrumental learning' consists in improvements and changes in policy instruments which are based on experience, better understanding of policy implementation and source of policy failure, or formal evaluation.
2. 'Social learning' entails a rethinking and a new definition of the policy problem itself, the scope of policy or policy goals. It is also based on experience and better understanding of policy problems, interventions or objectives.
3. 'Political learning' leads to changes in political strategy or to more sophisticated advocacy of a policy idea or problem. The foci are political feasibility and policy processes.

We also notice imitation phenomena at the level of technology policy. Indeed imitation of policies which have shown their efficiency in other contexts or countries is also a source of learning. Generally it is a matter of adaptive imitation which means that the policy that is imitated is adapted to the specific context and to the new objectives. For instance, this was the case with MITI which has greatly guided the success of the Japanese industry, thanks to long term policies and strong interactions between public and applied research. MITI has been at the origin of new technology policies in other countries, inspired by the Japanese model. These different types of learning, imitative or adaptive, are complementary and constitute the main forces driving the implementation and the evolution of technology policy.

An evaluation procedure integrated into the implementation of technology policy is necessary to assess their efficiency and to determine the improvements needed. We argue that the evaluation of technology policy is a necessary condition for learning. The main issue is to determine evaluation criteria that correspond to the objectives of the policy and allow the quantitative and qualitative effects to be measured. The additionality concept is often used to measure the effects of technology policy on innovative activities. In the case of R&D public funding policy Cameron, Georghiou and Buisseret (1995) define additionality as the extent to which public support stimulates new R&D activities, as opposed to subsidising what would have taken place anyway. Quantitative effects are evaluated on the basis of indicators on the inputs (R&D expenses, number of researchers...) and outputs (market shares, number of innovation, commercial impacts...) of the innovation process. It is also important to take into account the qualitative effects, particularly at the level of behaviours ('behavioural additionality'), such as the emergence of new modes of collaboration among firms, new relationships between university and industry, or changes in firms research strategies. Even if these effects are difficult to measure, it is necessary to incorporate them into the evaluation. The main difficulty lies in measuring the proportion of these effects which is due to technology policy and in taking into account indirect effects.

Thus the evaluation of technology policy constitutes the basis of the learning process that allows the adaptation and improvement of policy on the basis of experience and failures. It is no longer a question of evaluating policy on the basis of the sole criterion of social welfare, but of designing evaluation procedures with different criteria corresponding to the objectives of policy and allowing the different effects on the innovation process to be measured.

Selection and Evolution of Technology Policy

One can notice that certain traditional technology policies are maintained, while others are no longer used and new intervention mechanisms are implemented. Accordingly there are also selection mechanisms which guide the evolution of policy. We can differentiate between two types of selection mechanisms:

Internal selection: Certain factors and processes internal to public institutions play a part in the selection of technology policy. For instance, budget constraints of the government may lead to a decrease in R&D subsidies or to the abandonment of certain public research programmes. Political pressures of lobbies or international organisations can also affect the selection and the evolution of technology policy.
External selection: Firms constitute the main determining factors in the selection and evolution of technology policy. The efficiency of intervention mechanisms is determined on the basis of firms research activities and technological performances. To a certain extent, the evolution of private routines gives an insight into the efficiency of technology policy and influences the selection.

Moreover the evolution of the market and technologies, which may entail the disappearance of certain technologies, firms or industrial sectors, can be at the origin of the abandonment of certain technology policy. Generally speaking the selection of technology policy depends on variations in demand, changes in the environment and technologies, economic fluctuations and the international context. The selection mechanisms and the learning processes (adaptive or imitative) determine the evolution of technology policy and create 'political trajectories' which are characterised by stages of transition (emergence of new policy), development and decline. In a way, there are life cycles at the level of technology policy (Niosi, Bellon, 1995), or 'political paradigms' (Ruivo, 1994). The main features of the evolution of technology policy are the following:

- the abandonment of certain traditional policies at the national level. For instance, technology policies which aimed at developing 'national champions' have been given up after having shown their negative effects on the dynamics of innovation.
- the survival, adaptation and restructuring of certain technology policies. For instance, this is the case of public policies that aim at supporting technological change in military sectors.

- the relative decline of intervention mechanisms such as direct R&D subsidies.
- the emergence and development of new technology policy, such as technology transfer policies between public and private research, or european cooperative research programmes.

Insofar as firms take part in the selection of technology policy, the trajectories of technology policy evolution are strongly linked to the evolution of firms and technologies. Thus there is a co–evolution of technology policy, technology and industrial structure.

THE CO–EVOLUTION PROCESS

The analysis of industrial dynamics of Nelson and Winter (1982) emphasises the upward trend in industrial concentration due to innovative activities. There is a progressive domination of the most innovative firms, which invest the profits linked to their innovations in research activities, which tends to reinforce their dominant position. The characteristics of technological regimes have a strong influence upon the evolution of industrial structures. For Winter (1984), to characterise the key features of a particular knowledge environment is to define a technological regime. The trend in concentration is increasing with the intrinsic difficulty of imitation, the set of technological opportunities and the growth rate of latent productivity (in the science–based case) which represents the improvement of external scientific or technological knowledge. The evolution of industrial structure is strongly influenced by the technological regime and the outcomes of innovative activities. At the same time, the degree of competition in the industry implies a certain level of research incentives which also influences the process of technical change. There are strong interdependent relationships between technological regimes, innovation process and industrial structures.

Technology policies play a leading part in the configuration of technological regimes. For instance, patent systems determine the degree of appropriation and imitation of innovations, and technology transfer policies create new relationships between basic and applied research. Moreover information and diffusion policies, as well as public research programmes, tend to increase the set of technological opportunities. As a consequence technology policies directly influence technological regimes and, thus, the evolution of industrial structures. But to a certain extent technology policy must also adapt to certain characteristics of the technological regime, such as the type of knowledge and technology, or the degree of maturity of technologies. This is the reason why technology policy and technological regimes must be considered as a whole, determining the basic conditions for the process of technological change. In other words, technology policies influence technological regimes but must also adapt to changes in technologies and industrial structures. Therefore there is a co–evolution of technology policy, technology and industrial structure. This co–evolution can take two different forms:

- In an initial stage technology policies are adapted and improved according to the outcomes of evaluation procedures which depend on the evolution of the research activities and technologies of firms. For instance, in the field of the European Framework Programmes big companies have suffered since 1990 a decrease both in the number of participants and in their funding. Most of the cuts in big firms funding have been redistributed to research centres, higher education institutions and small firms. These modifications resulted from evaluations which have emphasised the existence of substitution effects at the level of big firms funding and the leading role of 'research institutions'. At this level of the co–evolution process, the learning of the policy maker is based on evaluation procedures and mainly consists in 'instrumental learning'.
- In certain cases the evolution of technological and scientific knowledge entails a deep restructuring of technology policy which is independent of the initial objectives of the policy. For example, the emergence of new technology can imply the setting up of new public research centres, or the adaptation of the intellectual property rights system (for instance, in the case of biotechnology). In other cases the decline of certain industrial sectors or technologies, due to the emergence of new technologies, leads to the restructuring, or even the abandonment, of technology policies directed towards these industrial sectors. At this level policy learning is based on the evolution of scientific and technological knowledge, and the co–evolution process may concern different scientific and industrial domains.

Generally we observe a timelag between the evolution of technology policy and that of technologies and industries. The evolution of policy is slower than that of private routines for the following reasons: the specific selection of policy, which is slower and less radical than the market selection, the lack of fluidity of the 'political market', a certain bureaucratic inertia and the difficulties in evaluating the outcomes and the efficiency of policy (Niosi and Bellon, 1995).

*Figure 11.1 The co–evolution of technology policy, technology and
industrial structure*

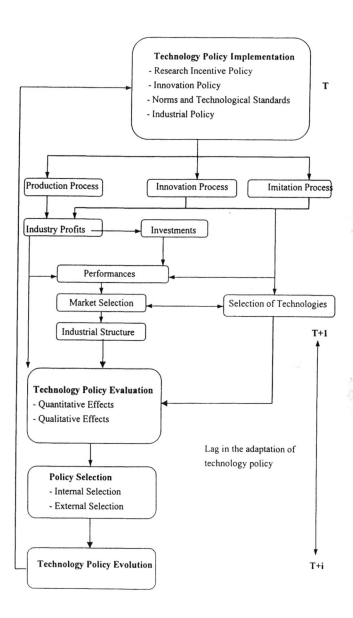

Figure 11.1 depicts the co–evolution process and sums up the different steps of our analysis. It emphasises both interdependent dynamics of industry and technology policy, each one being based on adaptation, imitation and selection mechanisms. While the evolution of industry (from the production to the changes in industrial structure) is sequential, the evolution of technology policy is divided into two steps: the implementation of policy, which influences the technological regime and the evolution of the industry, and the adaptation and evolution of policy, which is guided by the outcomes of evaluations and innovation processes.

CONCLUSION

In an evolutionary framework the main objectives of technology policy are to sustain the evolution of firms and technologies along their trajectories, to support variety creation and the emergence of new technological paradigms, and to guide the selection processes. Technology policies determine the basic conditions of the innovation process, by influencing technological regimes, and aim at supporting the evolution of private routines which, in turn, play a leading role in the determination and evolution of policy. This co–evolution of technology policy, technology and industrial structure is the main point of our analysis. Technology policies are presented as an evolutive pattern of interactions between public and private routines. The co–evolution process is based on learning, selection and variety creation mechanisms, and characterised by a timelag between the evolution of technologies and private routines and that of technology policy. This dynamics could be developed further in order to analyse more formally the interdependent relationships between industrial dynamics and technology policy.

The main implications of this analysis in terms of implementation of technology policy are twofold. First of all, it is necessary to consider policy as an integrated element of technological regime and to take into account the dynamic relationships between industrial structure, innovation and public intervention. As a consequence, it is also necessary to design evaluation procedures and more flexible intervention mechanisms, in order to adapt and to improve policies in the light of experience and failures.

REFERENCES

Cameron, H., L. Georghiou, and T. Buisseret (1995), 'What Difference Does it Make? Additionality in the Public Support of R&D' in Large Firms, *International Journal of Technology Management*, Special Issue on the Evaluation of Research and Innovation, 10 (415/6).

Cohen, W. and D. Levinthal (1990), 'Absorptive Capacity: A New Perspective on Learning and Innovation', *Administrative Science Quarterly*, 35.

Cowan, R. (1991), 'Rendements Croissants d'Adoption et Politique Technologique', in *L'évaluation économique de la Recherche et du Changement technique*, Editions du CNRS.

David, P. (1987), 'Some New Standards for the Economics of Standardisation in the Information Age', in P. Dasgupta and P. Stoneman (eds.), *Economic Policy and Technological Performance*, Cambridge: Cambridge University Press.

Dosi, G. et al (1988), *Technical Change and Economic Theory*, G. Dosi, C. Freeman, R.R. Nelson, G. Silverberg and L. Soete (eds.), London and New York: Pinter Publishers.

May, P.J. (1982), 'Policy Learning and Failure', *Journal of Public Policy*, 12 (4).

Metcalfe, J.S. (1993), 'The Economic Foundations of Technology Policy: Equilibrium and Evolutionary Perspectives', *Discussion Paper* 95, Department of Economics, University of Manchester.

Nelson, R.R. and S.G. Winter (1982), *An Evolutionary Theory of Economic Change*, Boston: The Belknap Press of Harvard University Press.

Nelson, R.R. (1986), 'Institutions Supporting Technical Advance in Industry', *AEA Papers and Proceedings*, 76(2).

——— (1994), 'The Co–evolution of Technology, Industrial Structure and Supporting Institutions', *Industrial and Corporate Change*, 3(1).

Niosi, J. and B. Bellon (1995), 'Une Interprétation évolutionniste des Politiques Industrielles', *Revue d'Economie Industrielle*, 71.

Ruivo, B. (1994), 'Phases or Paradigms of Science Policy', *Science and Public Policy*, 21(3).

Smith, K. (1991), 'Innovation Policy in an Evolutionary Context', in P.P. Saviotti and J.S. Metcalfe (eds.), *Evolutionary Theories of Economic and Technological Change*, Harwood Academic Publishers.

——— (1995), 'Interactions in Knowledge Systems: Foundations, Policy Implications and Empirical Mapping', Paper presented at the Lanzarote Conference, January 2022.

Soete, L. and A. Arundel (1993) (eds.), *An Integrated Approach to European Innovation and Technology Policy*, A Maastricht Memorandum, Commission of the European Communities, Brussels, Luxembourg: ECSCEECEAEC.

Winter, S.G. (1984), 'Schumpeterian Competition in Alternative Technological Regime', *Journal of Economic Behavior and Organisation*, 5(34).

INDEX